Jim Paulos

D1218511

Managing Creative People

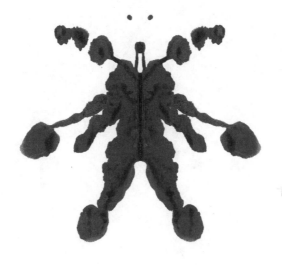

Someday someone will write a book explaining why so many pioneering enterprises, including Walt Disney, Hewlett-Packard, and Apple, were born in garages.

Organizing Genius by Warren Bennis and
Patricia Ward Biedermann

GORDON **TORR**

CManagingreative People

LESSONS IN LEADERSHIP FOR THE IDEAS ECONOMY

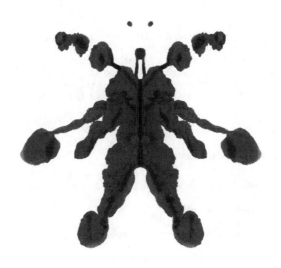

John Wiley & Sons, Ltd

Other Wiley Editorial Offices

John Wiley & Sons Inc., 111 River Street, Hoboken, NJ 07030, USA
Jossey-Bass, 989 Market Street, San Francisco, CA 94103-1741, USA
Wiley-VCH Verlag GmbH, Boschstr. 12, D-69469 Weinheim, Germany
John Wiley & Sons Australia Ltd, 42 McDougall Street, Milton, Queensland 4064, Australia
John Wiley & Sons (Asia) Pte Ltd, 2 Clementi Loop #02-01, Jin Xing Distripark, Singapore 129809
John Wiley & Sons Canada Ltd, 6045 Freemont Blvd, Mississauga, ONT, L5R 4J3, Canada

Wiley also publishes its books in a variety of electronic formats. Some content that appears in print may not be
available in electronic books.

Library of Congress Cataloging-in-Publication Data

Torr, Gordon.
    Managing creative people : Lessons for leadership in the ideas economy / Gordon Torr.
        p.   cm.
    Includes bibliographical references and index.
    ISBN 978-0-470-72645-7 (cloth)
 1. Creative ability in business.   2. Management.   I. Title.
    HD53.T67 2008
    658.3′14—dc22

                                                                                      2008007639

British Library Cataloguing in Publication Data

A catalogue record for this book is available from the British Library

ISBN 978-0-470-72645-7 (HB)

Typeset in 11/15 pt Times by SNP Best-set Typesetter Ltd., Hong Kong
Printed and bound in Great Britain by TJ International Ltd, Padstow, Cornwall, UK

For Bruce

Contents

Preface

This book is about how a few very bad ideas have got in the way of our ability to produce a lot of very good ones.

Those bad ideas have been accumulating slowly but steadily over the last hundred years or so, like lime-scale in the plumbing of an old building, and now they have reduced the free flow of new ideas to a tiny trickle.

In some areas, such as in the kitchen of popular culture, the faucets have run completely dry. You'll get a few drops out of them if you hit the pipes very hard with the heel of a heavy boot. Then you'll hear them grumbling and squeaking and in the attic, and the water that coughs and splutters into your cup will taste foul and bitter.

In the annexe at the back, newly built to accommodate the emerging sciences, the water still runs bright and clear. But the lime-scale will get there too, soon enough, unless we are vigilant and well equipped with the remedies for its removal.

*

The larger part of this story is devoted to identifying and understanding those bad ideas: where they came from, how we were seduced into taking them for granted, and why they have such a constricting effect on the free flow of creativity and innovation.

While many readers will be anxious to race ahead to the last few chapters in search of 'seven simple steps for the removal of creative lime-scale' they are urged to be patient, not because I wish them to hang onto my every word, but because the tonic that this book offers for the revival of the innovative spirit in creative sector organizations will not be easy to swallow without the sweetening palliative of understanding why we need it in the first place.

Some readers will find this book mildly upsetting. Some will find it deeply disturbing, very dangerous or profoundly threatening. With any luck, all readers will be provoked.

It is written for people engaged in creative businesses, or, more precisely, in that booming part of the economy that has come to be known as the creative sector. This describes the 15 major domains, from advertising to video games, that now employ as much as 30% of the workforce in the world's most developed nations. It includes the music business, film, fashion, publishing, broadcasting and software development. But it also encompasses those nominally 'non-creative' businesses that rely for growth on a constant stream of innovation from R&D or from new product development.

It is aimed specifically at that rapidly expanding cadre of executives, managers and agents who depend for their success on the performance and productivity of creative people, or who are in some way beholden to creative people for the furtherance of their individual or corporate ambitions. They could be marketing directors or brand managers seeking better ideas from their advertising agencies or their other communication partners. They could be film producers, commissioning editors, game designers, A&R executives, innovation managers or fashion buyers. They could be gallery owners, museum curators or sponsors of the arts. They could be editing houses, theatre directors or government ministries involved in furthering the creative industries in general. They could be publishers, newspaper editors, magazine owners or design agencies. Or they could be the human resource managers in any of the myriad businesses engaged in the creative sector. Anyone, in short, responsible in one way or another for developing or managing creative talent, or for commissioning, funding or selecting products of the imagination for commercial exploitation.

Shortly before going to press I happened to pick up a copy of *What Is Your Dangerous Idea?*, a collection of highly explosive views and observations by some of the world's leading scientists, psychologists, sociologists and philosophers, assembled by the legendary John Brockman, editor of *Edge*, and one of the most radical thinkers of our age. I mention this for two reasons: first, because it's such a bracing read, like an ice-cold shower for a mind made sluggish by too many warm layers of cosy assumptions, but second, because it reminded me just how difficult it is to have to reframe your thinking when confronted with compelling ideas that are not in accord with your own, or – worse still – with ideas you didn't think of first.

Keeping your mind open to new ideas is hard enough in relationships, politics and religion. It's harder yet when those ideas demand an immediate and drastic reappraisal of how you'll go about your business at the office tomorrow morning.

So here's the health warning . . .

If you're serious about making a significant, positive difference to the quality of the creative work or the creative thinking currently being generated in your organization or your business, be prepared to give up your most cherished beliefs about the way good ideas happen.

Be prepared, for example, to let go of the commonly accepted notion that we are all creative. Be prepared to forsake forever the counterproductive practice of brainstorming. Be prepared to give up the belief that teamwork is good for creativity. Be prepared to accept that good ideas don't sell themselves. Be prepared to reject once and for all the assumption that creative problem solving and creativity are one and the same thing, and along with it, the misguided idea that creativity can be taught. Be prepared to question whether your organizational structures are facilitating the production of good ideas or actively suffocating them to death. Be prepared to discover that the free market mechanisms of supply and demand, which are so good at driving up the quality and driving down the costs of everyday goods and services, like electric toasters and holidays in Jamaica, have the counterintuitive effect of driving down the quality and driving up the costs of creative products. And be prepared to learn that every single one of the management techniques commonly used to motivate the productivity of workers in the traditional commercial and industrial sectors has precisely the opposite effect on the productivity of creative people.

If a root-and-branch revision of everything we know about managing creativity is not dangerous enough, my really dangerous idea, the one that keeps me up at night in a state of frenzied foreboding, is that the bad ideas that are killing the good ones in the marketplace may also have begun to rot the foundations of art and culture, of our political and social aspirations, and of the values that prop up the entire edifice of our western liberal democracy.

Before you dismiss it as implausible, melodramatic or absurd you might want to remind yourself that all ideas, if they are to be of any significance at all, will appear at first glance to be implausible, melodramatic or absurd.

Just as fresh ideas are the lifeblood of healthy, dynamic organizations, fresh ideas in art, culture and politics are the lifeblood of healthy, dynamic societies. If, as I firmly believe, the mechanisms of libertarian economics are conspiring – quite paradoxically – *against* the origination of more, better ideas in creative sector companies, how long will it be before that same invisible hand moves on to throttle the imaginative life out of the body politic?

There was a time, not very long ago, when creative people pursued their ambitions outside of the commercial mainstream. If they were brilliant enough –

and lucky enough – they were drawn into the mainstream by wealthy patrons, or by the fortune of commercial popularity. We would never have heard of most of the great artists and writers of the past few centuries if they hadn't been born into money or, at least, into families prepared to support their talent.

That is no longer the case. Ever since Hollywood turned creativity into an industry there has been an increasing commercial demand for artistic talent in almost every imaginable form. By the end of the 20th century there was hardly a single expression of creativity that could not usefully be exploited for commercial purposes within a recognizable and respectable business sector. Who would have thought, just a few short decades ago, that an aptitude for animating digital dinosaurs, for example, could lead to a viable, fulfilling and lucrative career? For the first time in history the majority of people with creative aspirations have become wage-earners, just like everybody else, and the romantic view of the artist-as-outsider has been almost entirely dispelled.

On the face of things commerce and creativity have now become comfortable bedfellows, and we shall see just how profitable a partnership it has become. But strip off the duvet and you'll discover a perverse and dubious coupling that is irrevocably damaging their offspring at conception.

For all of these reasons it is no longer possible to critique creative outcomes without reference to the commercial environment in which they were conceived, just as it is no longer possible to discuss creative businesses without reference to the way in which they harness the creative spirit. So while I have been at pains to make this book as useful as possible to managers of creativity and innovation, hoping to improve the productivity of their creative resources, I will not be apologizing for drawing the reader's attention to the broader social and cultural implications of my argument.

The texts are intertwined throughout, just as our experience of creativity – on TV, at the movies, in the books we read, in the buildings we use, in the new products we buy – is intertwined, for so many of us, with the experience of making creative products or of managing them. We have become viewers and producers simultaneously. We are publishers of content and consumers of content at the same time. We live in a very different world, and it needs a very different perspective if we are to make out of it any meaning or magic.

Whatever other ambitions I might have for this work, not least of all the fervent wish that my children grow up in a world significantly more imaginatively fertile than the one they were born into, its principal objective is as clear as the title suggests, that is, to provide a simple and workable guide to getting the best out of creative people.

Acknowledgements

My thanks, first of all, to those friends and former colleagues at J. Walter Thompson who shared my belief that we were doing something more interesting than enhancing shareholder value. My thanks to John Furr for challenging me to shape my early convictions, to Teresa Amabile for lending them substance, and to Jeremy Bullmore for giving me the courage of them. To Jimmy Evans for embodying the new patronage, to Basil Mina and Eugene Strauss for keeping me honest, to Richard Block for making me think so hard, and to Dennis Ryan, Derek Day, David Lamb and Jon Steel for their unhesitating support when I needed it most. Heartfelt thanks to Charity Charity who knew exactly what I meant when no one else did, and who introduced me to exactly the right people and exactly the right books at exactly those times when I didn't know where to turn next. To Rae Burdon, prince among men and king among suits; to Harry Macauslan, who stood for everything that was best about JWT; to Mark Murray, the rarest of advertising animals, an account planner who is simultaneously brilliant and humble. To Miles Colebrook, my mentor. To my Mexican creatives for *la vida loca*, especially the magnificent Gloria Lopez, and to Rocio Fernandez for teaching me how to conjugate 'rain' in Spanish. To Rosemary Morton, Juliet Dewhurst and Jane Arton who knew what was coming and supported me anyway. To Jo Mawtus and Nigel 'Grubby' Foster for being right there. To my sisters Deborah Evans and Helen Field, the former for making sense of the text, the latter for making sense of my feelings. To the delightful people at Langland for the shelter from the storm. To Claire Plimmer at John Wiley & Sons for understanding how much it matters. And most importantly of all to my wonderful wife, Karine, without whose unconditional love and belief none of this would have any meaning at all.

The authors would also like to thank the following for material used in this book.

Extracts from *Source Book for Creative Problem Solving* edited by Sidney J. Parnes. Reproduced by permission of the Creative Education Foundation.

Extracts from *Cities in Civilization* by Peter Hall. Reprinted by permission of SII/Stirling Lord Literistic Inc. Copyright by Peter Hall.

Extracts from *Managing Creativity* by Howard Davis and Richard Scase. This material is reproduced with the kind permission of the Open University Press/McGraw-Hill Publishing Company.

Extracts from *Lights! Camera! No Profits!* in *The Economist*. Reproduced by permission of The Economist Newspaper Limited, London, January 2003.

Extracts from *Skunk Words*, an article used in Popular Mechanics website. Reproduced by permission of Popular Mechanics.

Extracts from *How to Kill Creativity* by Teresa Amabile. Reprinted by permission of Harvard Business Review.

Extracts from *Creativity Under the Gun* by Teresa Amabile. Reprinted by permission of Harvard Business Review.

Extracts from *Twelve Songs II*, *One Circumlocation* and *In Memory of W.B. Yeats* from Collected Poems by W.H. Auden. Copyright 1976 by Edward Mendelson, William Meredith and Monroe K. Spears, executors of the estate of W.H. Auden. Used by permission of Random House, Inc.

Extracts from *The Future of Ideas* by Lawrence Lessig. Reproduced by permission of Random House, Inc.

THE CREATIVE INDIVIDUAL

Creativity is its own punishment.
Anon

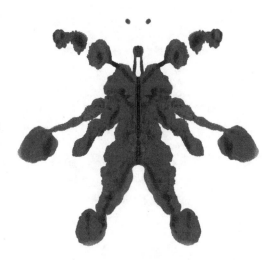

CHAPTER 1

The day the world ran out of ideas

A screaming comes across the sky. It has happened before, but there
is nothing to compare it to now.

Opening lines of *Gravity's Rainbow* by Thomas Pynchon

Along with several million other people I was in Manhattan on Tuesday,
September 11, 2001.

Ever since Friday evening, when my taxi dropped me off at the New York
Palace Hotel in Madison Avenue, a small crowd of people, mostly young women,
had been gathering on the kerb directly opposite the hotel entrance on 50th Street.
They were bored and restless, as though they had been there for some time. A
couple of NYPD officers hung around to make sure they respected the flimsy tape
barrier that kept them away from the traffic.

My room on the 15th floor looked directly down onto the nave of St
Patrick's Cathedral.

On Saturday night I was scheduled to meet up with an old friend from
Mexico, whom I had met while working there as creative director of J. Walter
Thompson in Mexico City.

The moment the elevator doors opened in the lobby I could hear the hys-
terical screaming of the crowd. I ran outside to see a white limo turning into the
vast concrete cavern of the delivery garage. The police and several bodyguards
were struggling to keep the crowd from streaming inside. A slight figure in an iri-
descent black suit was being hurried from the limo into the service elevator. I
caught a glimpse of a single white glove.

'Wow,' I said to Chris when we met up at the Thai restaurant somewhere
on the Upper West Side. 'Have I got something to tell the kids when I get back
home!'

*

On the Tuesday morning two planes appeared out of a clear blue sky and demolished all our certainties. Fukuyama was wrong. Far from having ended, history had been rewound to the beginning of the Crusades.

In the week I spent in a deserted Manhattan waiting for a plane to take me home to London I had plenty of time to think about how it could have happened, how we had been so tragically blind to its inevitability, and how the best brains in the world now seemed so bereft, not only of plausible explanations, but of the ideas we would need to take us forward.

The emptiness of the air above Ground Zero came to stand for that, the space where our ideas should have been.

A few weeks later I got a call from the *Wall Street Journal* asking me whether I thought advertising would ever return to normal. I said that I thought it would, and in due course it did.

But the emptiness stayed with me, and burrowed into my imagination like a worm.

*

As one of the global creative directors for J. Walter Thompson I had travelled regularly and extensively on behalf of my multinational clients, seeking out advertising ideas from our many international offices, or striving to manage the consistent application of those occasional few that originated from the global centres in London or New York. The first year or two were wonderfully exciting. The job was challenging, I was being very well paid, and I was visiting many extraordinary places and meeting some extraordinary people.

But after my seventieth or eightieth international flight things began to change. I grew numb to the novelty of each succeeding trip. Not jaded, just numb. I was staying in the very best hotels and eating in the world's finest restaurants. I was conferencing at the world's most exotic resorts, and getting front row seats to the world's hippest events. Perhaps there was a moment when I could have stopped and rebooted my numbing brain. But I was tired and stressed and carried along by the momentum of commitments like a straw in the wind.

The exciting cosmopolitan cities began to merge into one generically cosmopolitan city. The hotel rooms began to merge into one generic hotel room. The restaurants began to merge into one generic restaurant with the same generic menus, wines and waiters. The conversations at the generic restaurant began to merge into one generic conversation, and the people into shadowy archetypes entirely bereft of individual features, characters and points of view.

When once I was alive to the subtle differences of the locations and languages that surrounded me, I now was seeing only the similarities between things, the stereotype, no longer the thing itself. All the airports seemed to be the same airport. The stuff in the Duty Free was all the same stuff. The New York taxis were still yellow, of course, and the London taxis were still idiosyncratically black. But there seemed to me to be only one universal taxi driver, with the same-shaped back of the head and the same conversation. I went to crafts markets in the hope of finding interesting and exotic mementoes for my children.

I was excited, in Sao Paulo, to find a quaint wooden frog that struck me as truly original. It had a wooden stick, stored for convenience in its backside, which prompted an authentic *ribbit, ribbit, ribbit* when you ran it down the ridges of the frog's spine. A week later I found the same frog at Apt, in France. Then in Hong Kong, and later in Istanbul.

If this wasn't disturbing enough, the advertising ideas I was seeing from our network agencies began to take on an uncanny resemblance to one another. Here was an idea from Chicago that looked exactly like an idea from Singapore, an idea from Dublin that looked exactly like an idea from Amsterdam. Through exposure to the same sources of inspiration – the *D&AD Annuals*, the Cannes showreels, *Archive* magazine, the internet – the once rich diversity of local thinking had been replaced by the shallow homogeneity of globalism.

And that is how this feeling began; how I came to believe that there were no more ideas left in the world, and that the imaginative capacity of the whole planet had been infected too.

*

Down at Blockbuster, the special offer bins were full of DVDs that nobody wanted. I looked through them and I could see why. There wasn't an original idea among them. The movies that weren't remakes of old movies were part twos of box office hits or B-grade versions packaged to look like box office hits of the past. I wondered how *Pirates of the Caribbean* had become Hollywood's hottest property, and why it warranted not just one but two sequels.

Every movie seemed to be based on exactly the same plot, every book on exactly the same premise. In politics and in business, in sport and in the arts, the same handful of familiar tropes appeared and reappeared in transparently thin disguises, in the newspaper headlines, in magazine articles, on the radio, across the internet and on TV.

When I did see a good film, or an interesting one, I scrutinized the credits in search of the source of inspiration. Most of them seemed to be based on stories by Philip K. Dick.

Of course there were others, brilliant gems that gleamed in the dross. Almost without exception they were foreign films, small budget films, or films sponsored by independent studios.

Were there no more stories to be told? Or was it that interesting ideas for new scripts were being buried by nervous actuaries working in the bowels of the Hollywood machine?

There was another possibility, of course. Perhaps the new audiences, grown up on the schlock of poor TV, no longer cared whether they were watching something interesting or not.

I turned to the West End in the hope that Hollywood's apparent allergy to new ideas hadn't infected London's best and brightest.

Billy Elliot, Blood Brothers, Chicago, Dancing in the Streets, Guys and Dolls, Les Misérables, The Lion King, Mamma Mia!, Mary Poppins, Phantom of the Opera, The Producers, The Rat Pack Live from Las Vegas, Sinatra at the London Palladium, We Will Rock You, Dirty Dancing, Daddy Who and *Evita.*

The most popular of the lot was *Mary Poppins,* sold out for months. Only a couple contained material written in the past two decades. Music of 1950s, 1960s and 1970s was obviously still in huge demand, Abba, Diana Ross, Queen, Sinatra (going as 'live' but dead these 15 years) and the rest were tired old remakes of remakes of remakes.

Somewhere out there, in dark basements or dingy attics, in abandoned warehouses or unused cellars, the various muses of originality were being held hostage by unknown captors, for inscrutable purposes.

As for music itself, the crisis of originality was so public and so loud it was impossible to ignore. During their battle against Napster the big corporations that owned all the music almost succeeded in convincing us that they were the good guys, protecting musicians from the rapacious pirates of the internet. History proved otherwise.

Instead of anticipating the opportunities that the burgeoning internet would provide, the music companies had clung desperately to the tried and tested model that was making a mint out of the back catalogues. Instead of taking a chance on new music, or investing in new talent, they tried to shore up the crumbling walls of their entitlement in the copyright courts.

It took the Arctic Monkeys to prove, once and for all, that the old model was dead. The collapse of the rapaciously expensive CD system saw Warner Music and EMI dancing to the tune of the marketplace, where buyers eventually get what they want at a price they're prepared to pay. It used to cost £12.99 to get the track you wanted together with 19 tracks you didn't want. Now you can download the track you want for a few pence.

But it was a damaging war, and it left an entire generation without any music they could call their own.

Things were no different on the political front. The ill-conceived foray into Iraq had ended in a bloody stalemate as sectarian violence between Sunni and Shiite mocked the optimistic plans of Bush and Blair.

The intention was clear enough – to create a capitalist paradise in the oil-rich centre of Islam. All of the major corporations were lined up in advance. There were going to be Wal-Marts from Basra to Kurdistan. All the Iraqis needed to come round to democracy were Pantene and Coco Pops at really keen prices.

Among the collateral victims of this unfolding tragedy were ideas good enough to resolve it.

I began to see the same pattern in the business pages.

Skype was – and is – a brilliant idea. Free telephony across the internet. Why didn't BT think of that? I loved Skype, the simplicity of the branding, the ease of use, the free phone calls to South Africa. Skype proved what we'd always suspected – you didn't need to pay £100 a month to use the phone. The telecoms companies had been having a laugh all these years.

When Skype sold out to eBay for $2.6 billion many users feared the worst. Fresh and surprising new ideas like Skype don't come along very often. And no sooner had they arrived than they were snapped up by monster companies whose financial advisors identified them as opportunities for growth. What the critics forgot, of course, was that eBay, too, was a fresh and surprising idea when it first appeared.

eBay, Skype, Google, YouTube – the pattern was clear. The really good ideas were coming from individuals or small groups who worked independently of the major players, outside of the corporations or the existing business structures. The Arctic Monkeys, Brin and Page, the Skype guys, the auteurs, Berners-Lee himself.

The big companies seemed to be very good at exploiting ideas once they'd bought them, but pretty awful at coming up with them themselves. When was the last time you saw a good idea from an oil company or a bank? Why couldn't Microsoft have invented Google?

In film, theatre and music, in broadcasting and in advertising, in publishing, software development and now, apparently, in business in general, the organizations with the most resources, with the most talent and the most money were consistently failing to deliver the one thing their CEOs claimed to covet above all else, the ideas and innovations that would translate their steady curves of growth into quantum leaps of fortune and fame.

It would be easy enough to blame their risk aversion on shareholders who preferred steady growth to the chance of failure – even glorious failure. But the lack of imaginative adventure has somehow infected the non-commercial creative sectors, such as public broadcasting and state-sponsored cultural endeavours like the theatre, ballet and those other arts in the UK and elsewhere that benefit from public coffers.

In July 2007 that most venerable of creative public institutions, the British Broadcasting Corporation, was accused in a nationwide poll of viewers to be failing to deliver fresh and original programming. Rather than being sheltered by public money from the cold winds of commercial pressure, the BBC had become a bellwether of a steadily cooling creative climate. The BBC is a special case that we will go into in more detail a little later. It is the case that will prove that the imaginative malaise of almost all of the world's large organizations, including governments and the larger NGOs, goes deeper than a conservative regard for the bottom line. We shall see that it is rooted in a profound misunderstanding of the nature of creativity, and the way creative people have come to be managed.

Ever since 9/11 I had been marking the days when it seemed as though ideas had run out forever. The day that Leo Sayer's 'Thunder in My Heart' got to number one on the UK charts. The day that James Blunt got to number one in the US. The release of *Pirates of the Caribbean III*. The beginning of *How Do You Solve a Problem Like Maria?* on the BBC. The Harry Potter phenomenon for proving that there were no other books to get excited about. The sale of YouTube. The day Google sold out in China. The UK advertising industry's disastrous performance at Cannes in 2007. The bill to cut PBS funding in the US. The Danish cartoon madness. The 'surge' in Iraq. The Hamas debacle. The war in Lebanon. There were too many to count, and I gave up in frustration.

But then there were the exceptions that proved the rule: breakthroughs in genome research, extraordinary new drugs – if only for people who could pay for them; advances in astronomy, physics and technology in general. And the exceptions had a pattern, too. In every instance they were achieved by individuals or small groups whose specialist knowledge protected them from the organizational idea-killers. Or, in the case of exceptional consumer brands like Apple or Dyson, they were driven forward by CEOs with an emotional stake in the success of the company.

It wasn't, I realized after all, that the world had run out of ideas. It was simply that the world had forgotten how good ideas were created in the first place.

CHAPTER 2

The problem with creative people

I think the problem of the management of creative personnel is both fantastically difficult and important. I don't quite know what we are going to do with this problem because, in essence, what I am talking about is the lone wolf. The kind of creative people that I've worked with are people who are apt to get ground up in an organization, apt to be afraid of it, and apt generally to work off in a corner or an attic by themselves. The problem of the place of the 'lone wolf' in a big organization, I'm afraid, is your problem and not mine.

> A.H. Maslow (from a speech delivered at a Creative Engineering Seminar for the US Army Management School, Fort Belvoir, Virginia, 1957)

The job of creative director in an ad agency is very much like the job of a football manager; you buy the best talent you can afford and you strive to get the best performances out of the rest of them. Unlike Roman Abramovitch of Chelsea, I could usually afford to buy only a handful of A-list players, so the second part of the job became much more important to me. I began to wonder what the conditions were that made nominally average creative people perform so well at certain times and so badly at others.

It's fair to say, as the years wore on and the hiring budgets failed to improve, I began to obsess over it. I wanted to know how it was that you could buy a proven superstar from another agency and he or she would fail to perform in the new environment. Conversely, how could a certain creative person, regarded as average in one agency environment, move to another agency and suddenly perform miracles? I began to wonder whether it had anything at all to do with talent; and whether talent, perhaps, was the least significant of all the possible variables.

I began to experiment. I employed young people fresh out of universities and art colleges. I employed hacks whose careers were almost over. I put teams together and pulled them apart. I had them working in bigger groups and working singly. I put some teams in offices behind closed doors, and I put some teams into open plan areas with no privacy at all. When the money was available I hired people with sparkling reputations and gave them the toughest assignments in the agency. Then I gave them the softest and the juiciest.

I continued these experiments when I was transferred first to Mexico and later to London. As I began to move upwards through the agency ranks I found myself confronted by new challenges, managing multinational brands around the world, and overseeing some 50 or 60 regional offices for the agency network. I discovered that some offices produced consistently better creative work than others did, with the same brands, the same systems, and the same agency culture. I determined to find out why.

As my responsibilities increased in scope and complexity I began to take a more global view. I found myself being forced to look for patterns that made sense beyond the idiosyncrasies of culture and geography. When it became imposs- ible to manage the detail for the sheer abundance of it, I realized that I needed strategies, not tactics.

I had to redefine my remit. I could no longer hold hands with clients on spe- cific projects or intervene in the development of creative work in specific locations. I had to look at it – that is, the quality of the work coming out of the various offices around the world – the way a manufacturer would look at the quality of goods being produced in a hundred different factories. I could move or change people, I could rant and rave, I could philosophize and theorize, I could motivate and humiliate, but what I really needed was a total quality programme, like the ones our clients were using, to legislate a sea-change in our worldwide creative output.

Desperately, madly, and very secretly, I began to read management maga- zines, the *Harvard Business Review, Fortune, Fast Company* and the *Economist*. I read HR books like Peter Senge's *The Fifth Discipline*, coaching books like John Whitmore's *Coaching for Performance*, books on leadership like Jaworski's won- derful *Synchronicity*, and books that people said I should read, like David Whyte's *The Heart Aroused*. I read Drucker and Covey. I scoured the internet. And to my enduring shame I even bought a book by Tom Peters.

The more I read, and the more deeply I puzzled, the more I began to realize that traditional management theory had very little to say about managing creativity in organizations. There was plenty on innovation – absolute masses on innovation – but oddly, given the subject, nothing on talent, nothing on identifying talent, and nothing on managing talent. Everyone wanted innovation; the CEOs of major companies talked of little else. Innovation experts were in huge demand, and the territory was quickly claimed by the management consultants who flooded the business press with hastily written papers on the subject, interweaving quotes from Christensen with glowing case studies about Microsoft, Amazon and Enron. Innovation, it seemed, was code for exploiting new business opportunities, which allowed it to fit neatly into the conventional discourse on managing for growth.

Quite amazingly, or so it seemed from my first round of research, in the 50 years that had passed since Abraham Maslow first identified the problem of managing creative people in large organizations, not a single management theorist, academic or researcher other than Teresa Amabile of Harvard Business School had done anything at all to take up Maslow's challenge.

Given the extraordinary amount of literature on creativity and the extraordinary amount of literature on management, I found it hard to believe that only one person on the planet was interested in the intersection of the two.

I can't remember exactly when the horrible truth began to dawn on me. It took as long as it did, I suspect, because I found it inconceivable, like discovering 10 years later that the headmaster of the parish school is a paedophile, or that all those nice people at last night's dinner party voted for George Bush.

The reason why no one other than Amabile and myself were concerned with the problem of managing creative people was that *no one believed creative people were any different from anyone else*. The revelation was staggering.

Clearly if everyone is potentially just as creative as everyone else is, there is no need for a special class of theory devoted to managing them. If everyone is potentially just as creative as everyone else is, all one needs to do is train them to unleash that potential. If everyone is equally creative then Maslow's 'lone wolf' is a fiction and you can manage advertising agencies and film production companies the same way you manage a baked beans factory. It defied logic, it defied my own experience, and I was determined to discover the truth.

I plunged into the literature on creativity, the formal and the informal, the popular and the deeply academic. I trawled the internet, I spoke to experts in the field, I experimented in the laboratories of the ad agencies I worked with. I began to connect the dots of creative performance from advertising to other creative sector companies, and I began to understand how the commoditization of creativity was conspiring to limit the variety and quality of expression across all 15 of the creative sector industries.

This book is about my findings.

*

The truth is that creative people are different from other people – special, for better or worse, in a way that we're only beginning to understand. And everything we know about them suggests that they're creative because they're different, not that they're different because they're creative. It's a vital distinction.

Believing that everyone has the capacity to be just as creative as the next person is as ludicrous as believing that everyone has the capacity to be just as intelligent as the next person, yet it has become almost universally accepted as a truism. It's also relatively new, taking root only in the last 30 or 40 years, coinciding much too precisely to be accidental with the popularization of creativity as an essential ingredient of social and business success.

Before that, from the Palaeolithic era until the early 1950s, which is to say for almost the entire duration of human life on earth, the popular conception of creative people was that they were born that way, with unique gifts that obliged them to seek out and fulfil the singular vocations of their destiny. Ever since the first *sangoma* scratched out a picture of an eland on a cave wall, individuals with creative skills were treated with circumspect reverence in their communities. Often they were accorded magical powers of one kind or another, or given a special dispensation to behave as madly as they liked without regard to the traditions and taboos of the rest of the society.

They were shamans, priests, prophets, storytellers, poets, witches, troubadours, jesters, Giottos, da Vincis, romantics, lunatics, misfits, outsiders, strangers, village idiots, inventors, novelists, artists and, eventually, advertising people. They were vilified as often as they were revered, and reviled as much as they were respected.

Throughout this time no one bothered to question why they were different or how they were different. It was simply a matter of fact, as natural as the unpredictable markings on a cow. Psychology began to take a serious interest in creativity only in the 1950s when Maslow began to ask some difficult questions about the role of creative people in the workplace, and as the very first creative assessment tools were being drafted by people like Guilford and Torrance.

We will look at some of this research along the way, and examine the evidence on both sides of the argument about the distribution of creativity across the population. Even today the very best studies remain sketchy. But the rhetoric is becoming increasingly shrill, especially on the side of those who train creativity for a living and in whose interests it is to promote the idea of the creative genius lurking in all of us.

There are compelling social and political reasons why we cling so fiercely to the belief that we are just as creative as one another, or – at least – just as creative deep down inside of us if only we were given the opportunity, the training, or an expensive box of oil paints. The first and most obvious of them is that the word 'creative' has no socially acceptable antonym. If you are not creative you can only be 'uncreative', which is possibly even more taboo in today's politically correct climate than calling someone fat, short, ugly, old or stupid.

The really odd thing about this is that the word 'creative', when used to conjure up the stereotype of someone who spends his or her life with their head in the clouds, has strong shades of the pejorative. Then it suddenly becomes the opposite of rational, orderly, organized, deliberate, methodical, reasonable, disciplined and a hundred other adjectives used to describe decent, hard-working citizens whose feet are planted firmly on the ground.

This is especially true when we talk about 'creative people' (or 'creatives' as they are called in advertising and, increasingly, in many other business sectors) as a class. And here are some examples of what the raised eyebrow that accompanies that expression really means.

The problem with creative people is that they're unpredictable and unreliable. The problem with creative people is that they're morose, arrogant and impossible to manage. The problem with creative people is that they think they're always right. The problem with creative people is that you can't rely on them to get things done. The problem with creative people is that you can't tell if they're any good until it's too late. The problem with creative people is that you can't replace them with machines. The problem with creative people is that they think they're indispensable. The problem with creative people is that they don't know the meaning of money. The problem with creative people is that they won't listen, they won't cooperate and they won't toe the line. The problem with creative people is that they're impulsive, hostile and out of control. The problem with creative people is that they live in a dream world. The problem with creative people is that they think they're so different from the rest of us. The problem with creative people is that they think they're the only people who can be creative. The problem with creative people is that most of them can't even tie their own shoelaces. The problem with creative people is that they're anxious, unreasonable and antisocial. The problem with creative people is that they would rather be living on a different planet. The problem with creative people is that they have to be stimulated all the time. The problem with creative people is that there are so many bad ones and so few good ones. The problem with creative people is that they think they can change the world.

We all want to be creative. We just don't want to be creative *like that*.

None of this used to matter very much. Children who persisted with wild and uncontrollable imaginings even after a good Victorian education could be packed off to the country to live with Uncle Eric, or sent to fight Napoleon, or locked up in the attic.

Things began to change at the beginning of the 20th century. It was at about this time, while Edison was tinkering around with electricity and Henry Ford was tinkering around with the Model A, that the very first notions of productivity were postulated by one Fredrick Winslow Taylor, the father of 'scientific management'. Taylor's astonishing idea, which to this day informs all our thinking about efficiency in the workplace, was that businesses could be substantially more productive, and hence more profitable, if they could identify and replicate the 'one best way' of organizing the various tasks required to manufacture any given widget.

The famous management guru Peter Drucker once wrote, 'I do not think it extravagant to consider Frederick Taylor as the one relevant social philosopher of this, our industrial civilisation'.

Armed with a newly invented stopwatch that could record units of time to the accuracy of a second, Taylor began to measure how long it took a worker with a broad flat shovel to unload a ton of iron ore into a foundry cart, and then compared it to another worker doing a similar job with a small pointy one. Whichever method was found to be most time efficient was recommended to management as the optimal procedure. These 'time-and-motion studies' were soon recognized around the industrial world as the defining approach to worker productivity.

Among the other eminently logical recommendations of scientific management was the principle that all tasks that required any thinking should be allocated upwards to the management class, while all tasks that could be routinized should be delegated down to 'the lazy oxen' on the factory floor.

One of Taylor's greatest admirers was Joseph Stalin who was so struck by scientific management that he went on to formulate several Five Year Plans for Soviet workers based on its principles.

History has given Taylor a less glowing legacy than Peter Drucker thinks he deserves. Today we find Taylorism distastefully mechanistic. But we should remind ourselves that it was Taylor who first suggested that workers be given occasional breaks from the production line after being able to prove scientifically that a short rest did wonders to restore their appetite for rivet-bolting.

Taylorism and the mass production methods of Fordism combined to give us the dominant paradigm of productivity in the 20th century, and with the help of people like Drucker, conspired to pulp a forest the size of Bolivia into books on management theory.

But an interesting thing began to happen towards the end of the century, the phenomenon that has come to be known as the rise of the creative class, widely celebrated in Richard Florida's eponymous book. For the first time, at least in the post industrial world, as more and more people were becoming so-called 'knowledge workers' and the creative industries were becoming increasingly attractive engines of profit and growth, managers were confronted with the unexpected challenge of having to squeeze more productivity out of the human imagination.

It was only then that the problem with creative people became anything more than a curious social phenomenon. It became a management problem.

Without that new-fangled stopwatch Frederick Taylor could not have converted scientific management from theory into practice. The distinguishing feature of Taylorism and subsequent theories of management throughout the 20th century have been characterized, above all else, by measurement – measurements of time, of mass, of efficiency, of skills, of productivity, of motivation, of units, of value, of targets and of every other facet of production that is amenable to measurement or for which a unit of measure could be invented.

It is common practice today to bundle several of these measurements together into KPIs, or key performance indicators, which, when combined together, become the measurements of growth, and hence, without too much deduction required, the measurement of how long you are likely to stay in your current job.

As a logical corollary to the advance of measurement into every aspect of the workplace, underlined by the obvious performance benefits that were beginning to accrue to practitioners of the 'one best way', a belief began to emerge among the measurers that things that couldn't be measured accurately were probably of little importance, and that things that couldn't be measured at all probably didn't exist.

Unsurprisingly, one of the many things that turned out to be somewhat tricky to measure, as the management consultants turned their attention to the booming creative industries, was the size and shape of creative talent. It seemed, frustratingly, that the value of ideas could not be measured until *after* they had been realized. Even more alarmingly the likelihood of someone coming up with a good idea could not be measured at all. These findings suggested, according to the corollary above, that creative talent was either less important than it appeared to be, or simply didn't exist at all.

For those who were already deeply suspicious of the value of creative people, this latter conclusion clearly gave scientific credence to the view that creativity was a commodity as widely distributed across the population as hair, teeth and 10 fingers. And yet, with an obstinacy that they had come to expect from so-called creative people, the de facto evidence that good ones produced better and more valuable ideas than bad ones continued to stare the measurers in the face.

The inexorable march of measurement had come face to face with the unyielding truth of creative performance.

The resultant clash was keenly felt in all of the creative industries, but no more so than in advertising, which is where I happened to find myself at the time. By then the insidious myth of creative equality had become firmly established, so there was no better place to witness the collision between Taylorism and creativity than in the gleaming corridors of one of the world's biggest advertising agencies.

Taylor had nothing at all to say about creativity so it is probably unfair to accuse him of causing the current catastrophe in the imaginative life of the planet. But it is abundantly clear, even from the most cursory reading of his recipe for a more productive world, that he would have lumped today's creative workers together with the lazy oxen of the smelting plants. There is no room in Taylorism for anyone other than the managers to have ideas. How he would have reacted, therefore, to the challenge of managing workers *for* their ideas is a matter for speculation.

This is not a book about advertising, but readers will forgive me if I draw on my experiences in that business to illustrate how, in Maslow's words, creative people 'get ground up in an organization'. If I had been a shoe designer or a music producer I would have drawn my examples from the fashion business or the music business. I have compared notes with creative people in other industries and it is clear that they are confronted with the same issues and the same challenges as those that began to beset Madison Avenue and Berkeley Square as the 20th century drew to a close.

But advertising would be a particularly good laboratory in which to study creativity suffocating to death even if I didn't have an intimate knowledge of its labyrinthine ways.

It's at the sharp end of the claws of commerce and at the tail end of those pursuits with pretensions of artistic integrity. The pressures are intense, the stakes are high, and the pickings are getting leaner by the day. Most creative people who work in ad agencies are salaried functionaries with little or no claim to the profits made by the agency owners, especially since the recent consolidation of the network agencies that has concentrated management power in three of four holding companies. The exceptions prove the rule. Those creative people who have been brilliant enough or lucky enough to get their names on the front door lead lives of fame and fortune. But it's a short list, and getting shorter: David Abbott, John Hegarty and, uh...

Meanwhile, the names of the great luminaries of the past – Leo Burnett, David Ogilvy, J. Walter Thompson, Bill Bernbach, Young and Rubicam, McCann Erikson – have all been subsumed into the faceless corporate monoliths with names as meaningless as Accenture, Altria, Consignia or Omnicom, as is the current fashion with companies who don't care much whether we know what they do or not. At least WPP still stands for something.

All of this has had the effect of disempowering the creative voice within agency management, relegating creative people to the factory floor of idea production. It's taken a while, but the proper division of labour has been restored, just the way Taylor would have wanted it.

Advertising draws the elite stormtroopers of capitalism, the marketing people, into hand-to-hand combat with the Bolsheviks of business, the advertising creatives. This is always fascinating to observe though it's definitely not for the squeamish. Here the clash between the venal and the visionary is illuminated in graphic, slow-motion digital HD as every ringing thrust and parry echoes into the bitter divide that separates them. The marketers fight under the banners of predictability, precedent and profitability, the three handmaidens of the great god of growth. The creatives fight under the ragged flags of chaos and lost causes, of insight and inspiration, of romance and rhapsody, and they serve no gods but their own.

Stop the movie and examine it carefully frame by frame and you'll see, cleverly concealed by the magic of smoke and mirrors, the leashes that restrain the creatives from delivering the fatal blows.

As desperate as they are not to lose these battles, the agencies can no longer afford to win them. That would mean firing the client, walking out of the room, and looking for one with the balls to back the agency's brilliance. It used to work like that, and still does with those agencies with reputations big enough to sustain the courage of their convictions. But for the most part, local agencies and local businesses aside, client/agency agreements are negotiated between the procurement managers of the multinational clients and the management heads of the network agencies in chilly, smoke-free offices at the top of tall, glass-clad buildings a long, long way from the blood and thunder of the battlefields. Increasingly, these contracts will have to be sanctioned by the agency holding companies who must ensure that the Chinese walls they build between competing clients in the same network alliance are at least as robust as the emperor's outer garments.

This has served to concentrate even more power in the hands of the global procurement managers who can now negotiate for sizeable discounts from their suppliers because of the huge volumes involved. Procurement managers, or buyers as they used to be called, don't make much of a distinction between chassis components and advertising ideas, as long as the price is right. The pressure to discount goods and services is manageable only if the holding companies themselves have the scale to cope. From their centralized point of view a small discount on a massive number can easily be distributed across three or four agency networks and their seven or eight hundred offices. Of course, more funds are needed for the central bureaucracy that has to manage the individual network profitability, which means that more money is needed to fund the bureaucracies and network headquarters. So by the time it gets down to the office level, let's say to the office manager in Bucharest, the margins for servicing the relevant multinational have all but evaporated.

The same corporate take-overs and mergers have happened across many of the global industry segments, and the corporate agglomerates that have emerged are faced with the same issues and opportunities. But for most of them there are still costs that can be wrung out of areas like logistics, distribution and increasing mechanization, and the cascading effect of the margin squeeze can be compensated for in the kind of production efficiencies that Taylor recommended.

As we have seen, Taylorism recommends a clear division of labour between thinkers and doers, or, more precisely, between jobs that demand discretionary skills and jobs that don't. This idea has found its way into the lexicon of contemporary management thinking under the clumsy banner of 'deskilling'.

You can apply deskilling to any job that can readily be broken down into several different routines, especially those in which the thinking role can easily be divorced from the doing role.

In the creative industries these strategies are not an option, though it's highly likely that there are some procurement managers out there with dreams of mechanizing the creative process. When your basic unit of production is the imagination of a single human being, the savings to be gained from deskilling come to a sudden and abrupt halt.

As Davis and Scase put it:

> . . . personal creative abilities are difficult to bureaucratise and are highly resistant to managerial attempts to "deskill". If . . . the development of modern industry is characterised by a transformation in the nature and organisation of work, such that the all-round skills of craft workers have been subdivided into specific tasks that can then be executed according to routine procedures by deskilled employees, this is difficult to achieve with the work of creative employees.

If this doesn't explain everything, it certainly explains a lot.

It explains, first of all, why advertising agencies that prize ideas above service are prepared to pay for brilliance, put up with the vagaries of the creative temperament, and resist the temptation to routinize the creative process. By valuing the unpredictable nature of creativity these agencies continue to produce astonishingly good work year after year, attracting clients who themselves prize ideas above service, and defraying thereby the loss of margin from procurement pressure.

It explains, by contrast, why those agencies that adopted the Taylorist agenda and succeeded in deskilling their creative employees must now rely on speed, lower margins and efficiency of service – especially through global network structures – to compete. And as long as there are enough clients out there who are prepared to settle for the workable in lieu of the wonderful, compete they will.

The commoditization of creativity also explains the growing popularity of 'integrated communications agencies'. By offering a menu of services that include web design, customer relationship management, direct marketing, database management, promotions, event marketing and other non-advertising communications techniques, these agencies can avoid altogether the risky business of coming up with ideas. Craft replaces creativity, and process replaces passion. For clients and agency managers thoroughly fed up with dealing with creative egos, this is deskilled heaven. It is also, as we shall discover in due course, the perfect recipe for the commercial bureaucracies that now dominate the other 14 sectors of the creative economy.

But every now and then one of these Taylorist companies will employ a creative person by mistake. He or she will have an idea – a good idea – and a frisson of unrest will ripple through the organization. A senior manager will stand up in a meeting and say, 'Why can't we have more of these?' And someone will be dispatched to find the culprit, and she will be obliged to explain where that idea came from and how the company could design a process that would encourage other people in the organization to have ideas like that.

But the culprit won't know what to say because the truth is that the idea came from nowhere, it had nothing to do with the work she was supposed to be doing, and it happened on a Sunday while she was painting the garage.

It turns out that the three worst places to have an idea are in an office, in a group and in a hurry.

CHAPTER 3

Two guys in a garage

One man alone can be pretty dumb sometimes, but for real bona fide stupidity, there ain't nothin' can beat teamwork.

Edward Abbey

Creativity is the production of novel and appropriate ideas by individuals or small groups.

Teresa Amabile

The history of ideas teaches a very simple lesson: that two guys in a garage will beat a multi-million dollar corporation ninety-nine times out of a hundred.

Wozniak and Jobs, Hewlett and Packard, Brin and Page, Zennstrom and Friis, Lennon and MacCartney, Wieden + Kennedy, Smith and Wesson, Watson and Crick: these are the ones that spring instantly to mind. There are the loners, of course, the countless artists, writers, composers, programmers, philosophers and mathematicians pursuing their solitary dreams. And then the visionaries who attracted extraordinary disciples and galvanized them to share their purpose: architects, engineers, entrepreneurs – Brunelleschi, Brunel, Benjamin Franklin, Bill Gates, Richard Branson, Robert Oppenheimer, Tim Berners-Lee.

*

In just six years, between 1876 and 1882, Thomas Edison's Menlo Park Laboratory in New Jersey managed to invent the phonograph, the telephone carbon transmitter, improvements to the telegraph and, of course, electric lighting. Thousands of other mechanical and electrical patents came out of the same workshop in the same period.

There's a replica of the laboratory at the Henry Ford Museum in Greenfield Village, Detroit, which gives a good idea of how Edison and his colleagues went about inventing things, described here by Richard Donkin of the *Financial Times*:

> They worked long hours, often late into the night, stopping occasionally for sessions of drinking and singing around the organ at the end of the room. It was an informal, collegiate arrangement.
>
> 'Hell, there ain't no rules in here. We're trying to accomplish something!' said Edison at the time.

Donkin goes on to contrast Edison's approach to innovation with the idea-stifling environments of contemporary business practice:

> The problem with innovation is that it is often sparked by thinking or ideas that occur outside daily working routines. Edison himself was fired from his job as a telegrapher at Western Union 'for not concentrating on his primary responsibilities and doing too much moonlighting'. The problem was that his bosses paid him to be a telegrapher whereas Edison was never happier than when he had an opportunity to experiment with ways of improving the technology . . .
>
> . . . 'Idea assassination' has become a favourite bloodsport in some companies. This is a fundamental problem for creativity consulting, no matter how good the processes available in the marketplace. While there are plenty of people at the top of large companies who understand the need for innovation, there will always be tension between this need and the daily operational demands of the business . . .
>
> As one contributor to the . . . seminar put it, 'You can infect companies with ideas for a time but they tend to have strong immune systems that soon respond to get rid of creative thinking.'
>
> So how can companies avoid this immune reaction? One way, said Margaret Exley of Mercer Delta, the consultants hosting the forum, was to nurture a new project in a protected environment away from the parent . . . Sometimes, she said, the same kind of protection needed to be extended to individual employees.

I remembered Maslow, and what he'd said about the problem of the 'lone wolf' in organizations. I remembered the 'Imagineer' I had met at Disney. And I remembered the story I had read about the tender to supply the American and British governments with what came to be known as the Joint Strike Fighter.

*

This was a pitch and a half. At stake was the biggest military contract of all time, the right to build the new jet fighter to replace the ageing fleet of F-16s, Harriers and other fighter planes that had been around since the 1950s or 1960s. The idea was to have a single platform to be shared by the various arms of the US DOD and the British Air Force, and to sort out the disastrous procurement mess that the US had got itself into post Korea. The two major contenders were cash-rich Boeing and the somewhat fragile Lockheed-Martin.

The brief was a nightmare. The US Navy needed a plane suitable for its carriers, with short take-off and landing capabilities and room enough for a massive payload. The US Air Force needed a supersonic fighter with a low radar profile. And the Marines and the British wanted vertical take-off and landing. More than anything else, the clients wanted affordable mass production of the approved design.

Several countries had vertical take-off prototypes, but only the British Harrier and its variants had any kind of proven reliability. This is what Boeing seized upon, spending billions on upgrading the Harrier design to maximum efficiency. The rest of the Boeing pitch went into demonstrating its considerable credentials for cost-efficient mass production.

Lockheed was on a hiding to nothing. They didn't have the money to follow the Boeing strategy on the Harrier, and they couldn't tell much of a story around production efficiencies. Only one option was left – to have an idea.

The Harrier owed its hovering ability to the brute force of its jet engines thrusting towards the ground at a 90° angle. This not only blazed massive holes in the tarmac, or whatever happened to be underneath the plane at the time, it called for some very delicate work from the pilot as the turbines swung upwards into their horizontal thrust position. So vulnerable was the Harrier during this tricky procedure that a carefully aimed cricket ball could knock it out of the sky.

Meanwhile, as they say in the classics, a couple of American university graduates had been working on this precise problem, writing a speculative paper suggesting that the thrust of the engines could possibly be directed back under the wings of the plane for more stability and control. The idea was crude and untested, but to the Lockheed engineer who stumbled across it, it was the best chance they had.

Lockheed had enough sense and experience to know that ideas like these needed special protection. And they had just the place to do it.

Popular Mechanics tells the story of Lockheed's legendary 'Skunk Works' in riveting *Boy's Own* prose:

> The generals had botched it. Years before Pearl Harbor they had sneered at German plans for a new type of high-speed aircraft engine. Now in 1943, as the Allies began preparing for the D-Day invasion of France, intelligence reports revealed that the Nazis were ramping up production of a blistering fast fighter, a plane powered by the very same type of propellerless 'jet' engine they had rejected. The War Department needed a miracle airplane and turned to the one man it could count on to deliver it in six months, Clarence L. Johnson. At age 33, 'Kelly' Johnson had already established his reputation. His newest design, the twin-tailed, 400-mph P-38 Lightning, was the most maneuverable fighter – and arguably the most beautiful airplane – in the Allied force. To counter the new German threat, the War Department wanted Kelly to build a plane that could fly 200 mph faster, literally pressing its nose against the sound barrier. The scrappy, one-time dockworker who was often described as W.C. Fields without a sense of humor, knew exactly what to do: He rented a circus tent.
>
> Kelly pitched his tent on the sprawling Lockheed Aircraft complex in Burbank, Calif. Officially his shop was the Lockheed Advanced Development Projects Unit. The stench from a nearby plastic factory that wafted into the tent was so vile one of the engineers began answering the phone 'skonk works,' after the backwoods still in the then popular L'il Abner comic strip. Despite these less-than-ideal working conditions, Kelly's team of 23 design engineers and 30 shop mechanics delivered Lulu Belle, the prototype for the P-80 Shooting Star, in only 143 days. America had entered the jet age, more than a month ahead of schedule.

There are a few important things worth noting here. The first is the presence of an individual with enough of a reputation and sufficient strength of character to defy the status quo. Kelly carved out his own experimental space, outside of the corporate system, away from the concerns of the production line and beyond the reach of management. He would not allow anyone from outside the Skunk Works to communicate with anyone inside except through him. And he himself would only deal with specially designated individuals from Lockheed management – or from his client, the US Department of Defense. Kelly chose his own staff, set his own deadlines, and managed the process the way he saw fit.

> Kelly made no secret of how he worked his magic. He insisted his engineers get dirty on the shop floor. Working a lot like guys building hot rods in their garages, engineers and production mechanics created the hottest planes ever to cut through the air. This informal process produced the most important planes of the 20th century, including the Mach 2 F-104 Starfighter, U-2 and SR-71 spyplanes, and the stealthy F-117A. The Skunk Works' contributions to the creation of the F-22 Raptor and Joint Strike Fighter ensure its legacy in the shape of the Air Force of the 21st century. And its experimental stealth ship Sea Shadow means the Skunk Works will leave its mark on future navies as well.

Creativity works best when individuals or small groups are empowered by patronage. Sometimes patronage is bestowed. Sometimes it has to be demanded.

> The war ended before the P-80, later designated the F-80, would fire its first shot in anger, against Soviet MiGs in Korea. Eventually Lockheed would build about 9000. Kelly's team moved to more permanent quarters, in a windowless bomber-production hangar. The foul smell that inspired the design team's name became a memory but the name lingered. At least until the lawyers for the L'il Abner comic strip caught wind of it. In deference to the comic strip, the 'skonk works' was rechristened the Skunk Works.

This is American creativity at its best – practical and productive. A small group of 'muckers' led by an obsessive, headstrong visionary. *Popular Mechanics* draws the obvious comparison: 'Whatever the spelling, Kelly's Skunk Works is to aviation what Edison's Menlo Park was to electricity, a place where the daily pursuit of the impossible produces technologies indistinguishable from magic.'

This was NASA in the late 1960s, ordered by Kennedy to put a man on the moon before the Russians. And it was any number of small, aggressive companies, led by entrepreneurs with a passion for their subject, which built the American dream.

Passion is vital. So is challenge. Freedom to explore, sufficient resources, enough time. We shall see these ingredients of organizational creativity recurring again and again. And the power of patronage. For among the many other miraculous things it does for creativity, patronage allows for failure:

> That the Skunk Works thrived in those early years, let alone flourished to reach middle age, is all the more remarkable when you realize that its second and third major projects, the Saturn cargo plane and the XFV-1 vertical-takeoff naval fighter, were 'absolute clunkers,' according to Ben Rich, Kelly's protege and hand-picked successor. 'The open secret in the company was that Kelly walked on water in the adoring eyes of CEO Robert Gross,' Rich would later recall in his memoirs.

*

With well over 20 billion dollars at stake in the pitch against Boeing, Lockheed turned once more to the Skunk Works. The two young graduate students were ensconced among the best mechanical engineers in the world, given the workshop of their dreams, and challenged to make their idea a reality.

Now history, with a knowing smile, opens the sealed envelope.

Lockheed won the contract not only because they had a better idea, but also because they had the good sense and the experience to know that good ideas are best managed a long way away from the idea-assassins of corporate headquarters.

*

Walt Disney was a cartoonist first and a businessman second. You have to see those early Disney cartoons to remind yourself what the name stood for, because right now it's hard to tell.

Mike Vance, creative trainer, management consultant and author of the famously predictable *Think Out of the Box*, was a close associate of the Disney brothers in those days. His stories of Walt's enthusiasm for novelty, and his determination to make manifest an extraordinary vision of living entertainment for the American family, resound with the familiar echoes of the Skunk Works and Menlo

Park. Like Edison and Kelly, he had passion in spades, the charisma of a true leader, a small self-motivated group of highly inventive people, and the freedom from financial anxiety – courtesy of brother Roy – to make things happen.

When you visit EPCOT now it's difficult to believe that it was intended to be anything other than a collection of second-rate rides built around national clichés, though the nightly fireworks in the lake are truly spectacular. But Disney named it the Experimental Prototype Community of Tomorrow in all sincerity. He genuinely believed that it would become a model of how different people could live together in peace, harmony and fun. That's how big his dream was.

I came across Mike Vance on a company visit to the Disney Institute in Orlando. We were there to drink from the great well of Disney creativity, and Mike Vance was thrown in as an obligatory seminar. His anecdotal stuff about working with Walt, and subsequently with Steve Jobs, was fascinating in a celebrity gossip kind of way. And he had a great schtick with his Kitchen of the Mind, a creative living space with telescopes, pianos and easels. But on everything else he was as dull as ditch-water or just plain wrong. If you're ever looking for a dictionary of creative clichés get yourself a copy of his awful *Raise the Bar*, a follow-up to *Think Out of the Box*, co-written by Diane Deacon.

I had this nasty feeling about Disney even before the Mike Vance seminar. It seemed to me that the company's capacity for good ideas had been frozen along with Walt's body. I hoped that the trip to the Institute would prove me wrong. We were going to meet the creative director of the Disney creative department. And we were going to meet one of their famous Imagineers.

I was pretty excited. We were allowed a brief glimpse of Disney animators at work. They looked like Koreans in a shoe factory. Oh well, it can't all be fun.

We weren't allowed into the creative department as such but the creative director gave us a PowerPoint presentation of its activities. These consisted of designing Winnie-the-Pooh pencil cases, Winnie-the-Pooh erasers, Winnie-the-Pooh satchels, Winnie-the-Pooh strollers, Winnie-the-Pooh EZ-sip drinking cups, Winnie-the-Pooh stationery, Winnie-the-Pooh Interactive Bedtime Books with Sound Effects and, most exciting of all, the Winnie-the-Pooh Toddler Fashion Range. They were doing the same with Tarzan and Hercules.

Later we were taken to a large meeting room and briefed about the Imagineers, the people responsible for the really big ideas. We were told that they lived and worked off-site in an independent creative unit away from the day-to-day hustle and bustle of the resort itself. Menlo Park, I thought! Skunk Works!

The guy doing the briefing, a young good-looking man in a smart suit, was at pains to point out that the Imagineers were rather different. He seemed embarrassed, almost apologetic. He warned us that the particular Imagineer we were about to meet may not be able to explain himself properly, and that we were to refer any questions we had back to him, the briefing guy, not to the Imagineer himself.

Everyone who works at Disney is young and good-looking, and they all have exceptionally white teeth. All employees, including the garbage collectors, are called 'cast members', a designation meant to remind them that every day is another show and that they all have to play their part. I gathered from our briefing guy that the Imagineer was not a 'cast member', but a different kind of animal with a very different kind of job. I could hardly wait.

He had bleary eyes and a beard, and was wearing a Black Sabbath T-shirt and shorts. Think Comic Strip Guy in *The Simpsons*. Gasp! He didn't have a PowerPoint presentation and he mumbled a lot. Every now and then the briefing guy in the smart suit would interrupt and clarify.

The Imagineer told us that he and his colleagues were charged with thinking up ideas for the great new rides, interactive shows and other theme park attractions. For example, for the past two or three years he personally had been working on a ride that replicated the thrill of racing very, very fast. But he had run into a lot of regulatory and safety issues, and the suits were beginning to get cold feet. He was about to explain just how absurd the objections to his new ride had been when the guy at the back interrupted sharply, 'Tell them about the buses!'

The Imagineer sighed and looked down at his feet. Sometimes, he said, they had to think of clever ways to organize the theme park. Like, say it was raining, and, like, people had to have umbrellas. Well, all the umbrellas kept on ending up at the other end of the park. So we thought of, uh, putting umbrellas on all the buses so that wherever you were, like, if it rained, you would still be able to get an umbrella . . . sort of.

'How cool is that!' shouted the guy in the suit as he led the Imagineer from the room.

*

The word 'Imagineer' was apparently invented by the Union Carbide company during the heydays of its innovations in insulating materials, many years before it became synonymous with corporate greed and inhumane exploitation of workers. No one seems to be sure how Disney got hold of it and made it their own, though Disney's reputation for employing the sharpest copyright lawyers in the world may have had something to do with it.

According to the official Disney website Walt had handpicked the best creative talents in the organization in the early 1950s to help him design and build 'Disneyland Park' in Anaheim, California. This group, initially known as WED, after Walter Elias Disney, was later renamed Walt Disney Imagineering in 1984. By the end of the 1990s the group was expanded to include the company's property developers and real estate managers, bringing the number of people in this supposedly elite creative unit to around two thousand. That's a clue to why the history of Disney after Walt's death in 1966 reads like *The Decline and Fall of the Roman Empire*.

You can't argue with Disney's success as a global business, but if you read through the list of innovative projects in 'Technological Milestones' and 'Current Endeavors' on the company website it's difficult not to conclude that they ran out of ideas at about they same time they were putting Walt on ice.

The Mickey Mouse cartoons, *Snow White*, *Pinocchio*, *Fantasia*, Disneyland, the monorail, the 'animatronics' of the Enchanted Tiki Room and the inspiration for EPCOT all had Disney's sure personal touch, hilarity on the edge of horror, and a dark and mysterious magic.

Between 1963 and Space Mountain in 1975 there is not a single technological or creative achievement worth noting. And apart from the addition of 3D film photography for Magic Journeys (1982), Honey, I Shrunk the Audience (1995) and It's Tough to be a Bug (1998), the period from 1975 to the present is characterized, not by innovation, but by expansion into France, Japan, China and into the cruise ship industry. 'SpaceQuest' is mooted as being the next big thing.

Rolling out identical theme parks in Paris and Hong Kong and branding a couple of cruise ships doesn't strike one as an ineffable act of creation. And if you've ever been to a DisneyQuest you'll be hard pressed to tell the difference between it and a games arcade except, of course, for the ubiquitous presence of Winnie-the-Pooh.

It's clear that somewhere along the line the Disney passion for fun and entertainment was subsumed by the ideology of growth for growth's sake. And I suspect that the ageing bleary-eyed Imagineer was one of the few people who knew it and mourned it.

*

When the founder of a successful company dies or moves on to other things, the challenge for the next generation of leadership is to find a way to sustain and develop the original values, ideas and aspirations of the pioneer in response to a changing marketplace and a changing world: that is, to evolve the founder's brand of leadership in a way that remains true to the source of his or her primary inspiration while remaining relevant to new customers, new tastes and new social and economic arrangements. This is difficult enough for most companies to do at all, and only a handful have been able to do it well. So when Ford got into trouble they brought back a Ford, when Apple went astray they brought back Steve Jobs, and when Disney began to come off the rails they brought back Roy.

In creative sector companies the difficulty is compounded by the unique nature of the founding personality, which is invariably too complex to codify into a mission statement or an induction handbook.

The difference between first generation and second generation leadership has very little to do with skill, training, qualifications, competence, emotional intelligence, energy or any of the other qualities of effective management that HR experts and management consultants are so fond of touting, as the CEO merry-go-round has so vividly demonstrated. Indeed, on paper at least, the second generation manager is usually more skilled, better trained and more generally competent than the pioneer.

People like Walt Disney are successful because they love what they do. Second generation managers, if they love anything at all, tend to love the business more than they love what the business does. That's the difference. And it's as big a difference as drawing *Steamboat Willie* by hand and calculating the number of 'Steamboat Willie' pencil sharpeners you can sell in Taiwan.

*

Later that night, when the fireworks at EPCOT were over, three colleagues of mine – a Colombian girl, a Peruvian and a Venezuelan – and myself ganged together in search of Marlboros. It was dark, and most visitors were heading towards the exits. There were no cigarettes in America or France but we thought we'd probably find some in the pub in England. We got there as they were closing up for the night only to be told, in a voice as loaded with scorn as it was with racist undertones, that the sale of tobacco was against Disney policy.

We hurried around the lake towards the exit but, in nicotine-starved confusion, took the long way round. By the time we reached the giant silver geodesic ball, the gates had closed. We knocked on the doors of Canada, Norway and Morocco but to no avail. We decided that Mexico would be more sympathetic, but the staff had either gone home or were simply refusing to answer our cries of *Ayudanos*! Then the Peruvian spotted a light and some movement in China. We rushed over to the red wooden palisades and, *uno*, *dos*, *tres*, shouted again, in unison. An old Chinese woman opened the door with tentative suspicion. She was so perfectly stereotypical that I was convinced she was an animatronic. Even as she led us grumpily through the empty halls and the kitchens to the back lot I listened carefully to the sound of her joints, expecting the mechanical click-whirr of the Tiki birds.

Behind the facades of the nations of EPCOT, in a world without national borders, in tents and trailers and trucks and makeshift caravans, a peculiarly experimental community was indeed thriving. We saw five Mickey Mice, a few Goofys and several troupes of actors and actresses in face paint and national costumes, all in various states of undress. There were cleaners and cooks and sweepers and painters and electricians and drivers and wardrobe people, and more dwarves than I've ever seen in one place. Interestingly, despite the clogs, the geisha costumes, the kilts, the berets and the Mountie uniforms, everyone was speaking Spanish, most of it in giveaway Mexican sing-song.

Unlike the beautiful, shiny-toothed 'cast members' that populated the daytime world of Disney, this experimental community was comprised of people who looked as though they had been attending a massive fancy dress party in the Zocalo in Mexico City.

The first Mickey Mouse was a woman from Guadalajara. She had broken teeth, and four children at home. She explained that there were only two Mickey Mice that actually spoke. The rest, like her, did the casual meet-and-greet stuff at the various parks. They had strict instructions that two Mickey Mice never be seen together in case the kids twigged that there wasn't only one, which explained why it had taken Mickey so long to arrive at the official signing of our Disney Institute certificates earlier that afternoon.

She shared her pack of Marlboro with us and told us that the heat inside the costume was unbearable, but the money was good.

Someone was making a fire behind a caravan. I could smell chipotle. A young Puerto Rican dwarf invited the four of us, together with the Mickey from

Guadalajara, to share a few bottles of Dos Equis. We sat on fold-up chairs and talked about the Great American Divide long into the hot Florida night.

In deference to my poor Spanish they spoke in English for the first half an hour or so. But after a few beers the emotional temperature began to climb and they lapsed back into their native tongue to rage against the hypocrisy of the Land of Opportunity where they were simultaneously welcome workers and unwanted aliens.

The Colombian went to sleep on my shoulder. She smelled of dust and sweetcorn.

I thought about Walt Disney, the man, and wondered what he would have made of the syrupy confection that his name had become and I wondered if any-one in the company today would have the guts to kill Bambi's mother the way Walt did.

There was a darkness there that the makers of *The Lion King* didn't get. It was darkness that could only have come from a deeply personal vision of loss and despair, from one of those nightmares that haunts you until it is expressed.

Great leaps of the imagination are always personal, never collective.

They are always rooted in compulsion; always reclaimed from darkness and managed into light.

I thought about the barriers we create to keep out the things we hate and fear, unaware that they're the very things we need to save us from sterility and death.

> How else could it have occurred to man to divide the cosmos, on the analogy of day and night, summer and winter, into a bright day-world and a dark night-world peopled with fabulous monsters, unless he had the prototype of such a division in himself, in the polarity between the conscious and the invisible and unknowable unconscious?

That was Jung. And there was that flimsy Chinese wall, the only thing separating the clean white consciousness of corporate America from the fabulous monsters of its dreams.

Someone, somewhere, had turned off the darkness.

CHAPTER 4

21st century snake-oil

... ideas and beliefs are the same as hands: instruments for coping. An idea has no greater metaphysical stature than, say a fork. When your fork proves inadequate to the task of eating soup, it makes little sense to argue about whether there is something inherent in the nature of forks or something inherent in the nature of soup that accounts for the failure. You just reach for a spoon.

Louis Menand, *The Metaphysical Club*, describing John Dewey's version of pragmatism

The practise of Americans leads their minds to other habits, to fixing the standard of their judgement in themselves alone. As they perceive that they succeed in resolving without assistance all the little difficulties which their practical life presents, they readily conclude that everything in the world may be explained, and that nothing in it transcends the limits of their understanding. Thus they fall to denying what they cannot comprehend; which leaves them but little faith for whatever is extraordinary and an almost insurmountable distaste for whatever is supernatural.

Alexis de Toqueville, *Democracy in America*, 1840

I have decided to lay the blame for the worldwide crisis in creativity squarely at the door of Alex Osborn. But I do so with some reluctance; I know he was only trying to help.

Alex Osborn was the 'O' in the acronym of the global advertising agency BBDO, named for Batten, Barton, Durstine & Osborn Inc. His highly influential book, *Applied Imagination*, was published in 1953. In it he described a revolutionary approach to promoting creativity in organizations, a technique so universally embraced that it is now common currency in the English language. Yes, the 'brainstorm'.

Those of you who are impressed by this sort of thing should also know that a certain Prosper Vanosmael, Professor Emeritus of English at the University of Antwerp in Belgium, credited Alex Osborn with 'breaking the 2000 year old paradigm that creativity could not be deliberately developed'.

As founder and chairman of the Creative Education Foundation, an organization dedicated to furthering research and education in the application of creativity, he is widely regarded as the godfather of American creative studies, or certainly that part of it, at the very least, that believes that creative problem solving is the only part of creativity that really matters. He is also, by implication, directly responsible for the worldwide boom in creativity training that swept the world after the Second World War.

You can see immediately, on this last count alone, how much Osborn has to answer for. In the pages that follow you will also get to see how brainstorming has become such an effective management tool for exterminating ideas before they are born, and how Osborn's ill-founded belief that creativity can be taught has blighted the imaginative possibility of growth through innovation for companies, organizations and institutions in every field of endeavour, in all of the developed nations of the world, for more than half a century.

At the heart of this discussion is the crucial distinction that must be made between 'creativity' and 'creative problem solving'. In support of my view that they are two entirely different, mutually exclusive modes of thought and behaviour I will turn to the foremost authorities in the field of creativity research. As difficult and tiresome as this may be for some readers, I am aware that nothing short of the most detailed and rigorous analysis of the available literature will suffice to erase from popular belief the many dangerous assumptions that have arisen from the easy confusion of the two.

The point of departure could hardly be clearer or more fundamental. The American school of creative problem solving believes that *ideas do not, cannot and should not emerge from the unconscious mind or from unconscious processes.* This view not only abjures the unconscious as a source of inspiration, it denies the validity or usefulness of ideas that do not emerge from a fully conscious, rational process of deduction.

If this strikes you as just a touch insane, here's Osborn on the subject:

Daydreaming is the most common use of non-creative imagination. Sometimes called reverie, this is for some of us the usual form of our so-called thinking. It takes less than no effort. We merely let our imaginations join hands with our memories and run here and there and everywhere – without design and without direction, except as set by our prejudices, our desires, or our fears.

Doctor Josephine Jackson warns that daydreaming may become unhealthy when, 'instead of turning a telescope on the world of reality – as positive imagination does – this negative variety refuses even to look with the naked eye.'

With undiluted approval Osborn then quotes Victor Wagner describing daydreams as 'the rat-holes of escape from the stubborn realities of the workaday world'.

And then this extraordinary statement: 'But with children, daydreaming is natural and is less harmful than with grownups. The young gain innocent pleasure from merely imagining their desires to be gratified. But when this habit carries on into later life, such reverie is almost sure to grow into vicious phantasy.'

Like masturbation, one must assume.

*

Contrast Osborn with Joseph Campbell:

The unconscious sends all sorts of vapours, odd beings, terrors and deluding images up into the mind – whether in dream, broad daylight, or insanity; for the material kingdom, beneath the floor of the comparatively neat little dwelling that we call consciousness, goes down into the unexplored Aladdin cave.

There, not only jewels but also dangerous jinn abide: the inconvenient or resisted psychological powers that we have not thought or dared to integrate into our lives. And they may remain unexplored, or on the other hand, some chance word, the smell of a landscape, the taste of a cup of tea, or the glance of any eye may touch a magic spring, and these dangerous messengers begin to appear in the brain.

These are 'dangerous' because they threaten the fabric of the security into which we have built ourselves and our family.

But they are fiendishly fascinating too, for they carry keys that open the whole realm of the desired and feared adventure of the discovery of the self.

Destruction of the world that we have built and in which we live, and of ourselves within it; but then a wonderful reconstruction, of the bolder, cleaner, more spacious and fully human life – that is the lure, the promise and terror, of these disturbing night visitants from the mythological realm that we carry within.

Freud believed that creative expression was a way of sublimating the excess energies of the id, of resolving inner conflicts relating to sex and aggression in socially acceptable ways. Children play fantasy games as a way of dealing with the unnameable terrors of the adult world. Adults – healthy ones at least – use creative expression to deal with the unnameable terrors of their unconscious minds.

His famous dissertation on the creativity of da Vinci spawned a generation of artistic and literary critics who believed you could trace just about anything a creative person did to problems in their sex lives. This was always interesting, but seldom helpful.

Thankfully, this kind of pop analysis has now been discredited, not only by the post-modernists, but most importantly by the neo-Freudians themselves.

While the 'car-as-penis-extension school' of psychoanalysis has matured into richer and broader understandings of the role of the unconscious in both psychopathology and everyday behaviour, the neo-Freudian approach to creativity has been undermined by theorists bent on sanitizing the creative process. And they won't be happy until the door to Aladdin's cave is permanently sealed.

You can hear the welding guns at work in this paragraph from M.A. Collins and T.M. Amabile, even if it's tinged with some regret.

Although the psychodynamic approach has suggested a number of motives that may lead people to be creative, these ideas have been somewhat tangential to the development of more mainstream perspectives on motivation and creativity. Rather, the predominant line of theoretical and empirical work has arisen from the belief that creativity is motivated by the enjoyment and satisfaction that a person derives from engaging in the creative activity.

Bzzzz, frazzle, sp-sp-spitt-tt and the acrid stench of acetylene.

Amabile is undoubtedly the world's foremost authority on creativity in the workplace. Her research into creative motivation and her analysis of the organizational factors that stifle creativity are seminal to this book. But here she has neatly side-stepped the hazardous minefield of the subjective experience of the creative process, preferring to leave it to those prepared to tangle with Jung's fabulous monsters.

I am now going to make an outrageous generalization, a generalization so extreme, so ill-informed and so calumnious that I suspect I'll never ever be invited to the annual dinner of the American Association for Psychoanalysis. But no one else is going to say it, so I guess it's down to me. And here it is:

I don't think the Americans got Freud the way the Europeans did.

There.

Europe saw the id writ large. On European soil, in European homes, in European souls and in European nightmares. You couldn't repress it after that. You couldn't tidy it away, sweep it under the carpet, deodorize it. The stench of pure evil lingered long in the sewers and the salons, from Brighton to Belgrade, from Madrid to Moscow. You can still smell it in the streets of Budapest, in the St Petersburg subways, in the stations of Paris, in the Tuscan air, in the streets of Brussels – just a hint, a skin of molecules on cold stone walls.

The first time this generation of Americans saw evil was on September 11, 2001. 'Why do they hate us?' asked *Time* magazine. Instead of looking in the mirror Bush turned it into a battle between good guys and bad guys.

The point of all this isn't whether you believe in the gospel according to Sigmund or whether you believe they're the unhinged ravings of a sex-obsessed pervert determined to corrupt motherhood and apple pie.

Only one thing matters here and that's whether the idea of an unconscious mind teeming with the dark aspirations of our primal selves is in any way useful to our understanding of the creative process. Or, put another way, is it possible to have really good ideas without having to trespass into the shadows of the mind where the lights of conscious awareness cannot shine?

Clearly not if your definition of creativity, like Alex Osborn's, is confined to solving problems by using your head.

Should we locate the outlet of the factory's wastewater upstream or downstream of its clean water inlet? How can we get nurses to remember when to administer a patient's medicine? How can we make more profits without squeezing more hours from our underpaid workers? How do you join up these nine dots with just four lines without lifting your pencil?

He's absolutely right – you don't have to explore the deepest rat-holes of your psyche to come up with answers to these challenges. You may need some imagination, you may even have to use some intelligence, but usually a modicum of common sense will do just fine.

The Simpsons wasn't the solution to a problem. Nor was the Mona Lisa. Velcro, Google and the internet were solutions to problems we never knew we had.

We use intelligence to solve problems. When we solve problems in very interesting and novel ways we describe the process as imaginative, suggesting that some sort of inspiration was involved. Which in turn suggests that imagination is the very clever part of intelligence.

The entire creativity industry is built on the sandy soils of this premise – that is, that if we could learn to access this very clever part of our intelligence called the imagination we would all be very creative people.

It's difficult to estimate the size of the creativity training business but I'd hazard a guess that it's somewhere up there in the billions. Put 'creativity training' into Google and you get 49 300 000 results. Put in 'creativity training companies' and you get 25.9 million. Put in 'creativity course' and you get 58.4 million. Put in 'creative skills' and you get a whopping 125 million.

Put in 'mathematical skills' and you get a miserable 35 million results.

Mathematics can be taught – that is, you can teach people techniques for approaching and solving mathematical problems. Some people will learn more quickly than others will. Most people will get past addition, subtraction, multiplication and division with some degree of competence. Some will get through geometry and quadratic equations. A few will embrace calculus. One will end up solving Fermat's theorem.

You can induce pretty easily from this that proficiency in mathematics will reflect with some accuracy the shape of the intelligence Bell curve of the general population, with its bulging middle flattening out to the baseline on both left and right extremes. The assiduous study of maths by the whole population might help to push the mathematics proficiency curve along towards the right-hand side of the baseline as everyone develops better skills in the subject. Or it might expand the northeastern side of the bulge as brighter students find themselves able to progress more rapidly towards higher levels of mathematical competence. Whatever it does, it's not going to change the shape or position of the underlying *intelligence* Bell curve of the population.

You could, of course, teach the population how to answer IQ tests. That would undoubtedly improve the average scores, pushing the mean IQ from, say, 100 to 110. Once again, though, you couldn't credibly quote the improved figures as evidence that everyone had suddenly got smarter in any meaningful way.

Cross-cultural studies of IQ tests prove that some populations are better at answering typical IQ questions than others, results that have led to all sorts of notoriously chauvinistic conclusions. Moreover, the theoretical possibility of designing IQ tests that are entirely free of cultural bias remains moot. No one working in the field would claim that it's an exact science, but it's pretty much universally accepted now, in both academic and popular circles, that IQ tests measure something that correlates very highly with what we understand as intelligent behaviour.

We readily accept, even in these politically correct days, that some people are brighter than others and there's pretty much nothing that can be done about it after a certain age. We try hard to make stupid people feel as though they are not so stupid, and in some countries we try even harder to make very intelligent people feel as though they are not so intelligent.

We design our schools systems around what we know about the effect of nurture on maximizing the raw material of nature, and we try as hard as we possibly can to channel the resulting product, the incipient adult, into vocations appropriate to the level of intellectual development of the individual, while trying not to make it too obvious that we are doing so.

No one any longer campaigns for eugenics programmes to weed out the dimwitted. We have learned to embrace the differences and celebrate the diversity of the idiosyncratic hands dealt out by fate. And we concede that only the cruellest of dystopias – Cambodia under Pol-Pot or China under Mao – would wish it otherwise.

The unfortunate fact that some people are less intelligent than others has not given rise to a multi-billion dollar industry of consultants and intelligence experts claiming to be able to teach people to be smarter than they are. If there was any evidence at all suggesting that you could raise someone's IQ in a three-day workshop you could be pretty sure that every man and his dog would be clamouring for a slice of the global gazillion dollar training pie.

The fields in which we apply our intelligence are called domains. Electrical engineering is a domain skill. Software development is a domain skill. Operating a DVD player is a domain skill. Learning to paint in watercolours is a domain skill. These are things that can be taught, that bring rewards with application, that we use at work and that we develop our careers around. Several aspects of the advertising business require good domain skills. How to write a brief, how to interpret consumer research, how to use Photoshop, how to present ideas to clients, how to restrain yourself from strangling brand managers. Creativity is not a domain skill.

Improving your domain skills improves your competence and makes you more effective at what you do. We become professionals or specialists in our field by devoting ourselves to furthering our domain knowledge. If you want to be a rocket scientist the best thing to do is to study rocket science. If you want to be a fireman the best thing to do is to join the fire brigade. But what do you do if you want to be creative?

If creativity were about applying one's imagination to solve problems you could go on a problem solving course by signing up to one of the 158 million workshops that teach you how to join a grid of nine dots with four straight lines without lifting your pencil from the page. Soon you will become proficient. You will be able to balance a knife and a fork on top of a bottle at dinner parties. You will be able, instantly, to get your head around problems like the following . . .

Can you poke your head through a hole as big as the one made by touching the tip of your index finger to the tip of your thumb? Easy, touch the tip of the index finger of your right hand to the tip of your right thumb, place the circle thus formed flush to your forehead and with the tip of your left index finger poke your head through the hole. You have passed the lateral thinking test with flying colours. Soon you will be running a de Bono course in Vietnam. You are well on your way to becoming a creative genius.

We know that there is very little we can do about improving our intelligence beyond cheating on the IQ test. Yet we persist in imagining that we can enhance our creativity by disengaging the wooden ball at the end of the string from the spiral wire in the plastic box.

There is a rightful place for problem solving techniques and it is to be found in the new curricular of thinking skills that some of the more imaginative countries are using to accelerate learning in there schools. South Africa and Venezuela are notable examples of these. The Flexi-Think! Programme developed by Debby Evans and Belle Wallace is a brilliant example of this type of meta-learning, designed to enhance the new outcomes-based educational philosophy for South African children faced with the complex challenges of post-apartheid society.

Thinking skills programmes like these will undoubtedly help to equip next generation students with useful strategies for gathering information, adapting to new domains and being able to look at problems in different ways.

But inevitably you will find in the language of thinking skills the word 'creative' being used interchangeably with 'problem solving ability' as though they are one and the same thing. Indeed, this intellectual laziness, extraordinarily enough, characterizes even the most deliberate academic research into the field. R.S. Nickerson in his abstract entitled 'Enhancing Creativity' acknowledges the lack of clarity surrounding this issue.

> The relationship between creativity and problem solving is a very close one in the minds of many investigators. Guilford (1964) has argued that the terms refer to essentially the same mental phenomena. Some investigators have taken the position that creativity is a special form of problem solving.

Nickerson attempts to clarify the difference:

> I see the question of the relationship of the question between creativity and problem solving as dependent to a large degree on how one conceives of problem solving. If one's conception of problem solving is sufficiently broad to include solving problems algorithmically or by the application of well-known or memorized procedures, then

some instances of problem solving would be seen as creative, but not all. If one recognizes as instances of true problem solving only those that require some original thinking, then, by definition, all problem solving is creative.

And here are Runco and Sakamoto from *Experimental Studies of Creativity*:

Since not all problems require creativity for their solution, we can say that not all creativity involves problem solving. Problem solving may be a special kind of creativity, or creativity may be a special kind of problem solving. Both views can be found in the literature.

Hmmm . . .

Runco and Sakamoto point out that 'the most commonly used dependent measures in the experimental research on creativity seem to involve some kind of problem solving, perhaps because when problems are administered it is relatively easy to operationalize success'.

That's more like it. The point being that it's easier to tell whether a problem has been solved or not than to tell whether someone has just produced a great work of art or written a brilliant poem, which automatically biases the authors of creative psychometric tests to load them with problem solving type questions.

Runco and Sakamoto again:

Just as poor written examinations contain only questions concerning material that is easily described in writing, so too poor experimental research examines only the kinds of creativity that are easy to assess (e.g. problem solving) and ignores the other expressions of creativity.

If creativity testing is really measuring problem solving rather than creativity of the you-know-it-when-you-see-it variety, it's hardly surprising that the popular conception of creativity has more to do with the joining up of dots with a pencil rather than with, say, how Coleridge wrote 'Kubla Khan'. This point is seminal.

Problem solving is easier to measure. Problem solving does not have to rely on theories of the unconscious for proof of validity. Problem solving does not have to explore the rat holes of daydreaming. Problem solving does not have to acknowledge the existence of The Other. Problem solving is not subject to aesthetic judgements. Problem solving does not have a conscience. And, most important of all, problem solving is useful, i.e. instrumental.

A defining part of the legacy of positivism, empiricism and pragmatism – with its reductionist apogee in the behaviourism of B.F. Skinner – is the need for measurement. There can be no science without measurement, no engineering, no medicine, no commerce, no technology. If you can't measure it, it probably doesn't exist.

In this context, the impulse to define creativity through measurement – psychometrics, in other words – is unsurprising. The unfortunate fact that the psychometric approach has been unsuccessful in its attempt to pin down and quantify the precise variables of the creative temperament has secured the place of problem solving as the default component of creative testing. If you take away the only thing you can measure, the entire science deflates into a crumpled and embarrassing heap. So we're either missing some vital but elusive point, or creativity doesn't exist.

There are ways of studying creativity other than through psychometrics.

The psychodynamic model, which began so promisingly with Freud and Jung, found itself isolated from the mainstream of scientific psychology as structuralism, functionalism and behaviourism began to dominate the corridors and laboratories of the psychology establishment.

Freud's view, that artists produce creative work 'as a way to express their unconscious wishes in a publicly acceptable fashion', was further developed by Kris, Kubie and others. But, as Sternberg explains:

> . . . the psychodynamic approach and other early work on creativity relied almost exclusively on case studies of eminent creators. This methodology has been criticized because of the difficulty of measuring proposed theoretical constructs (such as primary process thought) and the amount of selection and interpretation that can occur in a case study (Weisberg, 1993). Although there is nothing a priori wrong with case-study methods, the emerging scientific psychology valued controlled, experimental methods. Thus, both theoretical and

methodological issues served to isolate the study of creativity from mainstream psychology.

The cognitive approach examines mental models of creativity and attempts to replicate them in computer simulations. The good thing about this approach is that it is soon very likely to yield software for solving problems, rendering the entire oeuvre of creativity training from Osborn through de Bono and van Oech entirely obsolete. But as regards creativity itself, I suspect the cognitive approach will become a lot more interesting when computers can dream.

The social–personality approach seems much more fertile right now. It is interested in the personality traits of creative people, the factors that motivate or demotivate them, as well as the social and cultural context in which they live and work.

Maslow identified boldness, courage, freedom, spontaneity, self-acceptance and other traits as typical of the creative temperament. Rogers found that the drive towards self-actualization was a powerful motivating factor, particularly in support-ive and evaluation-free environments. And several theorists, including Teresa Amabile, have conducted seminal research into intrinsic motivation and the vital role it plays in creative expression particularly, but not exclusively, in the workplace.

Sternberg himself, together with Amabile, Csikszentmihalyi, Gardner, Simonton, Weisberg and others, favours what he calls the 'confluence approach'. This is a much more holistic view, hypothesizing that 'multiple components must converge for creativity to occur'. These include strands of the social–personality approach as well as the interaction of variables such as education, intelligence, domain-competence, the environment and thinking styles. This approach results in creative models that quite closely approximate our experience of creativity in what we loosely call the real world. And hooray to that.

There's a third point to be made about the pragmatist view as represented by de Bono, Osborn and the 14.8 million creativity experts who populate the internet.

Training people to solve problems while pretending to them that they are learning to be more creative is almost certainly having a counterproductive effect. Apart from dumbing down the kind of creativity that would give us more interest-ing movies, art, music, TV, architecture, books, social ideas, political ideas, ideas about the usage of technology and so on – it is also, with exquisite irony, *actively undermining our ability to solve problems.*

If you wanted to be a copywriter at J. Walter Thompson back in those days at 40 Berkeley Square you had to pass the famous JWT Copy Test. In many ways it resembled the kind of tests you would find in psychometric creativity research such as Guilford's Structure of the Intellect divergent production tests, Torrance's Tests of Creative Thinking, and others. Though its authors would probably not have been conscious of this when they drew it up, the JWT Copy Test clearly sought to measure the same sort of factors as the SOI and the TTCT – fluency, flexibility, originality, divergent thinking and the elaboration of ideas. The biggest differences were that the JWT test phrased its questions as advertising problems (such as how to design a poster to attract recruits to the notoriously corrupt Mexican police force), and it had a sense of humour.

The following story, apocryphal or not, was told to me by the larger-than-life legend of London advertising Allen Thomas, for many years creative director of JWT London and later creative director of Europe and possibly the world.

One of the questions the Copy Test asked candidates was to describe a piece of toast to an alien in 25 words or less. Allen had seen many interesting attempts to answer this question. Some aspirant copywriters resorted to diagrams of wheat-fields and toasters, which was against the rules, or wrote streams of consciousness poems rhyming tasty and munchy with wheaty and crunchy, which were dismissed immediately as sycophantic and horrible. Most of them, reflecting the absurd tone of the test itself, simply took the piss out of the question in the hope they would get points for cynicism. Anyone who tried to answer the question seriously was automatically transferred to the head of client service for a second interview.

One day, flicking through the weekly mountain of tests, Allen came across an answer to the alien and toast question that he considered 'stonkingly good'. He reserved the word 'stonking' for ideas that were, in his opinion, genuinely and strikingly original.

Q: In 25 words or less describe a piece of toast to an alien.
A: Billi hubba boo bi bubba hoo boo bibbi hub bi boo hub billi boo.

On the strength of this answer alone he decided to employ the applicant immediately, then promptly forgot about him.

In those days the creative department of J. Walter Thompson was one of the biggest in London, employing scores and scores of writers, art directors, typographers, renderers, TV and radio producers and scores more people with odd titles that don't exist anymore thanks to the arrival of the Mac.

Several months later it occurred to Allen to find out how that youngster had been getting on.

'We had to fire him,' said the group head. 'I thought you knew.'

'Oh dear,' said Allen. 'What happened?'

'We gave him a brief to do a poster for Mr Kipling's new home-baked blackcurrant tarts and all he could write was billi hubba boo billi bubba hoo.'

R.W. Weisberg, in *Creativity and Knowledge: A Challenge to Theories*, explains:

> Well-known studies by Luchins and Luchins on problem solving ... have shown that individuals can easily be induced to perform inefficiently in problem solving situations, as a result of success with one specific solution. Experimental participants were sometimes so fixated on 'blindly' applying that previously successful solution to new problems that simpler solutions would be overlooked. The new problem might not even be solved by the experienced problem solver, although naïve participants solved it with no difficulty.

Paul Arden, the former creative director of Saatchi & Saatchi, describes the same thing in *It's Not How Good You Are, It's How Good You Want To Be*, the book that has fast becomes the creative wannabe's first-choice crib-sheet. In a chapter titled 'It's Wrong To Be Right' Arden says that experience is the opposite of being creative because, 'Experience is built from solutions to old situations and problems. The old situations are probably different from the present ones, so that old solutions will have to be bent to fit new problems (and possibly fit badly). Also the likelihood is that, if you've got the experience, you'll probably use it.'

There's even a name for this: negative transfer.

*

Despite the fact that modern psychometric testing for creativity has now been going on for close to 60 years, there is still considerable debate among researchers about whether the tests are measuring the right components of creativity – or whether they are measuring anything at all. There is still no such thing as a stable creativity quotient (a CQ) that academics or educators can agree on.

J.A. Plucker and J.S. Renzulli, in *Psychometric Approaches to the Study of Human Creativity*, confess that:

> While evidence of reliability measures for (list of the most well-known tests, including SOI and TTCT) and similar tests . . . is fairly convincing, the predictive and discriminant validity of divergent-thinking tests enjoys mixed support . . . The debate centres around the predictive validity of the tests and the apparent susceptibility of divergent thinking tests to administration, scoring, and training effects.

What Plucker and Renzulli are saying, in a nutshell, is that while the tests all seem to be measuring the same things, with some consistency and reliability, no one is quite sure if what they're measuring really is the same thing as what we call creativity, or even whether they are discriminating at all between high creative performers and low ones. And, worst of all, they are pretty awful at predicting anything about the future creative performance of the people they test.

There are a number of obvious problems dogging the psychometric approach. Though research indicates that most people know creativity when they see it, it's extremely difficult, when judging the results of the tests, to agree on whether some test responses are more creative than others.

The notion that creativity is some kind of subset of intelligence has also run into problems. It seems, from historical studies into highly creative individuals, that you need to have a reasonably high IQ to produce anything that most people would regard as creatively interesting, but the correlation between creativity (as measured on the standard tests) and intelligence breaks down at every other point of the IQ spectrum.

The relationship between education and creativity is also problematic. Studies by Simonton indicate that creativity peaks around about undergraduate level. Any more education, or any less, tends to inhibit the likelihood of highly creative behaviour.

*

It would be easier to summarize what we have learned so far if we could agree on a definition of creativity that held true in every case. We know, in some vaguely collective way, that it is about using our imaginations to create novel and original things. But the tension between the pragmatic view, that is, the Osborn–Parnes or CPS model, which insists that creativity is about solving problems, and the psychodynamic approach, which suggests that it is about reconstructing '. . . the bolder, cleaner, more spacious and fully human life . . .', betrays how deeply politicized the debate has become. The problem solvers eschew the role of the unconscious. Their opponents embrace it. The problem solvers believe in finding ideas through teamwork, processes and brainstorming. Their critics regard these techniques as mechanistic and counterproductive.

So when Jerry Hirschberg describes creativity as 'the mastery of information and skills in the service of dreams' or when Teresa Amabile describes it as 'the production of novel and appropriate ideas' they are clearly throwing in their lot with the problem solvers. When Einstein says 'The intuition is a sacred gift and the rational mind is a faithful servant. We have created a society that honors the servant and has forgotten the gift' he is clearly siding, as he does so often, with the absurd, the irrational and the poetic.

This is not a matter of taste. The way we describe creativity reveals what we want from it. More tellingly, it reveals what we want from the people we employ to do creative work.

As things stand in the early years of the 21st century, the problem solving definition is clearly in the ascendancy. And, consequently, creativity has been pressed into the service of the rational, the instrumental and the pragmatic. Creative training flourishes under the banner of productivity, and creative people who cannot solve problems find themselves marginalized by skilled craftsmen who can. Hardly surprising, then, if they have to retreat to the garage for inspiration.

And perhaps nothing divides the pragmatists from the poets quite as sharply as the nature of inspiration. Here is Nietzsche:

> Has anyone at the end of the nineteenth century a clear idea of what poets of strong ages have called *inspiration*? If not, I will describe it. If one had the slightest residue of superstition left in one's system, one could hardly reject altogether the idea that one is merely incarnation, merely mouthpiece, merely a medium of overpowering forces. The concept of revelation in the sense that suddenly and with indescribable certainty and subtlety, something becomes *visible*,

audible, something shakes one to the last depths and throws one down – that merely describes the facts. One hears, one does not seek; one accepts, one does not ask who gives; like lightning, a thought flashes up, with necessity, without hesitation regarding its form – I never had any choice . . .

In Chapter III of *Applied Imagination* Alex Osborn discusses what he calls '*Non-controllable* workings of the imagination'

> As a term, imagination covers a field so wide and so hazy that a leading educator has called it 'an area which psychologists fear to tread.' For imagination takes many forms – some of them wild, some of them futile, some of them somewhat creative, some of them truly creative. These forms, in turn, fall into two broad classes. One consists essentially of the kinds which *run themselves* and sometimes run away with us. The other class is made up of the kinds we can run – which we can *drive*, if and when we will.
>
> The less controllable group includes unhealthy forms such as hallucinations, delusions of grandeur, persecution complexes, and similar maladies. Delirium is a less chronic phase of the same form. Nightmares are akin to delirium.
>
> Inferiority complexes are still another form. Until recently, such ills were seemingly beyond control. But psychiatry has found ways of correction; and Doctor Harry Fosdick and Doctor Henry Link have helped by buttressing psychiatric therapy with religion.

At last, a way to get rid of those budding Nietzsches – venlafaxine, a Rorschach test, and a healthy dose of religion. And if you can't get it down with a spoon, use a fork.

Yes, folks, creativity can be cured.

*

The academic ambivalence surrounding the relationship between creativity and CPS has allowed the charlatans to flourish. We are back to snake-oil and phrenology as the boom in creative drowns out the reservations of those who really do know better.

Here is Sternberg, probably the most respected expert in the field of creativity, admonishing the lot of them in the strictest possible terms: 'Those taking . . . (the pragmatic) . . . approach have been concerned primarily with developing creativity, secondarily with understanding it, but almost not at all with testing the validity of their ideas about it.'

In the hard science of the creative brain we will now discover just how mistaken they really are.

CHAPTER 5

The biology of inspiration

A great poet is a man who, in his waking state, is able to do what the rest of us do in our dreams.

Schopenhauer

It's a shame there is no EEG record of Jesus's brain activity while he was composing the Sermon on the Mount. Colin Martindale and his studies into the cortical activity of creative people's brains suggest that it would make interesting reading.

Until Osborn and his disciples arbitrarily decided that all people were creatively equal, the rest of us had a pretty strong gut feeling that creative people were somehow different. The first scientific attempts to define exactly how and why they were different got going only in the 19th century. Someone called Morel formulated what came to be known as the 'degeneration' theory, which hypothesized that creative people (as we always suspected) were weak in the brain.

What he meant was that the higher, inhibitory brain centres, those areas of the brain that act as the policeman on the streets of our imagination, were not as alert in creative people as they might have been, allowing all manner of primitive thoughts to run rampant. Since Morel and other researchers at the time, like Lombroso and Nordau, did not have access to sophisticated modern equipment, they were obliged to speculate about how this actually happened. They put it down to environmental factors like diet, climate and toxins. They also thought that this degenerative condition was passed down through the generations.

If they turned out to be spectacularly wrong on the latter two points, history shows that the theory itself has some real merit. The fundamental premise that creative people are less mentally inhibited than normal people has been confirmed by Martindale and others in scientific trials. And the idea that creativity was linked with psychotisism also turned out to be fairly accurate in contemporary studies of the creative personality by people like Eysenck.

In 1895 Lombroso described the following creative or 'degenerate' character traits:

> Apathy, loss of moral sense, frequent tendencies to impulsiveness or doubt, psychical inequalities owing to the excess of some faculty (memory, aesthetic taste, etc.) or defect of other qualities (calculation, for example), exaggerated mutism or verbosity, morbid vanity, excessive originality and excessive preoccupation with self, the tendency to put mystical interpretations on the simplest facts, the abuse of symbolism and of special words which are used as an almost exclusive mode of expression.

A number of people spring to mind here, not all of whom work in advertising. Van Gogh, Janis Joplin, Don Quixote, the Reverend Jim Jones, Pete Doherty; pretty much anyone who has done something different and interesting. We don't know enough about Jesus to put him on the list, but I'd take a wild guess that these were some of the demons he was grappling with during those 40 days in the desert.

Nordau, writing at the end of the 19th century, added the following – an inability to focus attention and to differentiate the relevant from the irrelevant, a tendency to 'inane reverie', free associative thinking with an inability to suppress irrelevant thoughts, moral insanity, a rebellious inability to adapt to the environment, pessimism and egomania. Leonardo, John Lennon, Mozart, Jackson Pollock, Kafka; pick your favourite.

A hundred years later Eysenck described the traits of people who test high on psychotisism as aggressive, cold, egocentric, impersonal, creative, impulsive, antisocial, unempathic, tough-minded, and characterized by overinclusive thinking or 'wide associative horizons', a remarkable overlap with the conclusions of his 19th century predecessors.

We'll find out more about the personality characteristics of creative people in due course. It's a fertile field of study, and critical to our discussion of effective creative management. But brainwaves first.

*

Psychologists distinguish between two different kinds of thinking – 'primary process thought', which is the kind we experience in dreams and daydreams, and 'secondary process thought', which we use to deal with everyday reality. The latter is logical and abstract, helping us to get on the right train to work, to choose a decent wine for lunch and to compile those inventory reports before five o'clock. Primary process thought, which is also characteristic of abnormal states such as psychosis and hypnosis, is what happens when your computer screen blurs in front of you and you find yourself fantasizing about different ways to murder your boss.

These two modes of thinking exist on a continuum. We move backwards and forwards along it quite unconsciously most of the time. But when we're under pressure to get something done, like studying for an exam or compiling inventories before five o'clock, we may need to make a conscious effort to stay with the secondary process or suffer the consequences.

In 1952 a researcher by the name of Kris postulated that creative people find it easier to switch between the primary process and the secondary process than uncreative people do. In other words, creative people can move freely between one end of the continuum and the other, while less creative people tend to get stuck somewhere in between.

To come up with an original idea or an original solution to a problem, you need to be able to slip easily into a free-floating daydream of some kind. It's a space where thoughts and memories collide with half-remembered dreams and vague intuitions about possibilities explored and unexplored. When something interesting occurs to you in this state you then need to be able to slip out of it and return to world of logic and everyday reality to be able to test the feasibility of it in the cold light of day. If it doesn't work you need to be able to slip back into the maze of the primary process in search of something else.

Kris's theory not only makes an enormous amount of intuitive sense, it turns out to be well supported by a number of important scientific studies. Creative people fantasize more than uncreative people do, they remember their dreams more clearly and more frequently, and they are easier to hypnotize. Stories written by creative people contain more 'primary process content' – more absurd, dream-like and just plain weird – than those written by less creative people.

Interestingly, the studies also confirmed the close relationship between creative people and psychotics, the difference being that the psychotics have less control over where they are on the primary–secondary continuum at any given time. Schizophrenics, on the other hand, are stuck in the primary state and can't get out.

Other lines of enquiry suggest that creative people have something called 'defocused attention', an ability to mull over several things at the same time. Less creative people have a narrower focus of attention, tending to concentrate on only one or two things at the same time, an eminently useful faculty for heart surgeons and people who have to add up long lists of numbers.

Defocused attention is a feature of primary process thought. In the free-floating state of the creative daydream you can keep a lot of thoughts in the air simultaneously, like juggling three apples, a tennis ball, a chainsaw and a copy of *Gravity's Rainbow* in slow motion.

Things get even more interesting when you start digging around beneath the skull. It seems that the continuum between primary process thought and secondary process thought corresponds nicely with levels of cortical arousal, not in a linear way but in a U-shaped curve. That's not as complicated as it sounds.

When you're excited, tense, alert or anxious your brain patterns get excited too, and your cortical arousal is said to be high. When you're relaxed, daydreaming or feeling sleepy your brain also calms down, and your cortical arousal is said to be low. Both ends of the spectrum are good for primary process thought, frenzied madness on the one hand and 'inane reverie' on the other.

In between the extremes, at a medium level of arousal, you get 'alert wakefulness', which is the best state to be in for handling complex tasks, for learning efficiently, and for coping with day-to-day reality. Good for secondary process thought, in other words.

Conveniently enough for researchers, arousal can be measured by an electroencephalograph (EEG), so it has been possible to put Kris's theory to the test at the neurological level. The results are fascinating.

When you examine the cortical arousal patterns of highly creative people and uncreative people *during the conceptual process*, they head in opposite directions along the arousal scale. Say, for example, both groups are challenged to think of a very interesting story – not to write the story, but simply to think one up. The arousal levels of the creative people decrease, the arousal levels of the uncreative people *increase*.

According to Martindale, this is what's happening: '. . . when asked to be original . . . creative people exhibit defocused attention accompanied by low levels of cortical activation. On the other hand, uncreative people focus their attention too much, and this prevents them from thinking of original ideas.'

The question you then have to ask is whether creative people can control their own levels of arousal. If they can it might just be possible to teach uncreative people the same trick. The results are bad news for de Bono and everyone else who believes that we're all endowed with creative genius if only we could persuade it to get out of the bottle.

In biofeedback tests designed to measure this precise point, uncreative people turn out, somewhat ironically, to be fairly good at controlling the amount of alpha they produce, while creative people turn out to be completely hopeless at it. But we shouldn't be too surprised by this. Creative people, after all, are not very good at controlling anything.

*

In the light of all of this we should probably give Clark Hull more credit than has been bestowed on him by history. Hull was the arch-behaviourist who laid the foundations for the brave-new-world theories of B.F. Skinner. And Skinner, in case you haven't heard of him, was to scientific management what Timothy Leary was to the psychedelic pop culture of the 1960s.

Hull believed, the way Skinner did later, that it was theoretically possible to reduce the entire scope and substance of human behaviour to a simple series of stimulus and response protocols, eliminating the need for messy things like love, loyalty and liberalism. His experimental methodology of choice was the rat in the T-maze, which meant spending most of his life teaching small rodents to distinguish between their lefts and their rights.

Hull, as you can probably guess, wasn't searching for extraordinary new insights into the nature of creativity. So it's entirely an accident of fate that his Behavioural Law formulated in 1943 not only anticipated the findings of the arousal studies we've been discussing, but also led to several lines of enquiry in the field of creativity research that have produced some astonishing results.

The Law itself states, to quote Martindale paraphrasing Hull, that 'increases in arousal make behaviour more stereotypical and decreases in arousal make behaviour more variable'. Simply put – and you can readily appreciate the logic of this – when creatures like rats are subjected to a random sequence of electric shocks they're more likely to concentrate their minds on escaping from their torture chambers and less likely to consider doing the things that rats do in their free time, like grooming their whiskers or contemplating the nature of ratdom.

It seems obvious in retrospect, but so does nuclear fission.

A couple of decades later, as interest in the psychology of creativity began to gather some momentum, several researchers began to wonder whether Clark Hull's Behavioural Law could be applied to humans on the assumption that 'variability' of behaviour in rats approximated creative behaviour in homo sapiens.

Osgood in 1960 and Meisels in 1967 demonstrated that this was indeed the case by showing that '. . . written language becomes increasingly stereotyped under conditions of increased arousal'. The truth of this is self-evident if you've ever tried to write something under pressure, like a book about creativity with the wolf snuffling at the letterbox, the warm breath misting the polished brass.

Other studies of word association tasks and creativity tests '. . . have demonstrated that stress reliably produces decreases in originality'. On the same subject, but approached from an anthropological perspective rather than a neuropsychological one, Teresa Amabile makes precisely the same point in 'Creativity under the Gun'.

The evidence that stress is a effective way of killing creativity is now so comprehensive, so compelling and so incontrovertible that we must ask in astonished wonder just how contemporary management practice in the creative industries can continue to ignore it, or worse, as these next examples show, to fly contemptuously in the face of it?

White noise is a case in point. Back in the 1980s when the open plan office came into vogue as an inventive way of bringing the Taylorist productivity agenda to white-collar workers, interior designers were faced with the problem of controlling the cacophony of noise caused by so many people and so many ringing telephones in the same communal space. The solution was to flood the area with white noise, a mixture of all the sound frequencies audible to the human ear. It has the effect of deadening noises from more than a few metres away, creating an artificial silence.

You get the same effect on airliners since the noise of jet engines produces a similar multi-frequency hum. You can hear the passenger next to you whining on about the ineptitude of Heathrow security staff with crystal-clear garlic-scented Bose-quality clarity, but the conversation between the couple behind you, which seems to be about a plot to blow up the Statue of Liberty, is too muffled to make out in any detail.

What the interior designers didn't consider, however, was that white noise has the effect of stimulating cortical arousal. Which means that people working in large open plan office environments have a choice between learning to tolerate the noise of their co-workers or learning to function without a creative faculty. This is probably fine, perhaps even a good thing, if the office concerned is the Department of Statistics. But it's almost certainly less advisable in a design studio or an advertising agency.

By far the most egregious example of creative mismanagement is the brainstorm. There are several layers of irony to get through here. As we know, brainstorming was devised by Alex Osborn, an advertising man, as a technique for facilitating the generation of creative ideas. His timing could hardly have been more perfect. It was the late 1950s and Russia appeared to be winning every race that mattered, including the space race, the arms race and the 100 metres. America needed to catch up fast. Thinking of new ideas became the patriotic duty of every American, and brainstorming allowed them to do just that.

Taylor's dumb oxen were summoned from the factory floor, led into the boardroom, and encouraged to shoot the breeze. Scientists did it, engineers did it, government workers did it, the army did it, salesmen did it, dentists did it, and every single manager of every single office and of every single department of every single company from sea to shining sea did it, and then did it again, and again, and again.

Brainstorming spread to Europe, to Japan, and around the world. It became the default management strategy for every problem, every opportunity, every product innovation, every marketing challenge and every aspect of organizational change. It involved millions of people in billions of hours of meetings costing trillions upon trillions of dollars.

And it didn't work, it never had worked, it never will work, and there was proof that it couldn't work way back in 1965. If, during all this time, any ideas found their way out of brainstorming sessions and were implemented successfully to the great delight of all, it was in spite of the technique, not because of it.

*

If years of biting your tongue while drawing vicious doodles on your brainstorming pad hasn't yet convinced you that they're considerably more damaging than just being a waste of time perhaps the evidence will.

Tests show that the company of other people (let alone the presence of colleagues, competitors, bosses and strangers) has the effect of increasing levels of cortical arousal, thereby decreasing levels of creativity. Lindgren and Lindgren, among others, have shown that this is precisely what happens in brainstorming groups. Martindale, in *Biological Basis of Creativity*, states that

> A number of studies of word association tasks . . . and creativity tests . . . have demonstrated that stress reliably produces decreases in originality. Brainstorming techniques were originally proposed as methods of facilitating creative ideas. In fact, they decrease creativity . . . This makes sense in the light of Zajone's (1965) hypothesis that the mere presence of others increases arousal.

Nickerson quotes five studies done between 1958 and 1992 that show that brainstorming works better *when you don't do it in a group*, that is, 'when individuals generate ideas in the absence of the group and then subject those ideas to exploration and evaluation in group settings'.

This is not to say that brainstorming sessions have no useful purpose whatsoever. As David Brent has shown us so memorably, there is hardly a better way of humiliating your colleagues or of patronizing your juniors.

The cardinal rule of brainstorming is to reserve judgement so as to allow for the free flow of ideas within the group, and to encourage individuals to build on the ideas of others. In principle, this is a very good thing. We shall see later that the evaluation of ideas by anyone other than those qualified to make a judgement is one of the top creativity killers. In brainstorming sessions, however, the reservation of judgement serves both to damn those who remain silent in the face of rank stupidity and to embarrass forever those careless enough to proffer it. The difference between a brainstorming session and a committee meeting is that the committee will at least have the honesty to laugh in your face.

The only acceptable way out of a brainstorm is to endorse the most politically expedient option as soon as possible. That way no one gets hurt, no one gets embarrassed, and no one gets the blame. And if you do happen to have a good idea during the course of the session you're more likely to strangle it quietly to death than to allow the group to claim ownership of it.

*

It is standard practice in modern management to bribe people to work harder by offering them rewards of one kind or another. Robert Heller gives us this advice in *Motivating People*, one of the Essential Manager series from Dorling Kindersley:

> There are many incentives you can offer to help motivate people, and each has different effects. Some of those most commonly used include recognition, money, health and family benefits, and insurance. There tends, however, to be a dividing line between financial and non-financial incentives. If you are not in a position to offer financial incentives like pay rises and bonuses it is still possible to motivate staff by ensuring that the non-financial incentives you offer are attractive to the potential recipient. For example, you might allocate a parking space to someone who drives to work.

This is good, sensible advice if you're the manager of a large department of people whose job it is to stuff envelopes with junk mail, or if you're managing a group of salespeople selling double-glazing in south west London. But what Heller and the Essential Manager series fail to mention is that it is extremely bad advice if you're managing creative people, a theatre troupe, for example, or a studio of shoe designers. Considering that there are upwards of half a million people employed in creative services in London alone, and that gross revenues from creative industries now contribute a significant slice of the UK's GDP and the world economy in general, this is an unforgivable omission.

Incentives, bribery, the promise of rewards – even the intimation of possible rewards – every single one of those motivational sweeteners prescribed by management theory as ways to improve the productivity of workers has precisely the opposite effect on the productivity of creative people.

Not knowing whether or not you're going to be able to pay your mortgage at the end of the month is a guaranteed formula for stimulating cortical arousal.

But there's another less obvious explanation: creative people produce their best work when they do it *for its own sake.*

Amabile, who has done more work in this field than anyone else, calls this 'intrinsic' motivation. Its opposite is 'extrinsic' motivation, which comes in the form of the multifarious rewards and punishments that our parents used to get us to do our homework, that our teachers used to get us through our exams, and that scientific management uses to optimize the productivity of workers.

It's not that creative people are allergic to money. They love it as much as the rest of us do. It's when money or other rewards, like fame and parking spaces, are linked to the accomplishment of a specific creative task that things go pear-shaped.

In 1994 Amabile and her colleagues Phillips and Collins invited 29 professional artists, drawn from across the United States, to send them 20 pieces of work they had done in the past seven years. Ten of each artist's submissions had to have been commissions and the other 10 had to be non-commissioned works. The artists also had to send a detailed description of the conditions under which each of the pieces had been done, the nature of the commission, and how they felt while producing the artwork. The researchers then invited art experts to judge the quality of all the work without knowing which pieces had been commissioned and which had not.

Clearly there is an enormous amount of subjectivity going on in this kind of test and no one, least of all Amabile, would call it scientific. Nevertheless, the results were consistent with previous experimental studies. Overall the judges rated the commissioned works as less creative than the non-commissioned works, just as we would expect.

Anticipating the money you're going to get when you've finished your giant mural for those corporate headquarters in Canary Wharf is almost certainly going to arouse more cortical excitement than is good for the artist in you.

There were some notable exceptions. In the case of commissions which 'enabled the artist to do something interesting or exciting' the quality of the work was actually enhanced. For the managers of creative people working under pressure in the creative industries this is a very important finding. It resonates throughout history in the commissions of great artists and musicians, as we shall see, and it is one of the keys to unlocking the true potential of creative people in every field of today's creative economy.

*

Knowing what we do about the biology of creativity we can now begin to explain the behaviour of creative people, much of which strikes the rest of us as inexplicable, if not downright aberrant.

In a world that is constantly pushing our levels of cortical activity towards the red zone of mental and physical collapse it's unsurprising that many creative people have turned to drugs and alcohol in the hope of lowering their cortical temperatures. Unfortunately, although they may offer some temporary relief by numbing the psychic pain, most recreational chemicals induce more cortical arousal rather than less.

Laudanum, a mixture of opium and alcohol, apparently worked for Coleridge who claimed to have written the first part of 'Kubla Khan' under its influence. The poem also gives us history's most famous example of the cortical arousal needle jumping from primary to secondary state in mid-stroke. Coleridge blamed it on an unexpected and highly unwelcome visit from 'a man from Porlock', the neighbouring village. The first two hallucinogenic stanzas are probably the most hypnotic written in the English language. From the very first line, 'In Xanadu did Kubla Khan . . .' all the way down to, '. . . It was a miracle of rare device, /A sunny pleasure-dome with caves are ice!' Coleridge is in the sweet-spot of defocused attention, the cortical arousal level somewhere between zero and the last stop of the Poppy Express. Then suddenly you get this, 'A damsel with a dulcimer/In a vision once I saw: /It was an Abyssinian maid, /And on her dulcimer she played . . .' You can almost hear Coleridge gritting his teeth as the man from Porlock waves a cheery goodbye from the front gate. From the low revs of reverie the needle has climbed to the whining howl of intense irritation.

Isolation is more effective and less damaging than drugs. Finding a quiet retreat away from the bombardment of distracting stimuli is, indeed, a good way to lower cortical arousal. Proust apparently isolated himself in cork-lined rooms; Wordsworth found peace and quiet in a country cottage. Shelley retreated to Pisa and Lerici, Chekhov to the spas of the Black Sea, Gaugin to the South Sea Islands and Bob Dylan to Woodstock. J.D. Salinger disappeared soon after publishing his first story and Thomas Pynchon hasn't been seen in public for 30 years. Banksy is trying to do the same thing.

Of course, everyone works better in a quieter, less-stressful environment. But creative people, according to research by Martindale and others, are particularly sensitive to irritating stimuli, or 'physiologically over-reactive' as he calls it. They respond more intensely to beeps and electric shocks, and they don't get used to them as quickly as uncreative subjects do. So there may well be other good reasons why creative people seek to escape from the constant barrage of noise, confusion and other arousal-inducing assaults on the senses that are so much part of modern urban environments.

In spite of all this, and completely at odds with their constant search for states of low arousal, creative people also have a marked craving for novelty – not for adventure or extreme sports – but for new ideas, for the bizarre, the absurd and the shocking. It seems that it must be one or other of the two extremes, or probably, as Martindale suggests, one because of the other.

There are three more points to be noted about the way creative people's brains are wired.

The theory that they are more 'right-brained' than 'left-brained' turns out to be more or less true but not particularly useful. There is some evidence that small doses of marijuana and large doses of music increase right brain activation, but neither is guaranteed to turn you into a genius.

Creative people show lower levels of frontal lobe activation during creative tasks. It's generally understood that the frontal lobe acts as a cognitive inhibitor, like a schoolteacher in your head making sure you don't think bad or crazy thoughts. The schoolteachers in the heads of creative people are not quite as strict as the teachers that inhabit the heads of less creative people. Some days they don't even turn up for work.

Lastly, the question of whether or not the peculiarities of creative brains can be passed down from one generation to another appears to be moot. Some of the brain pattern characteristics of creative people seem to be shared by siblings, and some may be inherited. But you need all of them together, plus a mixture of intelligence and psychoticism, to be highly creative – just as you need all six numbers to win the lottery, three or four or five hardly count. Creativity does not run in families, contrary to the assumptions of romantic novels.

Unlike intelligence, which is highly inheritable and therefore spreads itself across in the population in a neat Bell curve, creativity happens when the genetic deck gets shuffled in your favour. You need some intelligence to be in on the game, but after that it's the luck of the draw.

So what percentage of the population gets blessed or cursed with high creativity? Here's the rub.

Compared to other species, such as fruit flies or golden retrievers, human beings are endlessly creative. They can dress themselves in the morning, remember their grandmothers' faces, roll their own cigarettes, programme video recorders, lay landmines, make broccoli taste palatable and remove obstructions, such as shrapnel, from major arteries.

This is the perspective of cognitive research, which is interested in how normal people solve problems in everyday life. Also known as the normative view of creativity, the starting point of this approach is that the human species wouldn't have got very far without the imagination needed to make a trap for mammoths. In this sense we are all equally creative, and the rest is simply a question of how well we use our creative faculties.

Taken at face value this view is eminently sensible, and salutary too. How easy it is to forget that we are more capable, more intelligent and more imaginative than fruit flies. And, unless we believe we have arrived at the long-sought Shangri La of human organization, we should indeed be spending time and effort learning to be more capable, more intelligent and more imaginative in the way we run our affairs.

This is creativity as survival, creativity as strategy, creativity as the opposite of idiocy. At it's best, it's building a better mammoth trap, or a better mousetrap. But it's still a long way from devising interesting and productive alternative careers for mice.

The contrary view, that creativity is a rare and precious gift won by only the charmed few in the lottery of meiosis, is supported by neurological researchers, historical studies and examinations of the personality characteristics of creative people. It is the underlying assumption of creativity testing and of developmental psychology. But no one in this camp seems prepared to put a figure to the percentage of highly creative people likely to be found in any given population. And this is despite the 285 studies quoted in Plucker and Renzulli's summary of creative psychometrics.

The underlying reason for this is, once again, the problem of definition. We can readily agree that a very high percentage of human beings are more creative than Labradors. It's much more difficult to predict how many of a class of 30 primary school kids will go on to achieve great things in one or other field of creativity. The Bell curve remains elusive, and the word 'creativity' is loaded with all sorts of political and personal agendas.

Perhaps it shouldn't matter if academics cannot agree on whom and how many among us are creatively gifted just as long as we are surrounded by the evident glory of their works. What does matter is that we understand once and for all that highly creative people are different from the rest of us. We have seen that they think differently. Now we will see how differently they behave.

CHAPTER 6

The creative personality

The lunatic, the lover, and the poet
Are of imagination all compact.

Shakespeare

Thus the creative genius may be at once naïve and knowledgeable, being at home equally to primitive symbolism and to rigorous logic. He is both more primitive and more cultured, more destructive and more constructive, occasionally crazier and yet adamantly saner, than the average person.

Frank Barron, 1963

Now that we know something about how their brains work it would be useful to know how to spot creative people at a dinner party, say, or among a thousand candidates applying for a job at an advertising agency. For this we must turn to personality studies, the favoured experimental technique of psychologists who can't stand white mice.

This approach attempts to explain or predict human behaviour by studying the differences between individuals' personalities. It is most famous for giving us tests like the Minnesota Multiphasic Personality Index (MMPI), the Myers–Briggs, the California Personality Index and many more.

The MMPI, developed in the early 1950s by the University of Minnesota, which continues to rake in a small fortune from its licensing fees, was designed to test for nine different kinds of psychopathology, including schizophrenia, psychosis, paranoia and hypochondria. The idea behind it was to enable psychiatrists to identify and label the condition of people who didn't adjust particularly well to normal life. But it was soon taken up by companies and institutions who used it to test job applicants, employees and anyone else they might want to subject to scrutiny. The US marines, for example, use it to identify the best candidates for their sniping academy. Counterintuitively, applicants need to fail the psychosis test if they want to qualify. Logic suggests that you would be eager to identify candidates who long to kill strangers at random, but clearly they need to be perfectly sane before they're allowed to. The MMPI is also used to screen recruits to police academies, fire departments and governmental secret services, clearly with mixed results.

The Myers–Briggs, on the other hand, is the preferred test of recruitment for business. Less clinical in orientation, it is designed to discover your personality type in the hope that prospective employers will be able to put you in the right pigeonhole. The MBTI, as it is known, is based on the four dichotomies of personality first postulated by Carl Jung. These are introvert versus extrovert, sensing versus intuition, thinking versus feeling and judging versus perceiving. Depending on how you score the bank of yes or no questions you will be identified as one of the possible 16 Types. So you could, for example, turn out to be an ISFP Type – an introvert, sensing, feeling, perceiving Type – or an ENTJ – an extrovert, intuitive, thinking, judging type.

The originators of the MBTI, Katharine Cook Briggs and Isabel Briggs Myers, had no scientific, medical or psychological qualifications. They simply made it up after reading Jung. Yet it has become one of the most popular and widely used ways of determining which people are fit for the business world and which aren't.

Despite their obvious flaws, tests like the MMPI and the MBTI have accumulated a lot of interesting data, simply because they are used so often and across such large and diverse populations. In the context of personality theory, therefore, they are able to give us some interesting insights into the nature and distribution of creativity.

Simonton has found a close relationship between creativity and the psychosis scale of the MMPI. As expected, the more creative you are the more likely you are to get high scores in this department. Using this as a starting point we are now able to predict with a high degree of certainty which of the various creative fields is most likely to result in mental disorder. Poets, at 87%, are by far the most vulnerable. They are followed by fiction writers, theatrical performers, artists, non-fiction writers and musical performers. Composers at 60% are next in line, followed by sports people, architects, social activists and businessmen and women. Professions with the lowest rate of association with mental disorder are explorers (down at 27%), natural scientists, the military and those who hold public office. A few hundred years after Dryden, the MMPI has confirmed that, 'Great Wits are sure to Madness near ally'd,/And thin Partitions do their Bounds divide.'

None of this is really surprising given the similarity of neural activity between creative people and psychotics that we have seen in the EEG tests. There is clearly a direct connection between the low arousal levels of the conceptual process and the personality characteristics of those tending towards psychotic or schizophrenic states.

By dividing people into 16 Types the Myers–Briggs explores the creative temperament from a different angle. Based on work done by David West Keirsey you now no longer have to read the MBTI manual to decode which of the dichotomies are most closely related to creativity. Very helpfully, he has given each of the 16 types a personality archetype, so an ISTJ is an Inspector, an ISFJ is a Protector and so on. He has two archetypes that approximate the creative people – an ISFP is a Composer, while an ENTP is an Inventor. We can deduce from this that the creative personality is most likely to be an Introverted, Sensing, Feeling Perceiver, which concurs quite nicely with common sense. Inventors are apparently more extrovert, intuitive and thoughtful than Composers. None of this is profound, but it does give us a clue to the breakdown of the percentages of creative people in the general population, or at least in the US. According to the demographic studies, 8.8% of the American population are Composers and 3.2% are Inventors. By way of contrast, 12.3% are Providers, 11.6% are Inspectors, 13.8% are Protectors, 5.4% are Crafters, 2.1% are Masterminds and, thankfully, just 1.8% are Field Marshals.

On the lighter side, personality theory has also given us hours of amusement in the form of those tests you get at the back of women's magazines – 'Are You A Compulsive Shopper?' or 'Is He A One-Woman Man?' You could, of course, be honest and simply answer 'Yes' and 'I hope so' but that would be to rob yourself of the fun of finding out just how compulsive or just how desperate you are.

Personality theorists have long been fascinated by creativity and the nature of the creative temperament. So too have many of the greatest writers and thinkers, including Socrates, Plato, Aristotle, Kant, Coleridge, Poe, Galton, Russell, Poincaré, Freud, Bergson, Einstein, Maslow, Rogers and Skinner.

'. . . few topics are of greater importance to psychology than creativity,' says G.J. Feist whose summary of the work done in this field will guide us through this discussion.

Universities, businesses, the arts, entertainment, and politics – in other words, all of the major institutions of modern society – are each driven by their ability to create and solve problems originally and adaptively, that is, creatively. Therefore, the ultimate success and survival of these institutions depend on their ability to attract, select, and maintain creative individuals.

For the time being we will forgive Feist for confusing originality with problem solving. Some of the institutions he mentions may well be looking for the former. But it is almost certainly the ones who want the latter who are funding most of this research.

The ability to solve problems is a subset of intelligence and has very little to do with creative aptitude. You need to be fairly intelligent to be highly creative, but no amount of intelligence guarantees it. As Feist tells us, Creativity is fluency, flexibility, usefulness, and originality of association, not speed at solving verbal and/or mathematical multiple-choice problems. It should come as no surprise, therefore, that creative potential and creative ability are better predictors of later creative achievement than is intellectual ability.

Rather oddly, most personality theorists don't regard intelligence as an aspect of personality, which means you have to look elsewhere to untangle the knotty skein of misunderstanding between the ability to solve problems and creativity in its purest sense.

But personality studies are able to pin down, with a very high degree of accuracy, those character traits typical of creative achievers.

The best place to get a flavour of the kind of work that has been done in search of the definitive creative personality is in the references section of Feist's excellent abstract, 'Influence of Personality on Artistic and Scientific Creativity'. Here are some examples:

'The possible different personality dispositions of scientists and non-scientists' by R.S. Albert and M. Runco; 'Creativity profile of university and conservatory music students' by J.B. Alter; 'Bipolar affective disorder and creativity. Implications and clinical management' by N.C. Andreason and L.D. Glick; 'Personality differences between young dancers and non-dancers' by F.C. Bakker; 'Personality of Australian performing musicians by gender and instrument' by L.M. Buttsworth and G.A. Smith. 'Do hostile and arrogant scientists become eminent or are eminent scientists likely to become hostile and arrogant?' by Feist himself; 'The creative spectrum of authors of fantasy' by R. Helson; 'Touched with fire: manic-depressive illness and the artistic temperament' by K.R. Jamison; 'Some correlates of creativity in engineering personnel' by C.D. McDermid; 'The making of a scientist' by A. Roe; and 'The personality of opera singers' by G.D. Wilson. There are hundreds more, but you get the idea.

Handily for us, Feist has summarized all of the literature and more to reveal the all-time top-17 list of traits most likely to tip you off that you're in the presence of genius. The first 10 refer to non-social traits, that is, those that characterize the mental or emotional life of the creative person; the inner dispositions as it were.

The first cluster consists of 'openness to experience', 'fantasy-oriented' and 'imagination'. There is something child-like about this set of qualities, and quite right too. The best creative people continue to see the world afresh, taking in everything around them with awe-struck wonder. Antoine de Saint-Exupery's *The Little Prince* is the classic example, an exquisite evocation of childhood's innocent wisdom.

Next we have 'impulsivity and lack of conscientiousness', most famously represented by the life of Leonardo, who plunged headlong into every conceivable field of creative endeavour and who never got around to finishing anything at all. In the words of Michael Levey, he preferred 'enquiry to exposition', becoming easily bored by repetition or the laborious attention to detail required to finish anything to perfection. If it hadn't been snatched away from him in the nick of time we wouldn't have the Mona Lisa as we now know it and love it. He was keen to experiment with another few layers on top of it.

Impulsivity is why El Greco is more interesting than Titian, and why Van Gogh is more interesting than Van Dyke. It's why Dylan was more interesting than Donovan, why the Stones were more interesting than the Beatles, and why John Lennon was more interesting than Paul McCartney and all of the Stones put together.

One of the thrilling things about Picasso is how much of the canvas he leaves entirely raw. Andy Warhol became so bored with his paintings he got his assistants to do them for him. In the right hands, lack of conscientiousness is the secret of greatness.

'Anxiety', 'affective illness' and 'emotional sensitivity' are the cliches of the suffering artist. But cliches only get to be cliches by being consistently true. Artists, writers and poets who lead lives of blameless domesticity are rare enough to prove the rule. 'Those who have become eminent in philosophy, politics, poetry and the arts have all had tendencies toward melancholia,' said Aristotle a long time before Jim Morrison.

'Drive' and 'ambition' are the last of the non-social traits. We underestimate these because they seem so at odds with our image of the anxious and introspective poet wasting away from tuberculosis and a broken heart. But strength of character, strength of belief, and an unwavering determination to pursue their own lights, no matter how faint or far away, are a necessary condition for creative achievement. Luck also helps, of course.

The first cluster of social traits consists of 'norm doubting', 'nonconformity' and 'independence', the stuff that most romantic heroes are made of. Given that creative people, if they are any good at all, will express themselves in a voice that's as original as it is unique, these traits are surely self-evident. But they make for good biography, and they're useful reminders for teachers and employers that little Jimmy may not have a learning problem and that Sandra in accounts may be put to better use elsewhere.

Lastly, the four ways that creative people make themselves unpopular long before you get the opportunity to find out what's inside their heads – 'hostility', 'aloofness', 'unfriendliness' and 'lack of warmth'. Which isn't to say that these traits are the exclusive province of the creatively minded. Many people are hostile and unfriendly without being in the least creative, or possibly because they know they're not.

It's certainly true of my experience in advertising that very few creative people came across as warm and cuddly, and the few that did seldom turned out to be any good. But I came to understand that their hostility was not just characteristic, but necessary. On the surface it seemed as though their egos were fragile and that the hostile barriers they set up around themselves were a way of protecting their self-importance. I realized, eventually, that this was generally not the case. Ideas are fragile, and it's ideas that need protection. Creative people nursing ideas are like animals nursing their young, and there's hardly anything quite as vicious.

Feist concludes:

Creative people in art and science tend to be open to new experiences, less conventional and less conscientious, more self-confident, self-accepting, driven, ambitious, dominant, hostile, and impulsive. Creative people in art and science do not share the same unique personality profiles. Artists are more affective, emotionally unstable, as well as less socialized and accepting of group norms, whereas scientists are more conscientious.

Considering how much painstaking research went into this it's a shame the conclusions aren't a little more surprising. It would be much more satisfying to be told that creative people have pointy ears or shorter legs. As things stand, we are obliged to come to terms with the knowledge that creative people conform almost perfectly to their popular stereotype.

Two dangers become apparent immediately. The first is that individuals wishing to pose as creative types can quite easily ape this set of character traits. And many do. Dress yourself weird, act sloppy, swear aggressively, and do strange and unpredictable things on the spur of the moment, and you too could land yourself a highly paid job in the creative economy. You will probably get found out in due course, but what fun while it lasts.

The second is the Forer effect. Except for the words 'hostile' and 'unfriendly' the language used to describe the creative personality traits is not as specific or as polarizing as it might be. Which means that just about anyone who reads through the list could believe that the attributes apply perfectly to him or her, particularly if the individual is disposed to believe – or wants to believe – that they are creative.

In 1948 the psychologist Bertram Forer gave a personality test to his students, and then gave them a personality analysis supposedly based on the test's results. Unbeknownst to the students, they all received exactly the same analysis. Here is an extract:

> You have a need for other people to like and admire you, and yet you tend to be critical of yourself. While you have some personality weaknesses you are generally able to compensate for them. You have considerable unused capacity that you have not turned to your advantage. Disciplined and self-controlled on the outside, you tend to be worrisome and insecure on the inside. At times you have serious doubts as to whether you have made the right decision or done the right thing. You prefer a certain amount of change and variety and become dissatisfied when hemmed in by restrictions and limitations. . . .

Forer then asked each of them to rate the analysis as it applied to themselves on a scale of zero (poor) to five (excellent). The average for the class was 4.26.

The entire text had been assembled from horoscopes.

*

Though personality tests like the MMPI and the MBTI remain in widespread use, there is a general consensus among personality psychologists that they are several sandwiches short of a picnic. One of the most important aspects of human personality was ignored by both of them, that is, whether you are a nice person or not. So in the past decade or so, employing sophisticated factor analysis on massive amounts of data, a more comprehensive view of personality has emerged in the form of the Five Factor Model, the FFM.

The proponents of FFM argue that there are five fundamental dimensions of personality – 'openness', 'neuroticism', 'extraversion', 'agreeableness' and 'conscientiousness'. Each of these dimensions has its opposite, with a spectrum in between. So you could be somewhat open, somewhat neurotic, somewhat extravert, somewhat agreeable, somewhat conscientious and very boring. Or you could tend towards the extremes of some scales and not of others. There are FFM tests on the internet that you can do in 10 minutes. But don't be surprised if you are not surprised by your profile. As with all of these kinds of tests you can see where they are heading from question one.

The real value of FFM, if it turns out to be as robust as many psychologists believe it is, is that we now have a comprehensive framework of human personality to work with. There is still some controversy about whether it is as relevant in Lusaka as it is in Lima, and such questions will no doubt continue to exercise the minds of personality theorists for years to come.

How FFM relates to creativity still awaits thorough analysis, but work on individual dimensions confirms most of what we know already. Creative people tend to be more open to experience, more neurotic, more introverted, less agreeable and less conscientious, though the strongest correlation is with the first of these – openness to experience. Whether FFM can take us a lot further down the road of understanding how and why creative people behave as they do, or what distinguishes them from uncreative people with any evidence more compelling than what we have already, remains to be seen.

We can hardly go much further without mentioning Hans Eysenck, the most prolific, influential and controversial of the scholars in this field. He was the first psychologist to bring rigorous statistical analysis to personality theory, developing several personality tests of his own, many of which are still in use. He is best remembered for his unfortunate and erroneous conclusions regarding IQ differences between race groups, as well as for his life-long scorn of psychoanalysis. Before his death in 1997 he published what Feist calls, '. . . the most ambitious and inclusive recent theory of personality and creativity . . .'.

Psychology is notorious for dividing up the study of human behaviour into ever smaller and more isolated ghettos of specialist knowledge. Setting aside the hostility that separates the behaviourists from the psychoanalysts, increasing specialization in the various subsets of psychological research has tended to narrow our appreciation of the depth and complexity of the individual human psyche rather than broaden it. So cognitive psychologists will take little interest in the work of personality theorists, and personality theorists will take little interest in the work of those who study learning theory. Bearing in mind, too, that only a handful of academics in each of these disciplines is interested in creativity per se, it's little wonder that multi-disciplinary theories of the psychology of creativity have been slow to emerge.

Eysenck is one of the few who have attempted to join the dots. The picture that emerges, as shadowy and tentative as it is, traces a path from 'genetic determinants' – the way your brain was wired when you were born – through the chemistry of the hippocampus to cognitive inhibition and psychoticism, which in turn lead to the development of creative personality traits resulting, finally, in creative achievement.

At the heart of Eysenck's theory is the phenomenon of cortical arousal and the remarkable role it plays in the creative process. We have seen that creative and uncreative people respond in diametrically opposing ways to the challenge of the blank page. As Martindale and others have shown, creative people automatically default to the low arousal state where attention is at its widest. Uncreative people respond with high arousal and its consequent narrowing of attention. This is the litmus test of creative potential, a fundamental difference in brain function at the deepest neurological level. And this, in Eysenck's view, is what goes on to manifest itself in the personality traits of creativity.

You are open-minded because your brain insists that you should be. You are anxious, neurotic and borderline psychotic because that's the price you pay for being able to juggle chainsaws and billiard balls in slow motion. You are hostile because your ideas need protection. You are introverted because that's where your work gets done. You are not as conscientious as you could be because elaboration requires different kinds of skills. You crave excitement and you demand solitude. And you can't do very much about it.

If this makes you feel that you're a hapless victim of biology you might take some comfort from the knowledge that Eysenck is a cold-blooded behaviourist with little sympathy for limp-wristed ideas like imaginative freedom and the will to choose. So you may well, after all, have some room to manoeuvre. If you can't change the way your brain is wired, you can probably work on that personality.

Anger management would be a good start.

CHAPTER 7

The survival of the weirdest

We'll carry on writing music forever, whatever else we're doing, because you can't just stop. You find yourself doing it whether you want to or not.

John Lennon, ITV interview, 1964

That their brains work differently is problematic enough. That their personalities are difficult makes them all the more egregious. But the thing that finally curses creative people to lives of disgrace is the compulsion to follow a distant drummer that the rest of us cannot hear.

One of the favourite examples of the self-promotional literature of creativity trainers is the invention of Velcro. It is quoted with clockwork regularity as evidence that ordinary people like you and me can come up with brilliant ideas if we'd only put our minds to it.

Here is Sidney Parnes telling us how you too could invent a Velcro if you only used his Visionizing process, a recent adjunct to CPS:

The heart of Visionizing's creative process is the breaking of habitual mental associations and forming new ones – including *remote* associations. Analogies can provide a powerful tool to promote this process. The sticky 'burr' you pick up on your slacks in the woods may provide a remote analogy to a desired closure process in buttoning or zippering – *if* you can redefine the problem in a new way. If we are able to view the problem as one of 'connecting' two pieces of cloth, we might suddenly realize that we might 'connect' them with something like the burrs. (His italics.)

On the face of it there's nothing much to argue with. The Swiss engineer George de Mestral had the idea for Velcro after taking a close look at the burdock seeds that stuck to his clothes and to his dog's fur on the daily walk in the Alps. He called it Velcro after the French words *velours*, meaning velvet, and *crochet*, meaning hook, and went on to make a sizeable fortune through international patents.

What Parnes and the rest of them don't tell us is that de Mestral was a compulsive inventor who spent his entire life fiddling with everything he could get his hands on. At the age of 10 he had already patented a design for a toy plane. If it hadn't been Velcro it would have been something else, something less marketable and less lucrative perhaps, but it would have been something. Velcro was lucky because it was the right product at the right time.

The point is that de Mestral wasn't just an ordinary Joe casting around for something to make himself a fortune after going on a course of Visionizing. He was compelled to pull things apart and put things together (as it were) because it was in his blood. That's who he was.

We are reminded immediately of Louis Pasteur's famous observation that 'Chance favours only the prepared mind.'

The stories of great inventors, scientists and entrepreneurs, with very few exceptions, are about 'turning chance to account', in the words of Bulwer-Lytton. We know that they share with creative artists many of the same character traits – openness to experience, drive and ambition, arrogance and hostility, introversion and independence. We know that they are more conscientious and more self-confident than creative artists. They are also less anxious, less impulsive and less likely to question prevailing norms. We also know that creative artists are more likely to be borderline psychotics than creative scientists or businessmen though, clearly, they are not immune, as Howard Hughes has demonstrated so vividly.

It all makes for fascinating biography, but none of it is instructive. Learning that Picasso was traumatized by an earthquake at the age of three is interesting but not very helpful. Knowing that most highly creative people are naturally curious may encourage us to be more diligent about asking questions but it can hardly make us naturally curious. Apparently most successful American entrepreneurs were more likely to have suffered some form of corporal punishment as children than non-entrepreneurs or less successful entrepreneurs. What can you do about that apart from beating up your own kids?

And does it matter, after all, whether it was nature or nurture that did it? The debate will go on for decades, as it has done with intelligence. In the end we will discover that it's a bit of this combined with a bit of that. Life can only be understood backwards, as Kierkegaard said, but it must be lived forwards.

We look back in awe at the lives of Mozart, Pasteur and Bill Gates. We turn over the pages of history with trembling hands, anxiously tracing the invisible hand of providence. We want it to reveal itself, somehow, somewhere. We look for clues to its presence behind the mundane details of genealogy, date of birth, family relationships, early education, signs of prodigy, adolescent love, chance meetings, influential friends, the geography, the climate, the average rainfall, the stars. We hope to discover a pattern that no one has seen before. We long for coincidences, for strange connections with our own lives. We pray for destiny to reach out from the ashes of the past and bless us or curse us with the mark of genius.

Fascination with fame makes primitives of us all, just as the presence of celebrity reduces us to savage superstition. Beneath our 21st century skins our blood beats with the rhythms of sacrifice and fire. Inside *Heat* magazine are the entrails of goats.

If the history of genius can teach us anything it is that genius cannot be learned by studying genius. Genius happens the way weather happens, with the stir of a butterfly's wing on a still day in Oaxaca. It occurs with the predictability of chaos, beautifully described by James Gleick: 'Somehow, after all, as the universe ebbs toward its final equilibrium in the featureless heat bath of maximum entropy, it manages to create interesting structures.'

The psychology of creativity is an attempt to recognize genius before it's too late. Psychometrics attempts to measure it. Personality theory attempts to describe it. Psychodynamics attempts to understand it. The cognitive approach attempts to replicate it. The biographical approach attempts to explain it. Biology attempts to record it at play in the natural habitat of the brain.

Some of these are more helpful than others. All of them point in the same direction, that is, towards the simple truth of Bulwer-Lytton's most famous observation, that 'Genius does what it must' and 'talent does what it can.'

Highly creative people are compelled to do what they do because doing anything else makes them miserable, neurotic, psychotic, suicidal or all of the above. More so than anything else, that is the mark of the creative beast.

*

Amabile describes intrinsic motivation as 'the reward of doing something for its own sake', which is apt enough, and true enough in the sense of distinguishing it from external motivation. But it sounds bloodless, anaemic, effete, like the pleasure of baking a cake for tea, or bricking the drive. There is something enormously satisfying about using the circular saw that you got for Christmas, not with the idea of making anything in particular, but just for the sake of hearing the teeth biting into the wood and seeing the sawdust fly – that would qualify as intrinsic motivation, at least technically.

It is surely true that people who love their crafts produce better work than those who don't. A potter who derives joy from the feel of raw clay coming alive on the wheel, who loves the smell of oxides and ash, who can't wait to see what the oven does with the glaze, will produce more work, and more inventive work than someone who does it to pay the rent.

But for the great potter, for someone like Bonnie Ntshalintshali of Ardmore, for example, whose work now commands the attention of the world's most famous auction houses, the intrinsic gratification is more than the feel of the clay and a love of the process. It's the release of the daemon, the full play of the senses, the reward of expressing the inexpressible, the dance with immortality, the sense that something deeply personal and profound, that desperately needs articulation, is finding its voice at last, and as it was in Bonnie's case, not just for her but the Zulu nation and a generation at the mercy of HIV/AIDS.

Nor is it simply a question of passion, though it was once a useful word. You can be passionate about football, or toy soldiers, without feeling compelled to put your soul on the line for them. The kind of intrinsic motivation experienced in true creativity, that is, in the way that it is necessary to understand creativity for the purposes of this discussion, is a compulsion. It is not something you can choose or choose not to put on, like a hat. It is something that must be done or that must be expressed, an all-consuming preoccupation, an incessant fiddling, a dog with a bone, an itch that needs constant scratching.

You wouldn't think you'd find it in someone who invented a bagless vacuum cleaner but it is in the case of James Dyson and you can tell it is as soon as you hear him speak. It's all there – the obsession with mechanics, the scorn for branding and marketing, the way he runs the company. It's not something he does, it's something he has to do.

Because the thing that distinguishes creative people from uncreative people is that they have to keep doing what they do, whether they make money from it or not, whether anyone cares or not, whether it's bad for the health or not, whether they're paid to do it or not, whether it's recognized in their lifetime or not. It's a river that will burst its banks if you try to dam it up.

It's the work of your life. And it's your life's work.

Talent isn't creativity - You can develop talent

Talent can do everything else. Talent is a facility with something, a sleight of hand, a supple wrist. Talent is great draughtsmanship, a good ear, a sharp tongue, a generous heart.

You can have a talent for the guitar, or a talent for ballet, or a talent for converting decimals to percentages and vice versa. You could have a knack for card tricks or for working with animals. You might have an eye for fashion, a good voice for radio, the perfect face for television, or a green thumb. You may be brilliant at crosswords, or at riding a unicycle on a tightrope. You may be a wonderful listener, a natural organizer or a good mother.

You can enhance you talent by practising or studying, or at the feet of a master.

If you're lucky you will find a job that puts your talent to good use. Your skill will be appreciated and you'll feel happy and fulfilled. You'll be doing what you do best.

If you're not so lucky you'll have to do nine to five in a job you hate or a job you simply endure. At night or on weekends or on holidays you'll give your talent free rein. Or you may be trapped in a life of domestic tedium, or of desperate poverty, with no margin at all for anything other than survival, and your talent will wither and die.

Within the constraints of circumstance, imposed or self-imposed, talent ends up doing what it can.

Talent amuses us in the absence of genius. Talent keeps the world ticking over. Talent fills the time on the TV screen between rare moments of genius, and the time on cinema screens between the movies that change your life. Talent fills books and bookshelves. Talent keeps us engaged in football matches while we wait for a glimpse of genius.

Talent populates the continuum between the trite and the transcendent.

*

The compulsion that drives creative people on is beautifully evoked in this passage from the brilliant literary critic George Steiner:

> . . . somewhere, at some moment, a man alone, or a group of men addicted to the drug of absolute thought, will be seeking to create organic tissue, to determine the nature of heredity, to produce the cloud-chamber trail of quarks. Not for renown, not for the benefit of the human species, not in the name of social justice or profit, but because of a drive much stronger than love, stronger than even hatred, which is to be interested in something. For its own enigmatic sake. Because it is there.

But why do they do it?

When human behaviour doesn't make sense the best thing to do is to consult Darwin. Considering that we've been standing upright, making tools, hunting and gathering, and living together in social groups for upwards of three hundred thousand years, we shouldn't be surprised to discover that most of what we think and do can be explained by what our ancestors had to think and do to survive for that long. This is called evolutionary psychology, a relatively new way of thinking about who we are – and why we are who we are.

The best introduction to evolutionary psychology has got to be Steven Pinker's eminently entertaining *How the Mind Works*, which tells us – among many other fascinating things – how we go about choosing people to have sex with. Once you've read it you can't help wondering why it's taken so long for the scientific community to appreciate the obvious merits of this line of investigation.

The logic of ev/psych (as they call it) is very simple. We behave the way we do because hundreds of thousands of years of Darwinian selection have weeded out behaviours which haven't been useful to our survival as a species, in just the same way that evolution has shaped our bodies and brains to be well adapted to our environment – that is, the environment of the savannah and the jungle, not the 21st century environment of driving cars, watching TV and working with computers. Cosmides and Tooby, the founders of modern evolutionary psychology, call this 'a stone age brain in a modern skull'.

Which means you can look at any set of typical human behaviours and the chances are high that it will have an adaptive purpose – that it would have been very useful for helping us to survive through all those millennia, even if it doesn't look all that useful today.

For example, why should a certain small percentage of people in a population, around 10%, always be left-handed? Geneticists are stumped because left-handedness is not a heritable trait. Cognitive scientists have found that left-handers tend to be of above average intelligence and very creative or, at the other end of the spectrum, to be cursed with a variety of mental, social and emotional difficulties. Neuropsychologists believe that the above-average creativity of left-handers is associated with increased activation of the right hemisphere of the brain (because the right hemisphere drives the left-hand side of the body and vice versa). Medical researchers have found a strong correlation between left-handedness and a low birth weight, but they don't know why. Anthropologists have noted a steady increase in the number of left-handers being born over the past century or so, but they put it down to the fact that in the past many left-handers were 'persuaded' to be right-handed by parents, teachers or cultural pressure.

It's been left to the evolutionary psychologists to figure out *why* there should be any left-handers at all. Considering that left-handers are more accident prone, apparently more violent, and have a shorter life expectancy than right-handers, the callous march of evolution should have got rid of them tens of thousands of years ago.

One explanation is that left-handers have a significant advantage over right-handers in physical combat because of their surprise factor, just as left-handers tend, on average, to excel at tennis, cricket and other sports that involve some sort of hand-to-hand competition. So it might have been very useful to clans of early homo sapiens to have had a few left-handers in the mix, especially against competing primates like homo erectus and other pretenders to the two-legged throne.

Another explanation may be that left-handers gave the hunter/gatherer tribes a creative edge by providing a right-brain alternative to the logical, left-brain-dominated style of all those right-handers. Perhaps the left-handers were regarded as having magical powers. Perhaps they were the shamans who inspired the tribe to courage in adversity, or to self-belief in the face of the dangerous odds stacked against their survival. Perhaps they were the musicians or the storytellers who gave the rest of the tribe entertainment, religion or hope. Even if the left-handers couldn't come up with novel ways of laying a mammoth trap, perhaps there was some equally vital role for them around the campfire at night when the right-handers came back empty handed, distracting them from grumbling hunger with legends of great hunts past or great hunts to come.

*

Though Charles Darwin himself, and William James a few decades later, were excited by the prospects of looking at animal and human behaviour through the lens of natural selection, early 20th century forays into the field were limited to studies of instincts and drives. As behaviourism and cognitive science began to dominate the mainstream of psychological research, interest in an evolutionary perspective was relegated to the extreme margins.

It was only the publication of Richard Dawkins's highly controversial book, *The Selfish Gene*, in 1976, that prompted scientists in all sorts of disciplines to review their assumptions about what made people tick. It wasn't at all what he intended, but most reviewers got the idea that Dawkins was implying that we were all helpless victims of our genes' ambitions to replicate themselves at any cost. It took 20 years for most of the dust to settle. By that time ev/psych had gained enough of a following to withstand the excoriating criticisms of Stephen Jay Gould, the famous American populist writer on Darwinian theory.

Of all the various ways of looking at creativity, evolutionary psychology seems to promise us the most useful insights into its nature and purpose. But so far it has asked more questions than it has answered, not only because it's such a new field, but also because it's still grappling with some tricky epistemological questions of its own. This gets very academic and very complicated, but it's well worth a brief summary.

Up until now there have been two broad approaches to understanding human behaviour – psychology that has focused on the workings of the mind, and psychology that has focused on the workings of the brain. This has split the entire field right down the middle creating an academic standoff exacerbated by the interminable nature/nurture debate. To make sense of how we got to behave the way we do evolutionary psychologists have had to join the dots between our genetic inheritance and our cognitive behaviour. And they have also had to connect the evolution of brain and mind in the context of broader cultural and social issues, factoring both nature and nurture into the same complicated equation. All of which means they have become a strange breed of generalists in a field dominated by specialists, opening themselves up to the kind of criticism that all generalists inevitably attract, that is, they make sweeping generalizations.

So when it comes to creativity Pinker, who is compelling on so many other subjects, takes the generalist's way out.

'And what about genius?' he asks. 'How can natural selection explain a Shakespeare, a Mozart, an Einstein, an Abdul-Jabbar? How would Jane Austen, Vincent van Gogh or Thelonius Monk have earned their keep on the Pleistocene savannah?'

A great question, deserving a much better answer than it gets.

'All of us are creative,' he says. 'Every time we stick a handy object under the leg of a wobbly table or think up a new way to bribe a child into his pyjamas, we have used our faculties to create a novel outcome.'

Which is hardly satisfactory on any level. It's the default response of the problem-solvers, confusing creativity with the most rudimentary kind of intelligence. And it leaves us to wonder, even more urgently than before, why on earth we would need an Einstein if my eight year old son is perfectly well equipped to stick a handy object under the leg of my wobbly desk? Pinker bottled out badly on this one.

In search of something less flippant I turned again to Sternberg's *Handbook of Creativity* and found it in the deeply erudite *Evolving Creative Minds: Stories and Mechanisms* by Charles L. Lumsden. I liked him immediately.

Despite its sterile and utilitarian undertones I had almost persuaded myself that there was no better definition of creativity than Amabile's 'production of novel and appropriate ideas by individuals or small groups'. Then Lumsden gave me this: '*Creativity* will refer to that tantalizing constellation of personality and intellectual traits shown by people who, when given a measure of free rein, spend significant amounts of time engaged in the creative process.'

¡Orale!

And elsewhere, '. . . a kind of capacity to think up something new that people find significant'.

¡Ijole!

It's a question of where you draw the line. Watching a monkey use a stick to retrieve a bunch of bananas hooked to the ceiling strikes us as charming, intelligent and creative all at once. And the monkey in question will certainly find it significant. But the only reason why we're impressed at all is because our expectations regarding monkey behaviour are so low. With a little training we could probably teach the monkey to wedge something under the wobbly leg of Pinker's desk, in exchange for some more bananas.

How low, or how high, are our expectations of human creativity? Where do we draw the line between the ingenuity that put man on the moon with a tenth of the computing power of an iPod and the kind of intelligence that gave us *Las*

Meninas? Where do we draw the line between the inspiration that produced Velcro and the inspiration that produced the cathedral at Chartres? Where do we draw the line between the intelligence that led Bush and Blair into Iraq and the kind of intelligence that will need to be engaged to get them out of there?

The artefacts of our intelligence surround us. The computer that I write on is an ingenious result of decades of research and development, of thousands upon thousands of minute refinements combined with the great leaps of imagination that took it from idea to production to distribution, through the complexities guiding the push and pull of our entire economic system, that led, finally, to the seven or eight pixels that make up the full stop at the end of this sentence.

There was a time when I would have been happy with a sharp pencil, let alone the miracle of a ballpoint pen.

We take it for granted, now, that we are capable of extraordinary manipulations of technology. We rightfully believe that the things we need to live with, or the things we want to live with, should be better and more accessible than they were in the past. We were impressed, five short years ago, by Google's ability to distinguish between an image search and a text search. Today we are frustrated by video clips that take more than three seconds to buffer.

But after Berners-Lee and the World Wide Web what have we seen in the advance of technology that we can call 'significant'? The digital camera? The iPod? The iPhone? Facebook? CCTV?

The hydrogen fuel cell is hugely significant, but its progress is constrained by the vested interests of the status quo. Stem cell research must be right up there on the list of modern breakthroughs, but narrow-minded superstition cuts off vital funding and pushes it into the shadows of basement alchemists. We look to the bio-techs for the next big thing, hoping against hope for something to sustain our vanity into old age.

Time and again we see a lack of imagination in our social organizations suffocating the life out of the possibility of true progress. As knowledge races ahead, wisdom lags behind, yoked to the service of commerce and chained to the ball of institutional self-interest.

What should we expect of human creativity when Rwanda reminds us how low we've set the bar? What should we expect of human intelligence when a child dies every second for the lack of clean drinking water? What will it take to produce something we recognize as significant while as long as we continue to prize talent ahead of imagination and fame ahead of creativity? How content should we be to accept that the destiny of our species is fulfilled as long as we are smart enough to bribe a child into her pyjamas?

Evolution psychology - Learnt survive
eyepsych

About four million years ago we learned to stand on our own two legs. About two million years ago our brain size had expanded to 650cc, compared with about 400cc in a chimpanzee and the 1200–1400cc we have today. Between 1.5 million and a hundred thousand years ago a rapid of burst of cranial capacity levelled off with the appearance of the first modern man, the homeo sapiens of southern Africa. It took another fifty thousand years to start using that brain creatively, producing specialized tools, fabricated dwellings, long-distance trade and masterpieces of cave art.

Lumsden believes that cultural evolution and biological evolution went hand in hand. As humans learned how to make things, say things, sing things and paint things, the genetic structure of their brains co-evolved at the same pace. This gives evolutionary psychology an interesting twist. If Lumsden is right, and everything I have come across seems to suggest that he is, we will have to interpret contemporary human behaviour not just in the context of our stone age brains, but in the context of the social and cultural ephemera of the Pleistocene age. Lumsden is now looking for a mathematical formula that will help us to understand how genes and memes collided to make us who we are today, an undertaking we will leave to those whose brains have evolved sufficiently to know what he is talking about.

But he is lucid enough on the major puzzle concerning the evolution of creativity – that is, why it took yet another fifty thousand years for our super-sized brain to get from the Bronze Age to the explosion of innovation that began in Mesopotamia four thousand years ago. There are all sorts of theories that attempt to explain what happened in the interim, including a few conjectures by Lumsden himself.

Perhaps, he suggests, it took that much time to evolve to self-awareness without which creativity is just a scramble for survival. Or, as William James concluded a century ago, that consciousness was 'an organ added for the sake of steering a nervous system grown too complex to regulate itself'. Perhaps it took that much time to engineer those last bits of DNA into ensuring we would be hard-wired for the kind of creativity we'd need once we took our evolution into our own hands. Or perhaps it was a fifty thousand year experiment with REM and the kind of dream states we would need to experience in preparation for future creativity. Finally, Lumsden reviews the rest of the current literature on the puzzle of the creative gap.

Some theorists, like Jared Diamond, believe it had to do with the development of language and the concomitant need for a larynx sophisticated enough to vocalize it.

Others, like John Pfeiffer, believe that the increasing human population began to require a more inventive approach to social structures, group survival and intergroup communication. As Lumsden puts it:

> The load of cultural information pressing down on ever more complicated networks of band societies, where people could not yet read or write, opened new opportunities for people adept at drawing; the underground sanctuaries at places like Lascaux became 'socialisation machines' in whose bowels rhythmic ceremony, sensory deprivation and exposure to 'virtual worlds' compellingly rendered on the cavern walls helped ingrain band norms and wisdom.

Or, in the words of E.O. Wilson:

> The Arts, while creating order and meaning from the seeming chaos of daily existence, also nourish our craving for the mystical. We are drawn to the shadowy forms that drift in and out of the subconscious. We dream of the insoluble, of unattainably distant places and times. Why should we so love the unknown? The reason may be that Paleolithic environment in which the brain evolved. In our emotions, I believe, we are still there.

Merlin Donald believes it was all of these, together with the invention of fire and – crucially – the freedom that walking upright gave us to use our hands for gestures, for acting out things, for re-enacting things and for planning ahead. You can still see this among the San today, the theatre of the hunt played out in the flickering shadows of fires lighted against the Kalahari dusk.

And right there, in those three key theories, you get the essence of it – language, art and theatre arising not only as a consequence of a bigger brain, *but arising as an engine of human evolution itself.* We are not creative because we are human; we are human because of our creativity.

We learned the joy and pain of consciousness. We learned to dream. We learned to speak and listen, to express our anger and our affection, to name the world around us, and to create the virtual world of the story and the song. We learned to live with each by experiencing, for the very first time, the transforming power of art. We learned to dance and we learned to act. And we learned to understand who we were in relation to the world in the power of gesture and performance.

*

The Darwinian perspective also illuminates the darkest mystery of all, what goes on beneath the skull as our brains struggle to make up their minds. The more we get to know about brain chemistry and the complexity of our neural structures, the more it seems likely that that same evolutionary process that helped to shape us over so many millions of years also operates at the micro level in the milliseconds that it takes for us to choose between one thought or another. This is survival of the fittest idea, guiding the way we think at the level of synapses and axon bundles.

There is a wonderful book called *How Brains Think* by William H. Calvin that posits a compelling case for the brain as 'a Darwin machine'. Calvin manages to make neuroscience as gripping as Le Carré and as entertaining as Bryson.

There's no point trying to get into the details of any of this because any kind of summary would do him a grave injustice. It's the implications that concern us, what it means to our understanding of creativity if we can conceive of our brains in this way – a restless struggle between thousands of cortical impulses competing with one another in endless chemical battles for dominance. Only the winner survives, the thought that emerges towards consciousness with the strongest claim for expression in action or idea. Most of the winning thoughts will be ones that have triumphed before, the default language of everyday speech, the impulse to make a cup of tea or to brush one's teeth. They will be repetitive and familiar, and they will get stronger over time.

These well-trodden neural pathways are what keep us sane, encouraging us to say, 'I'm fine,' in response to 'How are you?' rather than something more random, such as, 'My stripes are broken.' They enable us to socialize, to have more or less normal relationships, and to behave appropriately within our cultural norms. They also help us to deal logically with the simple algorithms of everyday life, making sure that every time we multiply 10 by 10 we get a hundred. It takes some mental effort to interrupt the natural flow of these habitual synaptic links. You can almost feel your brain resisting any other outcome, such as 10 times 10 equals 99.

De Bono based his 'lateral thinking' on this phenomenon, believing that by conscious effort we can trick our neural circuits into taking the road less travelled. The same presumption underlies creative exercises such as SCAMPER, which invite us to see familiar things in different ways, like imagining that a light bulb is a jet engine. Forcing associations between random words is another way of getting the needle to jump out of the grooves. You can amuse yourself for hours by choosing two arbitrary words out of a dictionary and turning them into a useful application for managing inner city traffic flows, for example.

As we shall see, the evidence that these kinds of tricks can produce anything more than 'non-trivial' results has yet to be delivered. And now that we know something about how our brains work it's easy to see why.

The neural networks of normal adult people are hard-wired to produce normal adult results, that is, thinking and behaviour that is more convergent than divergent. At the other extreme, the neural networks of adult psychotics are hopelessly scrambled, producing behaviour that is inappropriate, unpredictable and often extremely anti-social. Children and highly creative adults fall somewhere in between. Sometimes they behave with grown-up circumspection; sometimes they say and do the most outrageous things.

Children can be taught to think more convergently. Indeed, almost all of modern western education is designed to get them to do just that – to come up with the right answers in their maths, to spell correctly, and to behave appropriately in society. Though we no longer punish them directly for getting things wrong, we know that life will punish them sooner or later for any persistent failure to conform. Thanks to the efforts of people like Deborah Evans attempts are at last being made to teach divergent thinking within the school system. And it's true that we are much more tolerant these days of pupils who do not fit in easily with the codes and conditions whereby success continues, by and large, to be measured. Most kids will get through the system without too many emotional or psychological scars, and most of those will go on to be regular law-abiding, tax-paying citizens.

We now have ways of picking up learning difficulties fairly early on. In most decent societies there are safety nets for those kids who find it impossible to fit in, either academically or socially, with the requirements of the educational norm.

It's the naturally divergent thinkers who have the hardest time of it. They are bright enough to get through the system and to meet the standards that are required of them. But we know that they are never entirely comfortable in environments that reward convergence at the expense of everything else. The biographies of most great creative thinkers confirm, almost without exception, that they were seldom recognized as prodigies, and that they seldom made much of an impression on their teachers or their contemporaries.

For divergent thinkers wrong answers are just as psychologically comfortable – and often much more interesting – than right answers. The cortical inhibition that makes us feel a little queasy when 10 times 10 equals 99 is, for them, a lot more forgiving. It's as though their Darwin machines are faulty, or slightly out of tune. The fittest idea isn't always the one that survives the micro-evolutionary struggle in their brains. Often it's the awkward one, the peculiar one, the mutant one. It's the thought with the clubfoot, the six fingers, the conjoined toes.

Evolution throws up random mutations on the off chance that one of them may be of some use for the survival of the species if the environmental circumstances were to change in its favour. It's exactly the same with mutant thoughts. You never know when one will be perfectly adapted to the rapidly shifting sands of human debate and human uncertainty.

You can't teach psychopaths how to behave more appropriately. Drugs can help, of course, in the same way that drugs can help the chronically convergent to loosen up the shackles of the pre-frontal monitors. But these are not permanent conditions. When the drugs wear off you get back to the way your brain was wired together in the first place, divergent or convergent, sane or psychotic. And drugs, unlike dreams, often end up masking the brain's ability to retrieve the good ideas that you had while you were tripping, as Coleridge found out with 'Kubla Khan'.

When we dream, all bets are off. Thoughts that struggled to break through to the surface to the daylight of consciousness now find themselves free to frolic in the playground of self-expression, subverting the familiar, twisting the repetitive, mating with other aberrant thoughts in a licentious orgy of instant gratification. The Dionysian progeny, with their pointy ears and distended genitals, may grow up to be wonderful ideas that we find significant; or extraordinary images, dazzling poems, hilarious comments, life-changing revelations, new memes that whizz around the world with the speed of Google. It depends on how much we love them.

Tricking your brain into exploring new cerebral pathways will allow you to think of things you've never thought of before. As long as you can sustain the tricks you will continue to have ideas which are novel, at least to yourself. That's why you feel so stimulated in these artificial creative sessions like brainstorming or using the paintings of Monet to help you think up a new flavour of toothpaste.

The world appears to be opening up and expanding, the serotonin rushes in and your brain loves the taste of it. But when you're no longer in a safe environment, when the moderator is gone, the lights are off and the elevator rumbles ominously up and down the 37 floors, the creatures of mystery that you conjured up with such excitement only a few minutes ago begin to turn ghoulish and silly, and the default circuitry of your cerebrum rejects them the way your antibodies would reject a foreign heart.

Despite de Bono's best intentions, and despite some evidence that children can be taught to take a more divergent approach to problem-solving, we are, as adults, doomed to live with the neural pathways bestowed on us by nature and conditioned by nurture. We can continue to enrich them with further learning, we can fight off the IQ-diminishing advance of age by keeping them active – doing our crossword puzzles, playing bridge, joining a book club or playing the piano; we can soak them in barley grass and honey, exercise them with stimulating debate and BBC2, we can achieve great things by putting into practice the things we know and the talents we've acquired, but we can't change them or modify them or dig them up and replace them with new ones for the simple reason that we can't change who we are. At the very deepest level we are the matter that our minds are made of, the accumulated complexity of the way our brains are wired, by our personal histories, the shuffle of the genetic pack, and a few million years of evolution.

Connecting the neural dots to the work done by Martindale we are obliged to conclude that highly creative people – people who are compelled to think divergently whether they wish to or not – are wired to respond to creative challenges by stepping back into the alpha zone of the primary thought state. The rest of us are wired to resort to beta and the high GSR flutter of applied intelligence.

*

It strikes me that right- and left-handedness may be more than just a good metaphor for the evolutionary adaptation we call creativity. Maybe it's a simile. Maybe it's connected.

Evolution has distributed intelligence in a smooth Bell curve, making the majority of us reasonably smart, a decreasing percentage of us extraordinarily clever, and a similar decreasing percentage edging towards the lower end of the IQ scale. It may not be fair but that's the way it is. Luckily, IQ isn't everything. Some very smart people can't tie their shoelaces; some of the intellectually challenged are brilliant at doing other things.

Most human traits are distributed in same way across the population. What percentage of people can do the splits? What percentage can lick their elbows with their tongue? What percentage can sing in tune? If you took the trouble to research these things you'd almost certainly find a Bell-shaped curve of competence, with the majority of people in the swollen centre, not quite able to do the splits, lick their elbows or sing in tune, but capable, nevertheless, of coming reasonably close.

Left-handedness is clearly something different. While many left-handers use their right hands for certain things, and some right-handers use their left hands for certain things, there's a sharp and noticeable divide between the two groups. Most of us are either left-handed or right-handed, with a minute percentage of ambidextrous grey in the middle. Experts in 'handedness' will also take into account which ear we favour, we eye we favour, which foot we favour to kick with, which foot we favour to begin walking up stairs, which hand we use to brush our teeth etc. This adds some fuzziness to the edges of the divide because some right-handers will favour their left ears or eyes and some left-handers will favour their right feet and so on through all possible combinations. We can take all of these into account and still not arrive at any semblance of a Bell curve. We'll get a pie chart with around 10% of people showing up as left-handed, around 90% of people showing up as right-handed, with a fuzzy-edged slice of grey separating the black and the white.

Now what about right- or left-brain dominance? We know that brain centres involved in the perception and production of music, of visual art and of mental imagery are found in the right hemisphere of the brain. As for verbal creativity, Martindale tells us:

Based on research on split-brain patients it would seem that the right hemisphere possesses a rather comprehensive lexicon but that it is chaotically arranged. This is, it understands words but not how they go together in a grammatical or propositional manner. Access to such an 'alternative' lexicon could certainly be of use to a poet.

Or a writer like Joyce.

Most right-handers are left-brain dominant. Most left-handers are right-brain dominant. A few left-handers have their hemispheric asymmetry switched around, so effectively they are left-brain dominant, mirror images, if you like, of us right-handed left-brainers.

While left-handers, as we have seen, are disproportionately represented among high creative achievers, a small percentage of right-handers are right-brain dominant. That percentage, arrestingly enough, is more or less 10%. So the pie chart of brain dominance looks more or less the same as the pie chart of hand dominance. The big piece of the pie shows 90% of us as predominantly left-brained. The smaller piece of the pie shows 10% of us as right-brained. And there's a fuzzy grey area in the middle made up of ambi-brained exceptions, as well as those who are mainly left-brained but who have an active musical, visual or verbal hotspot in their right brains.

Now if we take our two pie charts and place them on top of each other while rotating the handedness pie slightly enough to account for the percentage of right-handers who are also right-brain dominant, an interesting picture emerges.

Evolution seems to be playing a peculiar game, covering its bets for both physical and intellectual survival. If the point of left-handedness is the surprise factor it lends to physical combat between competing groups, then the point of right-brain dominance appears to be the surprise factor it lends to the challenges that threaten our intellectual advance.

'The world of the future,' said Norbert Wiener, the inventor of cybernetics, in 1950, 'will be an even more demanding struggle against the limitations of our intelligence, not a comfortable hammock in which we can lie down to be waited upon by our robot slaves.'

Right-brainers are the jokers in the genetic pack, apparently useless for most of the game, but capable of trumping the ace of spades when all our chips are down.

CHAPTER 8

Towards a formula for genius

The real question is not whether machines think but whether men do. The mystery which surrounds a thinking machine already surrounds a thinking man.

B.F. Skinner

Right-brained, hostile, anxious, compulsive and ill-fitted for survival – it's unsurprising that creative people find it tricky to settle into the regime of institutional life, or that corporations have a difficult time deciding how best they should be managed.

Equally unsurprising, then, is the urge of the corporate technocrats to codify the behaviour of creative people as soon as they discover that they can be deskilled no further.

The search for the creative trick that will consistently deliver surprising ideas is especially intense in advertising. Since most good advertising ideas flirt with subversion in one way or another, the formula that usually ends up as everyone's favourite is the notion of the paradigm break, the unexpected overturning of convention.

Burt Manning of JWT called it 'abruption'.

But Jean-Marie Dru made it famous, first at BDDP in Paris, and later with TBWA, by calling it 'disruption'. What a difference a prefix makes. In his book of the same name he describes it as, '. . . finding the strategic idea that breaks and overturns a convention in the marketplace, and then makes it possible to reach a new vision or to give new substance to an existing vision'.

You can see what he's getting at. But for clarity of exposition it's not going to beat Koestler's 'creativity is the defeat of habit by originality'.

As with most of these books on advertising one can't help suspecting that the practice came long before the theory. Good advertising creatives make disruption work as a matter of course because they have a natural instinct for the subversive.

Everyone who stumbles upon it thinks that he or she has found the key to genius. James Webb Young clearly thought he had when he asserted, 'an idea is nothing more nor less than a *new combination* of old elements'. (His italics.)

The idea that creativity results from an unexpected collision between two competing frames of reference has been around as long as human beings have been telling jokes. Freud's classic analysis of humour, in *Jokes and Their Relation to the Unconscious*, makes the same point, as does Koestler's concept of 'bi-sociation'.

While the juxtaposition of contradictory or unrelated meanings appears to be the common denominator of all humour, most inventions and a great deal of art, it is by no means a necessary (let alone a sufficient) condition for true creativity.

Often it's just a cheap trick, like a pun.

But sometimes it can result in a very rich conceptual vein as in, to use another advertising example, 'Dirt is good', the underlying communications premise for a range of Unilever washing powders. This is compelling in all sorts of ways, not least in the reassurance (real or imagined, it doesn't matter which) that it gives to mothers that the dirtier the clothes of their little rascals the better they are expressing themselves, hence getting stronger both physically and mentally. Koestler could have done a couple of brilliant chapters on this particular 'bi-sociation', and Freud would have a field day.

Conceptually speaking, 'Dirt is good' is a direct descendant of the stroke of counterintuitive genius that led Edward Jenner to the discovery of the smallpox vaccine in the 1760s. Germs are good.

All outsider stories, in film and literature, operate on the same premise. The intersection of E.T. with a suburban American family is Gulliver retold with lashings of honey.

With some application, and a loose enough definition of bi-sociation, you could probably find it in everything you look at. In art you can see it as figure and ground, or in the intersection of the subjective with the objective. In music you can find it in counterpoint and, I'm led to believe, in many aspects of musical theory. It can be made into good drama, memorable poetry and interesting TV.

The public's evident fascination with shows like *I'm a Celebrity, Get Me Out of Here* surely derives from the intersection of spoilt brats and maggots.

For all of these reasons you'll find random word games and forced juxta-ⱻ positions are at the heart of most creativity exercises. But being able to identify bi-sociations and describe the way they operate in any piece of creative work is a long way away from being able to employ them to significant effect. For some time to come, gene splicing will remain more productive than meme splicing, except as a parlour game.

A less reductionist and much more helpful approach to the power of bi-sociation comes from Frans Johansson's recent book, *The Medici Effect*. The subtitle tells us exactly where he's coming from: 'Breakthrough Insights at the Intersection of Ideas'. It's Chapter 1 of *The Act of Creation* peppered with some contemporary case studies. Or Peter Hall lite for those who can't get through 'Cities in Civilization'.

Zooming out from the micro level of thoughts cross-pollinating in the human brain, Johansson uses the flowering of creativity in Quattrocento Florence to remind us that innovation happens at the intersections of different fields, disciplines and cultures.

For the better part of three hundred years a sizeable population of artistic and scientific wannabes was persuaded, lured, cajoled, attracted, invited or obliged to migrate to the Tuscan capital to decorate the city for the greater glory of God in general and the Medicis in particular. Their ranks would eventually include almost every one of the significant artists, sculptors, architects and thinkers of the Renaissance: Masaccio, Fra Angelico, Uccello, Fra Filippo Lippi, Castagno, Francesco de Giorgio, Pollaiuolo, Botticelli, Ghirlandaio, Piero della Francesca, Mantegna, Bellini, Leonardo da Vinci, Michelangelo, Raphael, Donatello, Ghiberti, Brunelleschi and Galileo.

What led to the unprecedented efflorescence of artistic and intellectual achievement during the Medici years, according to Johansson, was the sheer diversity of skills, perspectives and cultures rubbing shoulders together in a single concentrated community. His central thesis is that creativity tends to happen when ⱻ different disciplines intersect, quoting the example of Aquavit, the famous New York restaurant.

When the executive chef died suddenly in 1995 the owner had to find an immediate replacement. Out of desperation he promoted Marcus Samuelsson, a ⱻ newly hired assistant while looking for a suitable celebrity chef. Samuelsson began experimenting with new combinations of food from all over the world, such as mango curry sorbet and caramelized lobster with seaweed pasta, sea urchin sausage and cauliflower sauce.

Aquavit went on to become one of the most fashionable restaurants in New York, and Samuelsson became a celebrity in his own right.

Johansson writes:

> Samuelsson has accomplished this by breaking down traditional barriers in cooking. He has an uncanny ability to draw associations from almost any cuisine in the world and see how they connect with his base of Swedish ingredients and cooking techniques. This ability has placed him at the intersection of Swedish food and global tastes. ✗
> The solution to our mystery now seems rather simple. Samuelsson's creative genius lies in his ability to generate unique food combinations that surprise the palate.

It's a real shame that Johansson ends up with such a trivial example when the larger hypothesis of *The Medici Effect* seems to promise so much. Gravlax and tandoori smoked salmon is the most basic expression of bi-sociation where A plus B equals C.

Once again this leads us down the reductionist path with its logical conclusion that creativity is simply a matter of conjoining unlikely pairs, which only serves to undermine the very important lessons of Medici Florence. His recipe for innovation, it turns out, is much less imaginative than the Aquavit menu. The familiar admonitions are all there – expose yourself to different cultures, broaden your knowledge, encourage curiosity, reverse assumptions, randomly combine concepts, learn to be prepared to see opportunities at their intersections when they present themselves, look for connections in unlikely places, read as much as you can, listen attentively and – wait for it – brainstorm.

Oh dear.

In an interview with www.baconsrebellion.com Johansson is honest enough to admit that, 'Most breakthrough technologies and business models spring from passion on an individual level. There is no way that a group of political or civic leaders can predict who will succeed and who will not.'

There's real wisdom in that confession. First, because there is no substitute, in the end, for the compulsion that drives certain individuals to creative achievement. And second, because, implicit in that second sentence, there's an acknowledgement of the critical role of redundancy. In the same way that the human brain appears to neuroscientists to be much larger than would strictly be necessary for an adequate intelligence and all of our neural functioning, we shall see that an apparent 'redundancy' of talent is vital to successful idea generation in the creative workplace. And just as you cannot predict which particular part of the brain will come up with its next big idea, you cannot predict which individual in a creative community will find the innovation or artistic breakthrough you're banking on.

Buried under Johansson's enthusiasm for the 'intersection of ideas' is the notion of patronage itself, which he serves up badly undercooked. The liberating power of patronage has been largely ignored, or simply taken for granted, by the literature on creativity. As we begin to construct a shiny new model for the management of creative talent, both patronage and redundancy will be writ large on the blueprint.

*

If the production of novel ideas were a simple matter of putting two different things together in a new expression we would hardly need human beings to be involved, let alone talented ones.

This was precisely the thinking behind the steady stream of computer models of creativity that began to flood the halls of academe as soon as the day came that you didn't have to wait in line to use the university computer. To be fair, only the most optimistic of the early programmers expected to manufacture digital versions of T.S. Eliot. The rest were in hot pursuit of artificial intelligence, of which creativity was only a trivial subset.

Despite the exponential leaps in computing power of the last two decades, creativity programs have yet to produce anything as evocative as 'Twinkle, twinkle, little star . . .'. But by turning the bright beam of reductionism onto the creative process they have helped to illuminate some of the darker materials of genius.

The first problem that the early creativity programmers faced was the trivial matter of definition. On what basis would they evaluate the output of the computer? How would they know when it was being creative?

It was easy enough to get a computer to put billions of different words together in new arrangements but significantly harder to evaluate whether any of them were any good. They were soon obliged to accept that creativity involved substantially more than the novel combination of old ideas.

Margaret Boden, professor of psychology and philosophy at the University of Sussex, has thought about this more than most people. She has studied a wide variety of programs intended to mimic human creativity in one way of another. They include a program written by Philip Johnson-Laird of Princeton which can improvise modern jazz 'up to the standard of a competent beginner'; a program called AARON developed by Harold Cohen, an abstract artist, which produces some 'attractive' sketches and paintings; programs like AM and Eurisko that have been able to rediscover the fundamental laws of mathematics, and a series of programs variously known as BACON, DALTON, GLAUBER that use heuristics to discover new concepts in very tightly defined conceptual spaces such as chemical reactions.

A writing program called Racter, by William Chamberlain, has published a book called *The Policeman's Beard is Half-Constructed*.

There is even a program for telling jokes. Known as Jape-1, it was developed by AI researcher Kim Binstead at Edinburgh University. So far it's been able to produce some hilarious riddles, like 'What do you give a hurt lemon? Lemonade, of course!'

Boden's analysis has led her to propose several very different kinds of creativity. P-creativity (P for psychological) describes ideas that are new to the people who have them. H-creativity (H for history) describes ideas that are new in the context of human history. E-creativity 'explores' a particular conceptual space, like every possible configuration of jazz chords. T-creativity involves 'some transformation of one or more of the (relatively fundamental) dimensions defining the conceptual space . . .'. And ET-creativity includes both E and T.

Understandably, the most difficult kind to simulate is T-creativity. Picasso wasn't simply a great artist; he changed the way we look at art. Bach changed the way people listened to music. Einstein changed the way we look at the universe. A really great TV commercial changes the way we look at all TV commercials. *The Office* changed the way we look at soaps. In every conceivable field, the mark of true genius is its transformational power – not only producing something that people regard as significant, but something that changes the domain itself in some fundamental way.

In the real world, where time and ideas mean money, what we really need to know is whether creativity can be explained or, even more importantly, whether it can be predicted.

The various approaches to creativity that we have discussed so far, the psychometric, the personality theory, the biological and others, are attempts to explain it, to understand the underlying structures that generate it in the individual or in the community. Other approaches, particularly those dealing with the creative process and those dealing with creativity enhancement, are attempts to predict it.

Understandably, it's the latter type that has attracted so much commercial interest. For the owners and managers of the rapidly expanding creative industries some sort of replicable formula for predicting creative success would be the answer to many long nights of prayer. Which is why they have seized upon books like *The Medici Effect*, *The Rise of the Creative Class* and even *The Tipping Point* as signs of imminent salvation. And which explains why they have embraced the vacuous promises of people like de Bono, Parnes and Mr Plsek while ignoring the vast body of credible research that indicts them for what they are.

Computer models of creativity will clearly not be threatening to replace real, live creative talent for some time to come. But they do help to bring the issues of explanation and predictability into sharp relief. Boden sums up:

> With respect to creativity, there are many reasons for expecting that – in the general case – detailed prediction and explanation will not be possible. This is especially clear with respect to combinatorial creativity, but ET-creativity, too, is largely unpredictable (and H-creativity is by definition unpredicted). Although one can sometimes deliberately lead someone else to make a specific P-creative move (good teachers do this often), this is usually impossible. *Chance factors such as serendipity cannot be foreseen. When they happen, their effect may be mysterious (even to the individual concerned) because of the idiosyncratic, and largely unconscious complexity of human minds.* (My italics.)

In short, the outlook is bleak. We're back in the hands of luck, magic and the mysteries of the unconscious. This is bad news for organizations still hoping to eliminate uncertainty from the creative and innovation process. But it should be good news for creative people whose jobs are next in line to be deskilled.

We can be sure, however, that the disciples of scientific management will continue to seek out ways to routinize creativity. New technologies will continue to erode those areas of creative expression that are subject to replication, and there's no reason why they shouldn't. They will bring the divide between talent and true creativity into sharp focus, eliminating both the dilettantes and the craftsmen on the one hand while illuminating, for the first time in history, the authentic nature of creativity on the other.

We will soon reach a point where all creative skills have been commoditized except for those at the very core of conceptual originality. It will be a famous day for all of us. The Taylorists and their neo-Taylorist followers will be obliged to accept that progress is impossible without unpredictability, and creative people will find themselves valued and respected in an accommodation of interests that delights in their idiosyncrasies.

Douglas Hofstadter's groundbreaking book *Godel, Escher, Bach* puts forward an inspirational case for the undiluted thrill of approximating human consciousness in the body of a machine. Never mind the objections of the Luddites, the moralists and the sci-fi scaremongers. The closer we get to true AI the more likely we are to understand why normal human intelligence can be so unutterably stupid. And even more excitingly, our interaction with a real digital intelligence promises to create an intersection point liable to yield unimaginable creative possibilities.

As long as we have told each other's stories we have been fascinated by the notion of an alien intelligence. Over the years we have imputed one, or several of them, in rocks and trees, in the sun and the stars, in cosmic beings and in messengers from God. We keep hoping they'll arrive in flying saucers or on four black horses. We look for them in the patterns of gamma rays and the noises of deep space. But I can't help thinking that our best chance of meeting one is to construct it ourselves.

While the rest of us wait for an oracle from Oracle, the reductionists, the behaviourists and the pragmatists are busy with a program of their own.

CHAPTER 9

The barbel and the breadboard

BEVERLY: His artistic rages are awe inspiring!

SNOID: *!$!&!

BEVERLY: His untamed spirit roams the cosmos . . . he grapples with powerful unseen forces in the magic world of dark dreams!

SNOID: GRAHH!

BEVERLY: His tortured body is racked by the terrible battles raging in his soul!

SNOID: EEYAAAAHHH!

BEVERLY: I feel privileged to be a witness to this primal enactment of the creative process!

Robert Crumb, *Snoid Comics*, 1980

It speaks volumes that the two most illuminating books about the creative process refrain from reducing it to a formula.

Brewster Ghiselin's *The Creative Process*, published in 1952, is a compendium of the subjective accounts of 38 of the world's greatest creative thinkers describing how they came up with their ideas, or how their ideas came to them. Including the reflections of Nietzsche, Mozart, Poincaré, Gertrude Stein, Henry Moore, Van Gogh, Einstein, Henry Miller and others, it makes a fascinating read, not only for its historical interest, but for the glimpses it affords into those deeply personal corners of the creative psyche – much in the way that the divorce proceedings of major celebrities allow us glimpses into the grubby personal stuff that goes on behind the glossy photo spreads in magazine like *Hello*!

Despite clear similarities between the experiences of such a wide diversity of artists and thinkers, Ghiselin refrains from concluding that the patterns associated with creative inspiration can be imitated by those seeking creative immortality, or a job in advertising.

Arthur Koestler's magnificent exploration of creative thinking, *The Act of Creation*, first published in 1964, has yet to be surpassed in either the breadth of its intellect or the depth of its wisdom. It is so wide-ranging in its interests, so rich in detail, and so profound in the variety and complexity of its insights, that the only thing more difficult than reading it is attempting to summarize it. I suspect, in the end, it is to creativity what a unified field theory would be to physics, a Holy Grail of understanding that only a few mortals might ever get to appreciate in its fullness.

Many of Koestler's conjectures anticipate the findings of contemporary research, especially those dealing with the role of primary thought processes during creative conceptualization. For example, in his discussion of what he calls 'multiple attunements' we get a brilliant description of defocused attention as identified by Martindale and others, under sophisticated laboratory conditions, some 30 years later. This passage, which gives you some idea of the scope of Koestler's references, perfectly anticipates what we now know about the inhibitory function of the frontal lobe. He has been discussing the number of associations that spring to his mind when he hears the word 'Madrid' – the historical, the geographical, the personal experiences, the tastes and smells, and so on:

> Thus a concept is a member of several clubs, but it likes some clubs more than others. Its 'multiple attunements' may be represented as a line-spectrum of frequencies with a relatively stable energy-distribution. The frequencies of maximum energy – like the dominant partials in a sound-spectrum – would represent the concept's 'most-preferred' associative contexts. As the years go by, new lines would be added to the spectrum while others would fade away, and the energy-distribution of associative preferences would change – getting mellower perhaps, like an old Stradivarius, or croaking, like an un-tuned piano. The effort to 'concentrate' on an abstract problem is probably proportionate to the energy required to inhibit preferential associative contexts of high energy-potential – i.e. 'habit strength'.

One of the many wonderful things about *The Act of Creation* is that it is written for the sheer love of its subject. It is, in itself, as creatively expressive and beautiful as the objects of its interest. As intrigued as he is by the creative process, and as deeply as he understands it as both a historical phenomenon and as a gateway to a more profound knowledge of human behaviour, Koestler is manifestly unconcerned with any thought of translating his conclusions from theory into practical advice. Given the extraordinary breadth of his research we must assume he would have been aware of the work of both Herman von Helmholtz and George Wallas, both of whom were well known for their prescriptive definitions of the creative process. Yet neither is mentioned even once in his 750 pages. If it isn't oversight it must surely be contempt.

The difference between the approach of someone like Parnes and the approach of someone like Koestler is the difference between chess and pinball. At last count, Amazon listed 4704 books about chess, almost all of them aimed at helping us to be better chess players. At the same time, Amazon listed 84 books about pinball, not a single one of them aimed at helping us to be better pinball players.

With good coaching and a lot of practice, most people can learn to play better chess. While there is certainly no guaranteed formula for success, there are steps you can follow to help you improve your openings, tips to help you through the middle game, and plenty of instruction on the end-game. The more you study the better you become, even if you aren't blessed with the brain of a Kasparov.

There are no instructions to help you become a better pinball player. The more you play a certain machine the more you will get to know its quirks and character, what to aim for to get bonuses, tricks for keeping your ball in play, and just how much you can manhandle the machine without getting penalized by a *tilt*. At a conscious level there's not much more to absorb. Real learning takes place unconsciously, or even deeper than that. Your muscles must remember the weight and strength of the flippers, your eyes must learn to follow the ball without consciously looking at it, your brain must learn to anticipate the speed and direction of the ball without any conscious calculation. You have to learn to engage fully, with all your senses, in the randomness of the bounce, maximizing every chance opportunity in that peculiar reflex state that they call 'the zone'.

The Who understood it perfectly in 'Pinball Wizard'. And so does Mihaly Czikszentmihalyi, describing it like this in *Flow, the Psychology of Optimal Experience*:

> When all a person's relevant skills are needed to cope with the challenges of a situation, that person's attention is completely absorbed by the activity. There is no excess psychic energy left over to process any information but what the activity offers. All the attention is concentrated on the relevant stimuli.
>
> As a result, one of the most universal and distinctive features of optimal experience take place: people become so involved in what they are doing that the activity becomes spontaneous, almost automatic: they stop being aware of themselves as separate from the actions they are performing.

If they are not exactly the same thing there is clearly a strong connection between this trance-like state and the defocused attention of the creative mind in search of ideas. To play pinball well you need to be able to clear your mind of the logic of the secondary process and allow the ball and the bumpers and the lights and the sounds to be juggled with expert ease by an intuitive process that lingers below the level of conscious awareness.

In pinball, chance is everything. There is no predicting the bounce of the ball. Beyond the reach of your two clumsy little flippers, the field is a puzzle of aleatory events. To exert any kind of control the best you can do is to go with the flow of the ball, nudging the machine this way to keep it engaged in productive play in the hope of getting bonus balls. But there is risk in every move.

Chess, by contrast, is chance free. The gods of chess do not play dice.

You can teach people to play better chess, you can teach them how to paint with oils, you can teach them how to play the piano. You can teach them a thousand different crafts and skills for a thousand different creative applications; you can coach them to do passable imitations of Seurat, or passable renditions of Chopin. You can cajole them into thinking more critically, or writing more imaginatively; you can persuade them to express themselves more freely, to take more risks, to embrace the absurd, and to appreciate the beauty of chaos. You can make them wear green hats and whack them on the sides of the heads and teach them how to think outside the box and get them to make interesting new concepts out of random words drawn from a lilac teapot. But you can't teach people how to be more creative.

R.S. Nickerson has summarized all of the studies of all of the research of all of the techniques that have ever been used to teach people how to be more creative. This is his conclusion: 'To my knowledge, there is no easy, step-wise method that is guaranteed to enhance creativity to a non-trivial degree.'

Sternberg is even more damning: 'Equally damaging to the scientific study of creativity, in our view, has been the take-over of the field, in the popular mind, by those who follow what might be referred to as a pragmatic approach.'

He singles out de Bono, Osborn, Gordon, Adams and van Oech as chief culprits. There are many more.

The 19th century German physicist Herman von Helmholtz was, as far as we know, the first person to come up with a step-by-step method for producing ideas. He identified three phases – 'saturation', 'incubation' and 'illumination', based on his own subjective experience of coming up with some remarkable inventions (which include the ophthalmoscope), though he was also no doubt aware of many of the famous stories of inspiration among artists and scientists that Ghiselin was later to compile for *The Creative Process*.

'Saturation' was his description of the initial process of learning, struggling with, and anguishing about a particular problem that needed to be solved, or about the intimation of some sort of potential breakthrough that seems so annoyingly elusive when you first become aware of it. This is the part of the process that feels as if you're banging your head against the wall, though Helmholtz would probably not have put it into those words.

The second stage, 'incubation', describes that stage of the creative process when you allow all of your frustrations, and all of the issues associated with the challenge, to simmer gently on the stove of the unconscious. During this stage you could fall asleep in front of the fire like Kekule did, you could take drugs, like Coleridge did, you could go for a walk like Wordsworth did, or you could take a bath like Archimedes did.

Sometime soon after this period of letting go of the problem you will be struck by the third phase, 'illumination', which signals the arrival of the idea, almost fully formed, to the awe and admiration of the Nobel Committee and succeeding generations of admirers. Helmholtz, to give him credit, never prescribed his three steps as a technique for producing ideas. Like many great thinkers he was simply fascinated by the pattern he had observed and felt compelled to write it down.

In 1926, with the publication of *The Art of Thought*, Graham Wallas added a fourth stage to the Helmholtz formula, which he called 'verification', designed to test the appropriateness of the idea for application in the real world. Wallas's interest in the creative process was motivated by the belief that we could make a better world for ourselves if we stopped to think about it more a minute.

A remarkable character in many ways, Wallas not only helped to found the London School of Economics he was an influential member of the Fabian Society, along with such luminaries of the day as H.G. Wells, Sydney and Beatrice Webb, and George Bernard Shaw, which shaped the way socialist Britain continues to worship state institutions like the NHS.

Five years later, on the other side of the world, Joseph Rossman of the US Patent Office began tinkering with his own formula for creative achievement. Based on questionnaires completed by 710 inventors, Rossman took a much more practical approach, prescribing seven steps that now look ominously similar to the strategic planning disciplines of many advertising agencies:

1.   Observation of a need or difficulty.
2.   Analysis of the need.
3.   A survey of all available information.
4.   A formulation of all objective solutions.
5.   A critical analysis of these solutions for their advantages and disadvantages.
6.   The birth of the new idea – the invention.
7.   Experimentation to test out the most promising solution, and the selection and perfection of the final embodiment.

The contrast between the Wallas model and the Rossman model could not be starker. From the vague and idealistic notions of 'incubation' and 'illumination' we now have the no-nonsense language of pragmatism, a divide as vast as the Atlantic Ocean.

The Fabianist appeal to put our intellectual faculties to work for a fairer and more just society can be traced back to a long tradition of European Romanticism, particularly the German strand through Hegel and Goethe to its ultimate expression in Rudolf Steiner's *The Philosophy of Freedom*. The Rossman model is built firmly on the foundations of pragmatism laid down only a generation earlier by Charles Peirce, William James, John Dewey and Oliver Wendell Holmes. It is designed to be followed, to be used, and to get things done. Even so, as much as Rossman would have preferred it otherwise, step six is still shrouded in mystery.

Even the genius of Wikipedia can't tell us whether the creative process models of Wallas or Rossman inspired anyone, on either side of the Atlantic, to great feats of imaginative or inventive thought. Interest in the subject seems to have fallen dormant in the succeeding years as the world busied itself with the small matter of getting rid of Hitler.

It was only after the war that the bandwagon began rolling again, especially in the US where the post-war boom and Cold War fears combined to inspire a frenzy of investigation into how Americans could employ the full potential of their brains to create the most advanced and prosperous country on earth, and beat the commies at their own game.

Exhausted and cynical after two world wars, the Europeans were far less optimistic. The abiding mood was to put things together, not to take them apart. Psychologists embraced the Gestalt theories of Wertheimer (1945) and Vinacke (1953) in concluding that creativity could not be reduced to a series of linear steps or, indeed, be studied as something apart from the totality of human behaviour.

Their objections didn't bring the European study of creativity to a grinding halt, but it substantially altered the mood of the discourse. The thoughtful, holistic view was to be exemplified in *The Act of Creation*. Meanwhile, in the United States, its polar opposite was taking shape in the radical pragmatism of Alex Osborn's *Applied Imagination*.

Impatient with theory and deeply contemptuous of the 'uncontrolled' use of the imagination, Osborn's 'Seven-Step Model for Creative Thinking' deliberately avoids any mention of the role of the unconscious. Step four, 'ideation', is a coy substitute for brainstorming:

1. Orientation: pointing up the problem
2. Preparation: gathering pertinent data
3. Analysis: breaking down the relevant material
4. Ideation: piling up alternatives by way of ideas
5. Incubation: letting up, to invite illumination
6. Synthesis: putting the pieces together
7. Evaluation: judging the resulting ideas

Osborn had read Wallas but not Rossman, though in spirit and intent he is much closer to the latter. He downplays the role of 'illumination', which he got from Helmholtz via Wallas, by tagging it onto 'incubation', another borrowed concept. But he is deeply uncomfortable with having to rely on the chance appearance of an idea from the shadows of the mind, dancing gingerly around the subject of the source of inspiration. He advises readers to go for a walk, keep a pencil handy while you're in the bath, or go to church. Cold showers are optional.

We have seen the influence Osborn has had on the creative training industry around the world, and especially the way in which the 1953 publication of *Applied Imagination* doomed creative businesses to a mechanistic model of creative behaviour that came to be known as CPS, or creative problem solving.

Another advertising legend, James Webb Young, once of J. Walter Thompson, came up with five steps that strongly echoed the Wallas formula, though Young claims to have invented his independently 'one Sunday afternoon'. Oddly enough, considering they were in the same industry, Young also claims not to have been aware of the Osborn work.

In *A Technique for Producing Ideas*, first published in 1960, Young gives us the following:

1. 'Gathering raw material' in which he encourages us to find out everything we could possibly know about the client's brief, and simultaneously to keep an open and curious mind with regard to the world around us.
2. 'Mental digestion'. This is very similar to 'saturation', a concentrated struggle to fit the pieces of the puzzle together in a meaningful way. This is conscious work, which Young advises us to pursue to the point of exhaustion.
3. 'Letting go'. This is the equivalent of 'incubation', allowing the problem to drop from the conscious into the unconscious while you busy yourself with some other activity.
4. 'Illumination' – 'Now, if you have really done your part in these three stages of the process you will almost surely experience the fourth. Out of nowhere the Idea will appear. It will come to you when you are least expecting it – while shaving, or bathing, or most often when you are half awake in the morning. It may waken you in the middle of the night.'
5. 'The morning after'. This is identical to Wallas's fourth stage of 'verification', examining the idea in the cold light of day to make sure it checks out with the exigencies of the real world, including, in Young's case, the advertising brief.

I must confess that I was a great fan of Young. In the glory days of J. Walter Thompson people cared about this kind of stuff and encouraged young recruits like myself to think long and hard about the nature of ideas and how they came about. I thought Young's version was both sensible and elegant, as well as being a useful tool for the management of creative staff. At that time, when agencies still believed it was worth spending money on training, all senior JWT staff, from all over the world, were encouraged to attend the famous James Webb Young workshops, led for many years by the wonderful John Furr. It stirred the blood to be part of a huge enterprise that placed the exercise of the imagination at the forefront of its corporate ambitions.

It took me a few months of trying unsuccessfully to implement Young's five-step programme in my bewildered creative department before I realized that it worked perfectly only in retrospect. After that I let them get on with it, and put my energies into keeping Rhona, the ultimate traffic lady, out of their hair while they were in the middle of steps three and four.

After the 1960s the floodgates opened. Cursory research has unearthed well over a hundred different versions of these step-by-step guides to creativity, each one more determined than the next to erase the fallibility of the human imagination from the process. Listing them all would be an unproductive use of your time and of mine so we will sample only the most notable and the most egregious.

Koberg and Bagnall's Universal Traveler Model enjoyed some popularity after the publication of *The Universal Traveler* in 1981. It differs from the standard seven-step model only in stage one, which advises us to 'Accept the situation as a challenge'. This isn't bad advice if your next meal depends on whether or not your client buys your idea for his dog-food commercial.

Bandrowski's 1985 'A Model for Creative Strategic Planning' recommends 'Analysis, Creativity, Judgement, Planning and Action' which is alarmingly close to the process you would use if you ran out of milk at three o'clock on a Sunday afternoon.

Equally self-explanatory are Crawford's mercifully brief 'Attribute Listing' which advises, '1. List the attributes of the object to be improved and 2. Systematically examine each attribute in the search for modification', and John Arnold's 'Hypothetical Situation', which prompts us to 'develop a hypothetical situation with many unusual conditions' and then 'using this situation as a stimulus, design practical answers to fit the situation'. Or, in other words, think about what you want to do and then do it.

The 'Work Simplification Model' is refreshingly direct: '1. Select a job to improve. 2. Get the facts. 3. Challenge details, list possibilities. 4. Develop better methods. 5. Install improvements.' Or: 1. Kitchen sink. 2. It's leaking. 3. Could be blocked pipe or loose connection. Call the plumber? Fix it myself? Ignore it for as long as possible? 4. Yes, I know I should have turned off the mains. And of course I'll help you to mop up. 5. What do you mean you can't squeeze us in until next Friday?

Contrast the five stages of Zwicky's 'Morphological Analysis': '1. Problem statement. 2. Selection of independent variables of the problem. 3. Develop the sub-classification for each independent variable. 4. Construct a matrix that provides a "cell" for each of the relationships between the sub-categories. 5. Search the combination from the matrix for new directions.'

That's not as easy as it sounds, especially if you're trying to come up with an idea at the same time. But dig a little deeper and you'll find an exquisite circularity as beautiful in its own way as the apocryphal recipe for barbel, the ugly yellow-grey catfish that bottom-feeds in the dirty spruits of the South African highveld. Its diet of *E. coli* and rotting garbage, together with a texture of bullet-proof rubber, has given it a reputation for being as disgusting as it is inedible. But you can make a delicious meal of it by following these simple steps:

1. Nail the barbel to a wooden breadboard.
2. Score several times lengthways with a hacksaw, exposing the skeleton.
3. Cover with a thick paste of garlic, Mrs Ball's chutney, limejuice and black pepper.
4. Grill for 40 minutes in a hot oven.
5. When done, remove the barbel and eat the breadboard.

There are a bunch of creative interventions that do what they say on the tin – Random Input, Problem Reversal, Thinkertoys, Forced Analogy, Storyboarding, Role Playing, Draw-a-Picture, Squeeze and Stretch, Assumption Reversal and so on. And there are a bunch that don't – Lotus Blossom Technique, Fishbone Diagram, Lion's Den and King of the Mountain.

There are the obscure ones like Hiroshi Takahashi's NHK Method and the Basadur Simplex Process, and there are well-known ones like de Bono's 'Lateral

Thinking' and Tony Buzan's 'Mind Maps'. Some of them, like the 'Kepner-Tregoe', make brain surgery look like an inviting alternative. And some of them, like William Gordon's 'Synectics', are more like secret cults than creativity programmes.

Truly, we are in the land of gods and gurus. Religions flourish when hope gets the better of reason, and when faith has more currency than common sense. In the same way that prophets and charlatans prey on the fears of the masses, the gurus who invent these techniques for creativity prey on the anxieties of all those companies and institutions who don't know where their next idea is going to come from.

By asserting the privilege of a closer connection to god, all the priests and imams and teachers and gurus of the religions that continue to tolerate them, by the very nature of their designated functions as intermediaries between a higher power and the pitiful aspirations of the great unwashed, actively disempower the spiritual progress of the faithful. Creative prophets have the same effect on creativity, their reckless interventions muddying the waters of inspiration's fragile stream.

It's a human truth that applies as much to corporate entities as it does to individuals, that the more desperate you are the more superstitious you become. And since all companies and institutions are more desperate than ever for ideas, superstition about creativity is at an all-time high. Into this climate of ignorance and fear, the self-styled creativity gurus can sell just about anything, even if it's based on a barefaced lie. Of course, knowing the truth about something has never stopped anyone from believing that it might be otherwise. Knowing that walking under a ladder will not bring you bad luck won't stop you from walking around it, just in case. And knowing that creativity cannot be taught won't stop people buying creativity training, just in case.

Apart from these two underlying premises – that creativity is teachable, and that superstition has a magical power to separate idiots from their cash – there are a few more important observations to be made about this analysis of creative processes.

From Helmholtz at the end of the 19th century to 'TRIZ' a hundred years later their evolution appears no less logical than the evolution of finch varieties on the Galapagos Islands. But a closer reading reveals two distinct species, as different from one another as lions and leprechauns.

I probably wouldn't have noticed it if it hadn't been for Mr Paul E. Plsek and his 1996 'Working Paper: Models for the Creative Process' at www. directedcreativity.com.

Early on in the game we saw Helmholtz's model expanding from three steps to Wallas's four to Rossman's seven in what looked like a linear progression. We noted how Rossman's pragmatism found a champion in Alex Osborn, and how his *Applied Imagination* led in turn to the creative problem solving school known as CPS. The distinguishing feature of this branch of the evolutionary tree was its disdain of chance and its outright contempt for the notion that ideas emerge from the unconscious in random Darwinian fashion. This line of thought culminates in the zero-imagination models of morphological analysis that we've been looking at.

By reducing creativity to a six-step algorithm, adherents of the CPS model have been able to cleanse idea production of the smallest trace of randomness. And by redefining creativity as a problem solving skill they have shut the door firmly in the face of the irrational and the unreasonable.

CPS is a huge commercial success. Founded by Sidney J. Parnes, it has been taught to thousands of disciples through its Creative Education Foundation in Buffalo, NY. In his introduction to the foundation's 1992 *Source Book for Creative Problem Solving* Parnes pays obeisance to the messiah of American creativity:

> The 1992 50th anniversary of Osborn's disseminating his discoveries about creativity development is also coincidentally, the 500th cele-bration of Columbus's discovery of America. I have on my desk a cube anchored on a pedestal like a normal globe of the world is held. Its six faces carry the distorted map of the world. On the base of the pedestal is inscribed, 'And then came Columbus.' Now I want a similar symbol of the old distorted view of creativity being an inborn, unchanging quality. The inscription on the pedestal will read, 'And then came Osborn.'

There's something very creepy about this, something decidedly cultish and fetish-ist. Parnes isn't just gloating over the apparent demise of 'inborn' creativity, he is celebrating the birth of a new religion. Morris I. Stein, one of the many acolytes of CPS, goes even further, '. . . insofar as brainstorming is concerned, the human being has a God-given potential for creativity and a God-given right to fulfill this potential and to bring forth creative works.'

Here the tablets that Osborn brought down from the mountain are rewritten by Parnes to make sure the heresies of 'incubation' and 'illumination' are forever erased from the faith:

1. Objective finding.
2. Fact finding.
3. Problem finding.
4. Idea finding.
5. Solution finding.
6. Acceptance finding.

Thou shalt not worship the false idols of Darwin, Freud and the Pin-Ball Wizard.

The second branch, which looked to have died out after the Second World War, placed the emphasis on the workings of the unconscious, treating 'illumination' the way Koestler did, as the quasi-magical result of productive dreaming. Just when we thought that Freud was dead along comes Frank Barron, in 1988, with his 'Psychic Creation Model', which in four simple biological metaphors – 'conception', 'gestation', 'parturition', and 'bringing up the baby' – places the creative process firmly back in the dark shadows of the unconscious mind where the silver ball bounces haphazardly off the bumpers of ontogeny and phylogeny. Oh, heresy of heresies!

Now Mr Plsek, who for some time has been trying to found his own church of creative pragmatism, gets a little twitchy. With badly disguised scorn he tells us: 'The tone of Barron's model supports the popular view of creativity as a mysterious process involving subconscious thoughts beyond the control of the creator.'

He goes on to quote David Perkins, another fan of brainstorming, in arguing that:

> ... subconscious mental processes are behind all thinking, and, therefore, play no extraordinary role in creative thinking. Just because we cannot fully describe our thought processes does not mean that we are not in control of them. For example, we cannot begin to describe all of the subconscious mental processes that are engaged in the simple act of picking up a coffee mug. But we are certainly in control of the overall act. Further, Perkins argues, just because random events

play a part in some acts of creation, this should not be taken to imply
that random events are the source of all acts of creation.

This isn't about creativity anymore. This is about the politics of control. Mr Plsek
makes it clear that the cornerstone of his new church of 'Directed Creativity' will
be the avoidance of risk: 'Directed creativity simply means that we make purpose-
ful mental movements *to avoid the pitfalls associated with our cognitive mechanisms* at each step of this process of searching for novel and useful ideas.' (My
italics.)

And here, at last, the mantra of the technocrats is revealed in the glorious
oxymoron of risk-free creativity. Now the door is open for creativity without creative people, for ideas without inspiration, for imagining without imagination, for
life without dreams.

We have reached the point in this discussion, and in the history of the planet,
when we must decide whether we want creativity with a small helping of imagination on the side or a large helping of imagination garnished with the spice of all
its attendant risks. We must decide whether creativity is possible without creative
people, and whether we can give over the responsibility for creativity and innovation to Mr Plsek and Mr Podsnap.

We must decide, in the end, whom to believe.

If we go with the pragmatist view, that creativity is just another version of
rational thought, we must be prepared to consign any aberration from the norm to
the scrap heap, and we must widen our definition of psychosis to include all those
unfortunate miscreants who trust their dreams more than they trust the easy com-
placencies of the status quo.

If we believe, like Koestler, that there is after all some strange magic to be
discovered in the untapped realms of the unconscious, there may still be hope for
us all.

Process really doesn't matter. If we're smart enough we will solve problems. If we're even smarter we will allow for the illogicality that has brought us
this far.

THE CREATIVE ORGANIZATION

As business learns to compete in the new creative age, the efficient exploitation of the imagination will be as critical to success as the exploitation of coal once was. And it would be good to think that some of the management skills and tricks that its communications advisers have painfully accumulated over the years could be brought more usefully and centrally to bear.

Jeremy Bullmore

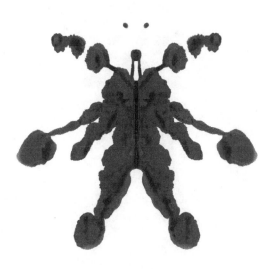

Introduction to Part II

All great things are done for their own sake.

Robert Frost

A belief in creativity for the sake of creativity is a necessary condition for the success of creative companies.

Perhaps this isn't as explicit as it could be, so I'll say it again:

For a creative company to succeed it must celebrate its creativity as an end in itself. This is not because creativity has any lofty moral purpose, or because it is somehow more worthy than other human activities. It doesn't, and it isn't. It is because creativity is self-consummatory, non-instrumental. It is its own purpose.

But how do we harness the power of creativity, which refuses to do anything well except for its own selfish gratification, to the drive-train of the profit motive, which refuses to do anything at all except for its own selfish gratification? How will society deal with their irreconcilable differences? How can companies do it?

In 1952, at about the same time that Osborn was telling the world to stop daydreaming and start brainstorming, Maslow was pondering these same questions. Osborn was an ad man who needed to get on with the business of making ads. Maslow was the patriarch of humanistic psychology, the grand old master of self-actualizing, and he saw what was coming.

I don't know how an organisation manager is going to work these things out. I don't know what would happen to morale. This is not my problem. I don't know how it would be possible to use such characters in the middle of an organisation which has to do the orderly work that ensues upon the idea. An idea is just the beginning in a very complex process of working out. That's a problem that we'll be working out in this country more than any other place on the face of the earth, I guess, during the next decade or so. We've got to face it. Huge sums of money now are going into research and development. The management of creative personnel becomes a new problem.

However, I have no doubt that the standard of practice which has worked well in large organisations absolutely needs modification and revision of some sort. We'll have to find some way of permitting people to be individualistic in an organisation. I don't know how it will be done. I think it will have to be a practical kind of working out, just simply trying out this and trying out that and trying out the other, and finally coming to a kind of empirical conclusion. I would say that it would be a help to be able to spot these as characteristics not only of craziness but also of creativeness. (By the way I don't want to put in a good recommendation for everybody who behaves like this. Some of them actually *are* crazy.) Now we've got to learn to distinguish. It's a question of learning to respect or at least to look with an open eye on people of this sort and trying somehow to fit them into society. Customarily today such people are lone wolves. You will find them, I think, more in the academic situation than you will in large organisations or large corporations. They tend to be more comfortable there because they are permitted to be as crazy as they like. Everybody expects professors to be crazy, anyhow, and it doesn't make much difference to anyone. They're not beholden to anyone else, except for their teaching, perhaps. But the professor has time enough ordinarily to go off into his attic or his basement and dream up all sorts of things, whether they are practical or not. In an organisation you've got to give out, ordinarily. I don't know how you can put these necessities together in your situation. That's your problem.

That was 50 years ago when the world was a very different sort of place. Eisenhower was in the White House; the Cold War and McCarthyism combined to freeze the intellectual life of Americans into a state of paranoid conformity. Beautifully captured in *The Wonder Years*, these were the days of the Company Man, the automaton who sold his soul to the corporation for a life of dull but predictable drudgery.

We like to believe we have moved on from there, that we have finally liberated ourselves, in this so-called Creative Age, from the constraints of social and political repression that shackled our fathers and our grandfathers to the treadmill of corporate compliance. We like to think that the counter-cultural detour of the 1960s and 1970s was enough to liberate us forever more from mute obedience to the prevailing social code, that the interregnum of sex, drugs and rock 'n' rock has distanced us from the conformism of past generations, and that a combination of media studies, mobile phones and MySpace will protect us henceforth from meek deferral to the status quo.

But as we now turn our attention to the great issues and opportunities of the creative economy, and in particular to the issues and opportunities that now confront creative sector companies, we must take clear and objective stock of how much progress we've made towards that Nirvana of free expression that was promised by Woodstock, R.D. Laing and Jonathan Livingston Seagull.

Whether we like it or not, the truth is that creativity is still tainted by the politics of the 20th century, and in particular by the clash of conservative and liberal politics in the 1950s. It was during that time that creativity first began to be associated with the reckless ideologies of the political left. It was not an accident that the McCarthy witch-hunt focused on Hollywood, and on the writers and poets who were beginning to espouse dangerous ideas like freedom of expression, civil rights and alternative lifestyles.

In 1954 the American artist Jasper Johns painted his famous American flag out of newspaper and pigmented wax, brilliantly subverting apple pie patriotism and upsetting both the art world and the social establishment all in one go. At the same time Le Corbusier was saying that 'everything must be started over again from scratch', and Hilla von Rebay, director of the New York Museum of Non-objective Art, was saying that 'still not enough bombs have been dropped on our old museums'.

Elvis, probably one the most politically naïve singers in world history, was managing to offend the conservative right by the way he moved his hips. So music, too, was soon to be implicated in the liberal plot to undermine family values and the American way of life. You wouldn't have suspected it from the most popular shows of 1953. *Paint Your Wagon*, *Guys and Dolls* and *The King and I* played to vast and appreciative audiences on both sides of the Atlantic, while Arthur Miller's *The Crucible* failed miserably after a few nights on Broadway.

In a few short years, probably between 1955 and 1965, all forms of creativity had suddenly become the province of left wing politics, deeply anti-establishment and profoundly anti-corporate. Dylan's 'Masters of War' wasn't so much a pacifist anthem as a scathing attack on big business. And big business wasn't doing much to help. In an act of astonishing corporate hubris General Motors spent $100 million on its new headquarters in Detroit. When it opened in

1955 the architect Eero Saarinen described the building as 'an expression of the great precision and capacity for mass production'. A massive, featureless expanse of glass and steel in five identical blocks, it set the tone for the kind of architecture that was to drive creative people out of city centres for the next five decades.

If the Spanish Civil War was the first global event to suggest a direct connection between artistic expression and political allegiance, the lines of demarcation began to clarify only after the defeat of Hitler and the several years it took for the creative community to realize that Stalin was not a reincarnation of William Blake. Vietnam, the civil rights movement and the Rolling Stones exacerbated the great divide between the creative left and the anti-creative right. In Soviet Russia, Latin America and South Africa, wherever restrictive regimes outlawed political dissent, it was the artists and writers who were most vocal in opposition.

So we are inclined to think that the creative temperament has always been politically aligned against the social, political or religious establishment. But history tells us quite clearly that this is not the case. Koestler's definition of creativity as 'the defeat of habit by originality' holds true for all circumstances, whether the 'habit' in question is the consequence of autocratic ignorance or democratic enlightenment – whether it was the rigid style of International Gothic or the canonical style of expressionism. Creativity, just like intelligence, is morally neutral. The only thing that creativity cannot abide is entropy, the tendency towards uniformity.

Despite the History Channel, we have very short memories. So, it is difficult to imagine a time when creativity could be patronized as fervently by the political right and by the political left. Unfortunately, since the 1950s and early 1960s creative people have been unable to escape their perceived affiliation with political subversion, while the political right has never been able to reclaim the affections of art and artists. Every four years we witness a parody of this as Republican and Democratic contenders for the American presidency attempt to recruit notable creative people to champion their cause. The Democrats always get the A-list creative celebrities, but they should know by now that they are more of a hindrance than a help, since conservative America has been trained in these last three generations to be deeply suspicious of the creative impulse.

To the extent that creativity is always about upsetting the status quo, then, of course, all creativity is political. Creativity wants to make things that change things, not because the status quo is right or wrong, but simply because it is the status quo.

This is not the same thing as saying that creativity despises instrumentalism because it is the favoured tool of the political right. Conservatism generally attempts to preserve the status quo – that's the meaning of it. And in this respect creativity is more likely to rub against the grain of a conservative agenda than against the grain of a libertarian one. But creativity will abhor instrumentalism no matter where it comes from, and the 20th century has proved that it is just as likely to be employed in the interests of the political left.

Creativity is allergic to instrumentalism in all its forms. It cannot operate when the reward for its results becomes more significant than the gratification of doing something for its own sake.

It's notable, for example, that the Jewish diaspora has generally been over-represented among creative achievers in so many communities around the world. Yet in Israel itself, despite a record of remarkable technical achievement, very few artists or writers have managed to find a global audience. Judaism clearly isn't inimical to inspiration; it's just possible that Zionism might be.

Similarly, one is obliged to compare the extraordinary cultural achieve-ments of the Baghdad of Haroun as Raschid with the limited artistic output of fundamentalist Islam.

In western liberal democracies, as politics move ineluctably to the centre, ideologies have given way to a mild-mannered pragmatism leavened occasionally by Christian moralism or neo-socialist rhetoric. Governments don't run things anymore, they make the arrangements whereby companies do. It's an accommoda-tion that suits everybody, as long as you live in a country where governments reciprocate the goodwill of corporations by providing them with an educated population of future employees and the kind of stability and law and order that facilitates their operation.

It's the accommodation that Paul Bremer wanted to achieve in Iraq by force of arms before everything went so horribly wrong. It's the accommodation that the International Monetary Fund, the World Bank and other global institutions desire of Africa, Latin America, China and the other emerging economies. It is opposed only by ideological zealots from the left and the right, by people like Chavez and Khomeini. To these ideologues it looks like a competing ideology, but it isn't. It's just the pragmatism of post-Keynesian economics, as natural as natural selection.

Without the moderating effect of public opinion, as expressed through the institutions of democracy, free enterprise has the nasty habit of eating its young, overexploiting natural resources and leaving behind a horrible mess. Without the energy and inventiveness of free enterprise, on the other hand, governments have a nasty habit of stifling progress, limiting opportunity and manipulating the gene pool in favour of turgid conformity. The net result is Darwinism with a conscience: nature red in tooth and claw but with some of that blood, at least, from a bleeding heart.

As the reputation of artists and musicians was sliding down the slippery slope of social acceptability, the reputation of scientists, chemists and engineers was moving rapidly in the opposite direction. The stereotype of the mad inventor, with his wild white locks à-la-Einstein, his exploding test-tubes and his Heath Robinson machines, was at least as deeply rooted in the popular imagination of previous generations as the Ozzie Osbourne image of creativity is entrenched in the popular imagination of today. And possibly even more so. Moreover, the mad scientist was most often portrayed as an evil genius, or a dangerous and irresponsible fool. Yet his rehabilitation is now almost entirely complete. Even the bioscientists working on the ethical fringes, in fields like human cloning and gene manipulation, receive a more favourable press than artists such as Damien Hirst or writers such as Martin Amis.

The British public now regards Brunel as a greater Briton than Shakespeare. And someone like James Dyson, the vacuum cleaner guy, is certainly accorded a great deal more respect in the media than someone like Tracy Emin, the controversial creator of the Turner Prize-winning unmade bed.

If creative people have always been viewed as different from the mainstream of society, there is nothing in the historical record suggesting that they were subject to the kind of universal disapprobation that we are seeing today. They may frequently have run foul of the church, or the state, or censorship laws. They may have shocked and offended the sensibilities of the bourgeoisie. Occasionally they were persecuted as heretics, mocked for their eccentricity, or disgraced and humiliated for their refusal to conform. But there is a sense that these transgressions were somehow expected of them, that there was a tacit understanding among great societies that creative people had some sort of special and mysterious role to perform, that they should be given some social latitude at least, if not active encouragement. It helped, of course, that many of them came from rich or aristocratic families, so the indulgence they received was often financial as well as emotional. Even the Victorians understood, in their own peculiar way, that aspiring artists and writers and poets and scientists and philosophers deserved a moratorium from judgement, a time of experimentation and excess during which the normal rules of conformity were relaxed. And the people who understood that best were the patrons.

Creative people today live in a state of permanent disgrace that can be redeemed only by celebrity. Perhaps that has always been the case.

*

It is not an accident that the beginning of their fall from grace coincided with the rise of the Company Man. During the golden dawn of mass production that began with Ford and that ended with the triumphal opening of General Motors' monument to conformity, the period that took in the two world wars, the rush to urbanization, and the first blush of the suburban dream, our notions of the role and value of creativity underwent a sea change.

By 1950, mad scientists were no longer mad, they were necessary. Werner von Braun was no longer an evil Nazi collaborator, he was the architect of America's future in space. Corporations opened their arms to scientists, chemists and technicians with interesting ideas. They were given laboratories and workshops and massive amounts of R&D funding. But there wasn't much use, in the new corporate establishment, or in the increasingly technocratic corridors of government, for creative people who didn't have a useful technical skill.

The creativity of science found rich and powerful patrons competing for its products. Creativity of the arts found its patrons buried under the rubble of Berlin and Cologne, banished to the gulags of Siberia, or distracted and confused by a new social order obsessed by technological, rather than artistic, ingenuity.

Vacuum cleaners first, art later.

Creativity doesn't have a conscience. Nor does the market. Creativity resists regulation, defies moderation and despises conformity. So does the market. They are natural bedfellows – indeed, closer than that, since in the larger view of things they are indistinguishable. The operation of the market, free of the constraints of conscience, is a living definition of creative behaviour. This is inescapably true in the grand macro-economic sense, and we wouldn't wish it otherwise without denying the market the very inventiveness from which it draws its vigour.

But in the sense in which it matters to us, that is, in the efficient operation of creativity within a single corporate entity, in a company seeking to prosper and grow through the success of its creative product, creativity and entrepreneurship find themselves bitterly and paradoxically divided.

This is baffling to both sides: to the entrepreneur whose hopes for success hinge on the liberated play of the creative imagination of the people he or she employs, and just as baffling to the creative person who finds himself or herself suddenly and unexpectedly constrained by those very same ambitions.

*

If the world ran out of ideas in the fall of 2001, the obituary had already been written in the autumn of 1952.

The occasion was the Conference on Creativity hosted by the Ohio State University in Granville, Ohio, one of the two earliest such meetings that followed J.P. Guildford's appeal, in 1950, for the academic community to take the subject more seriously.

The author was not an expert on creativity, and nor were many of the other speakers. So few people were working in the field in those days that the conference organizers were obliged to spread the net across a wide variety of disciplines. He was a young Princeton sociologist and anthropologist by the name of Melvin Tumin. If his name doesn't ring a bell it's only because you weren't paying attention to sociological theory in the 1980s and 1990s when he rose to prominence for his work on social stratification.

But in 1952 he had little to go on, no research to back up this thinking, and nothing to consult except his instincts. This is how he began:

> Since this is a conference on creativity, I feel it important that the central term, creativity, receive at least a work definition if there is to be any order introduced into our thinking about it. In trying this definition, I would follow Dewey's lead and view 'creativity' as the esthetic experience, which is to be distinguished from other experiences by the fact that it is self-consummatory in nature. This is to say, the esthetic experience is enjoyed for the actions which define and constitute the experience, whatever it may be, rather than for its instrumental results or social accompaniments in the form of social relations with others.

Sidney J. Parnes, who, in mitigation of his other crimes against creativity, reprinted this speech in his 1962 publication of *A Source Book for Creative Thinking*, acknowledges that it was a cry in the wilderness. 'He was like a pioneer environmentalist trying futilely decades ago to get people's attention. The same environmentalist today would find eager audiences.'

You can see the audience in Granville, Ohio, quietly nodding off, eyes glazing, chins dropping onto tie-knots, unaware that they're missing one of the great prophecies of the age.

*

There are several remarkable things about the short speech that Melvin Tumin made that day. The first is that he chose to use John Dewey's definition of creativity – the notion of the self-consummatory aesthetic experience – when there were plenty of other definitions he could have latched onto, all of them much less obscure than Dewey's. This could hardly have been an accident. Dewey died in 1952, which would have been big news at the time. And Tumin, the sociologist, would have been very well acquainted with his work.

He would certainly have been an ardent fan of Dewey's views on education. The latter's highly influential book, *Democracy and Education*, promoted the radical notion that schools should teach children to think rather than learn by rote. (In a list of 'The Ten Most Harmful Books of the 19th and 20th Centuries' compiled by a Republican think-tank, *Democracy and Education* came in at an admirable fifth place.)

And Tumin would have gone along quite happily with Dewey's instrumentalism, at least philosophically. But now it occurred to him, as he looked around and read the signs that all pointed to the coming age of materialism, that the pragmatic view had been hijacked by a generation of opportunists who would use it to justify the ends they sought, no matter the means.

It is clear from his opening sentences that instrumentalism had taken on an entirely new meaning, and that this new meaning set it in direct opposition to creativity. This is an extraordinary insight, and not just for 1952.

Arthur Koestler, who read more widely and wrote more thoroughly on the subject of creativity than anyone else on the planet, didn't get it. Howard Gardner didn't get it, nor did Czikszentmihalyi. The problem solvers like Osborn and de Bono clearly didn't get it, but nor did the great pioneers of creativity research like Torrance and Sternberg.

Teresa Amabile got it in spades, but she had to reinvent it from scratch, and it took her another 40 years to prove it. Her principle of intrinsic motivation is the same thing as Dewey's self-consummating aesthetic experience, while extrinsic motivation, as she describes it, is essentially the same thing as Tumin's 'instrumental results'. Quite remarkably, as it turns out, she was unaware of the work of either of them.

Tumin continued:

> Much of human striving . . . can fruitfully be viewed as striving for a favourable place in the social order. This place may be marked by family, or wealth, or power, or physical appearance. But whatever the criteria by which persons are distinguished from each other, it seems clear that the vast majority of persons in any society are deeply motivated to strive for a favourable place.
>
> All of this striving seems to have few, if any, *necessary* connections with those types of experience which we label aesthetic or self-consummatory. What this is saying, in effect, is that societies seem quite capable of surviving without paying any specific attention to the problem of insuring that their members have deep creative experiences. We may not like the quality of a society which pays little or no attention to these facets of man. But the fact remains that societies *can* get along perfectly well without any attention to them, or at most, with a meagre amount of attention.
>
> The attitude of the society at large, then, so far as any individual member is concerned, is primarily instrumental. And the individual members have to learn the lesson that they must demonstrate their valuable instrumentality if they are to receive social recognition and reward. To the extent that the instrumental orientation is hostile to the self-consummatory (though it need not be), to that extent it may be said that society by its very nature is fundamentally hostile or at least indifferent to human creativity and far more friendly to the conception of man as an instrument of the social order.

To 21st century ears this is shocking stuff. We are used to thinking that we live in an age of boundless creative expression, that our post-industrial liberal democracies are a paradise of self-consummatory playfulness. We blame the anomie of our daily lives on the weather, on the price of avocado pears, on global terrorism, on the trains and the traffic. We dissolve away our alienation in doses of Prozac, citalopram, cocaine, librium and ecstasy. We cannot accept, or we refuse to believe, that we are instruments of the social order, and that our collective despair is a direct consequence of the same system that blesses us with so much material wealth.

We cannot see, or we refuse to see, that society's hostility to the creative impulse affects every one of us, whether we regard ourselves as creatively inclined or not, by driving a wedge between the way we live and the way we dream, severing the healing power of the unconscious from the pain of living without self-esteem.

But Tumin went even further, anticipating the curse of celebrity that blights our cultural landscape by condemning the unfamous and the unglamorous to eternal obscurity, no matter how creative they might be:

> . . . throughout (America), there runs the idea that scarce and rare talents must be especially rewarded with highly disproportionate amounts of the desired social goods and services if the possessors of these talents are to be motivated to make them available to the service of the public. Accompanying this is a patently marked disregard for the possibility of motivating persons at *all* levels of talent with something other than material rewards as bait. An expected corollary of this is the tendency for the talented elite to become encrusted in positions of high power and prestige, and to limit access to those positions to an equally rarefied elite in succeeding generations. (His italics.)

Here is the last great obstacle to creativity, pin-pointed with extraordinary prescience decades before anyone had the faintest idea how much it would matter. It's the all-or-nothing conception of creative talent that has come to dominate our view of the arts, of popular culture and, most destructively of all, of the commercial value of creative employees. The corollary of Tumin's analysis that creativity has no value unless it is shown to have instrumental value, it follows that creative people who have been able to demonstrate their instrumental worth are, de facto, worth everything, while creative people who have not been able to demonstrate their instrumental worth are, de facto, worth nothing, and therefore, by implication, not really creative at all.

You're hot or you're not. Or as the old lions of advertising always tell the young creative cubs, you're only as good as your last job.

We can read Amabile as a kindly corrective; we can address her obstacles to creativity with common sense and hard work. But we can't read Tumin without being shocked by how deeply embedded those obstacles are in the very fabric from which our creative organizations are made.

Now we can see why creative organizations are being torn apart and remodelled as commercial bureaucracies. It's not for more efficiency, or creative productivity. It's not simply the assertion of administrative control over the indeterminacy of creativity. And it's not because of the temporary pre-eminence of marketing mumbo-jumbo over common sense business practice. It's because creativity *cannot demonstrate its instrumental value* – not to itself, not to the organizational hierarchy, and not to society at large.

The implication of this is profoundly disturbing. Against hope and expectation, against history and logic and all the evidence to the contrary, creativity in contemporary society, and in contemporary business organizations, has no demonstrable worth.

*

It's little wonder, then, that the delegates to the 1952 Ohio conference failed to take much notice of Tumin's speech. They were there to hear creativity being celebrated as the great wave of the future, as the desideratum of long and lucrative research contracts. And it's little wonder that Tumin himself gave up on the creativity lark and devoted the rest of his working life to theories of stratification and the sociology of peasant economies.

But Tumin's thoughts were saved from complete extinction by Fredrick Hertzberg, one of the founders of industrial psychology, whose 1959 book *The Motivation to Work* acknowledged Tumin's startling idea that people would be more productive if they enjoyed what they were doing.

Hertzberg gave us the 'hygiene factors' that are often still referred to by management theorists and HR people, factors that are not themselves motivations to work harder, but things that get in the way of working harder, like undrinkable coffee and the noise of a hundred telephones ringing all at once in your new designer open-plan office space.

CHAPTER 10

The muse's ransom

Software is an idea; hamburger is a cow.

Peter Coy, *Business Week*

In 1997 America produced $414 billion worth of books, films, music, TV programmes and other copyright products. Copyright became America's number one export, outselling clothes, chemicals, cars, computers and planes.

John Howkins, *The Creative Economy*

A culture persists in time only to the degree it is inventing, creating and dynamically evolving in a way that promotes the production of ideas across all social classes and groups.

Shalini Venturelli, *From the Information Economy to the Creative Economy*

Now that everyone knows that you can make more money out of ideas than you can out of hamburgers, will someone please explain the following. On the eve of Christmas 2006 UK music retailers were complaining that sales – including downloads – were down by as much as 30%, blaming it on a very bad year for music in general, and specifically on the disturbing news that the holiday season charts were topped by an album called *Beautiful World* by Take That. For those readers who didn't have to live through Take That's rise to musical notoriety in the 1990s, the kindest way to describe their anodyne version of R&B/pop/rock is that they were designed to appeal to the market – and they did. Imagine Justin Timberlake without the charisma.

Something is clearly going wrong.

In numerical terms there is little doubt that we have crossed some sort of structural threshold. The US Patent & Trademark office is handing out 70% more patents than it did only a decade ago. US capital spending on information technology has tripled since 1960. The Microsoft Corporation with just 31 000 employees has a market capitalization of $600 billion compared to McDonald's Corporation with 10 times as many employees and only one tenth of the market capitalization.

The shift of value from the industrial sector to those businesses dealing in intellectual property have been well documented by Richard Florida who, somewhat disturbingly given his definitions of creativity, has rapidly become the leading authority on the new paradigm. John Howkins is much more specific about the industries and the kind of people who are making the new economy tick. His book, *The Creative Economy*, is subtitled 'How People Make Money from Ideas' and it does what it says on the cover. He identifies the four most significant legal mechanisms for turning ideas into cash – copyright, patent, trademark and design, and provides a handy primer for describing how and why they work. For most of us these concepts are as arcane as the gospel of St Thomas, which is rather unfortunate because they represent the real levers of power in the world of creative value. It is no accident, therefore, that the big winners in the intellectual property game are also the ones with the best lawyers. We shall see the effect of this in due course.

Howkins also identifies the 15 sectors that make up the creative economy. In alphabetical order they are advertising, architecture, art, crafts, design, fashion, film, music, the performing arts, publishing, research and development, software, toys and games, TV and radio and video games. The top five, in order of global value, are R&D, publishing, software, TV and radio and design. The smallest is art followed by fashion, video games and architecture.

He estimates that the total value of the creative economy in January 2000 was around $2.2 trillion and growing at 5% a year. He projects the figure to rise to $6.1 trillion in 2020.

The sudden increase in awareness of the shift in economic resource and value is actually the conflation of four separate but interrelated elements. The first is the recognition by the media of the sheer size of the creative market; the second is the realization among the traditional industrial sectors that creativity and innovation are the hot buttons of future growth; the third involves a renewed determination by the creative industries themselves – especially the larger stakeholders – to protect current and future value by lobbying for tougher copyright enforcement around the world; and the fourth is a belated acknowledgement, by those who care about these things, that culture itself is part of the equation.

With so much money sloshing around it's hardly surprising that the creative economy has attracted the attention not only of investment bankers, financial analysts and a whole new generation of idea entrepreneurs, but also of governmental think-tanks and economists charged with figuring out how it can best be managed to the advantage of national interest.

In 2003 the European Parliament set out a policy document calling on 'Member States and the Commission, in consultation with professionals in the sector, to identify *priority actions to promote cultural industries*'. (Their italics.)

In Singapore, New Zealand and the UK government funding has been set aside for specific research into the factors underlying the growth of the creative sector, while in Australia it has been raised to the level of a national priority. Hardly a day goes by without the announcement on the internet of yet another conference of experts assembling in some exotic tropical hotel to discuss new ways to exploit this extraordinary boom. These will most usually be convened by businesses already engaged in one or other of the creative sectors, but increasingly we are beginning to see the appearance of NGOs and governmental ministries representing departments like tourism, sport and culture, the short straws of the cabinet lottery.

The reason for this is very simple. More and more countries are waking up to the fact that their cultural legacies are no longer immune to the proliferation of ideas flooding in through satellite TV, the internet, radio, foreign movies and so on. In Europe as a whole, for example, the ratio of locally produced films to imported films is down to one in five. In Africa it is as low as one in 40, and even in Latin America it is as low as one in 15.

This is disturbing news for governments spending money on museums and art galleries in the hope of protecting their national cultural identity, and it is raising some serious questions about the relationships between, and the definitions of, culture and the creative industries.

Carmen Marcus, in a report commissioned by the European Commission, has attempted to hack her way through the jungle of politics that surrounds these issues. Quoting the work of David Throsby, T. O'Regan, Stuart Cunningham and others, she points out how the creative industries are slowly but surely usurping the place of those 'pure' artistic activities that used to be central to our concept of culture, just in case you hadn't noticed that Kylie Minogue's wardrobe was attracting bigger queues at the V&A than the greatest collection of Ming vases ever assembled in one place.

We are used to imagining music, dance, theatre, literature, crafts and the visual arts as the most significant aspects of our cultural experience. Around them we visualize those newer forms of artistic expression that include things like performance art, video art, installations, computer and multimedia creations. The next layer consists of things like book and magazine publishing, television and radio, newspapers and film, with an outer layer made up of advertising, architecture, tourism, design, video games and fashion. On the outer peripheries we might imagine hardcore scientific and commercial applications such as software development and the various fields of research and development that require a high degree of creative and technical competence.

Underlying this way of looking at culture is the romantic assumption that the activities at the centre are somehow worthier than those at the circumference because they are less tainted by commercial ambition. But even if they are, the harsh reality of the way in which we consume culture these days is that they are becoming increasingly peripheral. They have been replaced at the core of contemporary cultural experience by TV, advertising, films, magazines, newspapers and fashion, and even to some extent by the artefacts or market-led R&D: iPods, mobile phones, designer drugs, cosmetics and plastic surgery.

The trend is clear. The high-end cultural stuff that survives only through the beneficence of state or municipal subsidies – the ballet, opera, national theatres, public galleries and museums, public service broadcasting and others, which in some countries includes publicly funded journalism, literature and poetry – has had to make way as the products of the creative economy claim centre stage. And because high culture tends to be more local in origin and flavour, the cultural shift is clearly also towards increasingly global content.

The UK Creative Industries Task Force defines the creative industries as those 'that have their origin in individual creativity, skill and talent and which have a potential for wealth and job creation through the generation and exploitation of intellectual property', which would be very reassuring if only it were true.

In the real world a dozen or so massive conglomerates dominate the film industry, the record business, book publishing, and the toys and games markets. In 2003 Walt Disney, Sony, Viacom, Vivendi Universal, Time Warner, News Corporation, Bertelsmann, The Direct TV Group, General Electric and NHK recorded a combined turnover of approximately $140 billion, representing well over 90% of the total turnover of audio-visual commerce in the western hemisphere. Their dominance extends to music, publishing, the internet, the cable business and a very large slice of media ownership. Which means that nine out of 10 of the things you see or hear in the media today are likely to have been processed by one of these companies.

The Creative Industries Task Force would probably argue that somewhere along the line, even in these huge corporations, 'individual creativity' must have had at least something to do with the genesis of the media output. But you can be sure it isn't what they had in mind when they wrote the definition. Perhaps they were thinking of some imaginary world in which individual creative talents, working in feverish excitement in their garrets or sheds, inspired by passion alone, come up with brilliant ideas for films or books or TV shows, or sensational demo albums recorded in their kitchens, which are lapped up by hungry A&R people and film producers, which go on to win Emmys and Oscars and platinum sales, which make everyone rich and famous and happy and provide years and years of stunning and profitable creative content to the companies that buy them and the networks that distribute them, which in turn make the readers and viewers and listeners who consume them ecstatic with praise and admiration. Or perhaps they were just thinking of J.K. Rowling.

There's a fascinating pie chart in Carmen Marcus's document showing a breakdown of cinema admissions in the EU market in 2002 according to the origin of the film shown. The US takes by far the largest share, at around 65%. Next comes France with 10%, then Britain with 7%. The fourth largest piece of the pie, coming in ahead of Italy, Denmark, Spain, the rest of Europe and the rest of the world, is a country called 'Harry Potter' at almost 5%.

The story of how a single mother at the end of her financial tether sat down to write, in sheer desperation, the children's books that would become the publishing phenomenon of our time is at least as well known as the stories themselves, probably more so. Harry Potter is the exception that proves the rule. What is truly extraordinary isn't that one single individual author could have been responsible for such a significant percentage of Europe's cinema admissions, it's that so few others weren't. This is not to deny J.K. Rowling's imaginative genius or to question the scale of her achievement. It is simply to make the point that a host of other very talented writers are clearly being buried in the corporate bureaucracies that are now responsible for so much of our media content. That's the real message of these figures.

Like all of the stories of unknown authors made good, it took an exceptionally perspicacious publisher to take the initial risk, but not before she had been turned down by others. Those commentators who continue to believe that the market is the most efficient mechanism for optimizing the selection and production of creative goods often quote the success of Harry Potter as proof of how well it works. Actually, it proves the opposite. J.K. Rowling was not just brilliant, she was lucky.

The market is dumb, deaf and blind when it comes to creative quality. We have already seen, at the level of creative individuals working in closed environments, how competition inhibits creative ambition. It is no different at the macro level.

If any evidence were needed to prove the point we need look no further than The News Corporation. It's not that Rupert Murdoch deliberately sets out to produce the tackiest and most facile TV programmes, news programmes and newspapers on earth. It's that Rupert Murdoch understands that the market is deaf, dumb and blind to creative quality. That's a critical distinction. The case of O.J. Simpson's mooted book about how he would have murdered his victims if he really had been guilty, sponsored by Rupert Murdoch, is an example of just how horribly egregious the product has to be before someone intervenes. Interestingly, it wasn't the market that did. Indeed, we can be fairly confident that the market would have lapped it up and come back for more. There would have been movies and another TV series and all the other collateral that goes with it.

The real crime isn't that Rupert Murdoch should have commissioned such a book, it's that it would have been commissioned in favour of so many other ideas that must surely have reached the desks of his publishers, the proposals for which could not possibly have been worse.

*

You don't have to be an economist to realize that something's wrong. The laws of supply and demand and the way they operate in a free market economy have brought us to the very brink of paradise, and it's easy to see how. The market gives us the right to choose which products we want to consume and which ones we don't. The people who make the products we want to consume make lots of money and make more products that we might want to consume. The people who make products we don't want to consume go out of business. As more competitors enter the market making the things we want to consume the price of those things goes down or the quality goes up or both.

Ever since Adam Smith and *The Wealth of Nations* we have been reaping the benefits of this free market efficiency. When we began producing cultural products to be bought and sold on the same basis, we assumed that there was no distinction between industrial goods and cultural goods. But we missed one small thing. Cultural goods don't disappear once you have consumed them. Quite the contrary. The more you consume them the more valuable they get.

When you eat a hamburger, the hamburger disappears. When you use software, the software is still there after you have used it. If you want another hamburger someone has to make it all over again from the cow to the patty to the griller to the plate. The person who made your software, Bill Gates for example, doesn't have to make anymore software to make more and more money. All he has to do is find new buyers for it. As soon as everyone has his software he changes it and makes it better, obliging you to buy it all over again if you want to keep up with your neighbours, your competitors or the latest applications. But that's your choice.

As Thomas Jefferson famously observed in a letter to Isaac McPherson in 1813:

> If nature has made any one thing less susceptible than all others of exclusive property, it is the action of the thinking power called an idea, which an individual may exclusively possess as long as he keeps it to himself, but the moment it is divulged, it forces itself into the possession of everyone, and the receiver cannot dispossess himself of it. Its peculiar character, too, is that no one possesses the less, because every other possesses the whole of it. He who receives an idea from me, receives instruction himself without lessening mine; as he who lites his taper at mine, receives light without darkening me.

With remarkable foresight, Jefferson went on to caution future generations of lawmakers to be extremely mindful of balancing intellectual property rights with the notion of 'fair use'. He realized, two hundred years ago, that a zealous regime of copyright and patent protection would pose a serious threat to enlightenment in general and creativity in particular:

> That ideas should freely spread from one to another over the globe, for the moral and mutual instruction of man, and the improvement

of his condition, seems to have been peculiarly and benevolently designed by nature, when she made them, like fire, expansible over all space, without lessening their density at any point, and like the air in which we breathe, move and have our physical being, incapable of confinement, or exclusive appropriation. Inventions, cannot, in nature, be a subject of property.

This is strong stuff, especially when you consider that he was America's first patent commissioner. Jefferson's warnings have gone largely unheeded, and we're now beginning to pay the price.

Long before 1997, the watershed year when copyright goods took over from manufactured goods as the major contributor to US wealth creation, the conglomerates whose primary assets were in intellectual property began a vigorous and highly successful campaign to lobby governments around the world for the strongest possible legal enforcement of copyright protection. They argued, and continue to argue, that without it there would be no incentive for artists to create or for companies to innovate since they would have no guarantee of just reward for their efforts. On the face of it this seems compelling, especially since their aggressive media campaigns have manipulated us into thinking that it's the poor and vulnerable creative people who will suffer most from copyright theft, illegal downloads and the like.

I wouldn't have realized how specious this was without the help of Lawrence Lessig whose book *The Future of Ideas* should be prescribed reading for everyone aged 12 and upwards. Lessig, a professor of law at the Stanford Law School, is particularly concerned about the way the free flow of ideas on the internet is in danger of being stifled for good. The best possible summary of his argument comes from the blurb on the inside cover.

The explosion of innovation we have seen in the environment of the Internet was not conjured from some new, previously unimagined technological magic; instead, it came from an ideal as old as the nation. Creativity flourished there because the Internet protected an innovation commons. The Internet's very design built a neutral platform upon which the widest range of creators could experiment. The legal architecture surrounding it protected this free space so that culture and information – the ideas of our era – could flow freely and inspire an unprecedented breadth of expression. But this structural design is changing – both legally and technically.

This shift will destroy the opportunities for creativity and innovation that the Internet originally engendered. The cultural dinosaurs of our recent past are moving to quickly remake cyberspace so that they can protect their interests against the future. Powerful forces are swiftly using both law and technology to 'tame' the Internet, transforming it from an open forum for ideas into nothing more than cable television on speed. Innovation, once again, will be directed from the top down, increasingly controlled by owners of the networks, holders of the largest patent portfolios, and, most invidiously, hoarders of copyright.

There are two separate points here, both of which Lessig goes on to elucidate with admirable clarity and a wealth of irrefutable evidence.

The first is the idea of 'the commons', which he describes as 'a resource to which anyone within the relevant community has a right without obtaining the permission of anyone else'. A place like Wimbledon Common is a good example because the notion is captured in the name. Or you can think of Central Park, Chapultepec Park, Joubert Park, your favourite beach or any other place where you are allowed to go without fear or favour. It doesn't have to be free to qualify as a commons but it certainly helps. A toll road is an example of a commons you have to pay for. As soon as the price of entry gets too steep it clearly begins to favour people who can afford to pay for it, so Coombe Hill Golf Course is only a commons for those with buckets of money.

You also get an intellectual commons, which is the one we're most interested in. Lessig cites Einstein's theory of relativity as a commons because it is a way of understanding the universe 'that is open and free for anyone to take'. Public domain writings, like the works of Shakespeare, are also a commons because we can use them and distribute them without any constraint.

It follows that the wider and more open the commons the more creative people can draw on it for inspiration and new ideas. The artists, sculptors and architects working in Quattrocento Florence were able to experiment freely not only with the ideas that came down to them from the rich cultural legacy of the preceding centuries, but also with the abundance of creative ideas that were emerging from the pool of extraordinary talent that surrounded them.

Advertising is another good example of the commons in action. There is an unwritten code of conduct among advertising creatives that you can borrow freely from any idea in any imaginable domain as long as you use it in an interesting way. Sometimes this is very controversial, such as when Wieden+Kennedy won the Cannes Grand Prix for a commercial for Honda called 'Cog', which was based on a 30 minute film produced in 1987 by artists Peter Fischli and David Weiss who subsequently threatened legal action.

It isn't quite as fair a commons as it might be. Since most of the big advertisers have deep pockets they can usually afford to buy the rights to songs and other well-known creative properties to use in their advertising assuming, of course, that they trust the recommendations of their agencies. Which allows agency creatives to buy those ingredients that they can't legitimately borrow, parody or steal, biasing the commons in favour of clients with bigger budgets.

The second point follows from the first. The erosion of the commons by property developers, intellectual or physical, will clearly restrict the kind of activities that can take place within it. Let's take a physical example first.

It is becoming popular practice in big cities to sell off open spaces and parkland to corporations, not necessarily for development, but on the understanding that they will take better care of them than local government can. The corporations agree to keep them neat and tidy, to plant shrubs and trees, to mow the lawns and provide such facilities that people would expect from a public area. So they look like parks, and they operate like parks. The neat corporate buildings are surrounded by neat green spaces, the local council doesn't have to pick up the tab, and everyone is happy. Except the skateboarders, the fire-eaters, the frisbee throwers, the dog-walkers and everyone else who poses any kind of risk to the liability insurance of the corporations. So it becomes a commons in name only, a kind of pseudo-commons that at some deeply unsettling level is worse than having no commons at all.

Excessive copyright regulations are doing exactly the same thing to the intellectual commons, and it's difficult to say which is the most pernicious. Without the freedom to play – even if it's rough and dangerous play – the red blood of creativity is diluted with the anaemic drip of conformity in both instances. This should be making us very angry and very fearful, if only we realized just how quickly it's happening.

The 'hoarders of copyrights' see it otherwise. By closing down the intellectual commons, by restricting the discourse of the internet, by starving artists and musicians of the diversity required for inspiration, by limiting innovation only to those companies that can afford to pay the legal fees, they are happy to drag us all into a new Dark Ages in which we will have to pay through our noses for every glimmer of sweetness and light.

Since YouTube sold out it has gone from a multimedia version of Speaker's Corner to a strip mall festooned with Shockwave banners and policed by copyright lawyers representing the global media conglomerates.

*

So vital are these issues to the fate of ideas that it's nonsensical to discuss the creative economy without them. Yet that doesn't stop most commentators from going right ahead, their columns ringing with hallelujahs of thanks to an economic model that no longer requires messy factories or equally messy unskilled workers.

In an interview with *Business Week* an economist at the University of Chicago's Graduate School of Business, Raghuram Rajan, rather gave the game away by admitting that, '. . . in the Creative Economy, the power to exert influence is nearly unlimited because there's no ceiling on how many people can be made to depend on idea-based assets'.

Received wisdom has it that without the rewards guaranteed by copyright and patent protection there would be no incentive for companies to innovate, no incentive for authors to write books, no incentive for dancers to dance, for cartoonists to make comics, for musicians to make music or for artists to make art. If that were entirely true we would have had no Athens, no Florence, no Paris, no Mozart, no Shakespeare, no Picasso and no internet. It completely misunderstands the nature of creativity, ludicrously conflating the motivation of creative people with the grubby motivations of the technocrats.

Which isn't to say that creative people don't need to be rewarded. Of course they do, and handsomely too. The Renaissance is over, history has ended, the market rules, it's the 21st century, and there's no going back. We are now supposedly in a position to organize the affairs of civilization in a more considered and reasonable way. But we still haven't grasped, as Lessig points out, that the way we legislate for the production of cars and coffee is no longer the appropriate way to legislate for the production of ideas.

The critical distinction, to use his words, is between rivalrous resources and nonrivalrous resources. A rivalrous resource is one that 'does not permit your consumption without lessening mine', like the apple that Adam and Eve ate, a meadow being grazed by a flock of sheep, or Russia's gas reserves. A nonrivalrous resource is the one that Jefferson describes – a secret divulged, an idea expressed, or a rampant meme:

1. If the resource is rivalrous, then a system of control is needed to assure that the resource is not depleted – which means the system must assure the resource is both *produced* and not *overused.*
2. If the resource is nonrivalrous, then a system of control is needed simply to *assure the resource is created* – a provisioning problem . . . Once it is created, there is no danger that the resource will be depleted. By definition, a nonrivalrous resource cannot be used up.

And Lessig goes on to say:

The system of control that we erect for rivalrous resources (land, cars, computers) is *not necessarily appropriate* for nonrivalrous resources (ideas, music, expression). Indeed, the *same system for both kinds of resources may do real harm.* Thus a legal system, or a society generally, must be careful to tailor the kind of control to the kind of resource. (His italics throughout.)

If more than a handful of commentators have come to the same conclusion they're certainly not saying so. And if they are, one can only conclude that their voices are being drowned out by the uncritical hype of the oligopoly of media owners in whose interest it is to maintain the status quo.

It's not the first part of Lessig's analysis that's the problem. There are more than adequate systems in place, both governmental and commercial, to assure that rivalrous resources continue to be produced. We are spectacularly efficient at making things like washing machines, cameras, paint, printers, mobile phones and so on. America now produces more cars than it can sell. We're also extremely good at agriculture, making much more food than white people could ever eat.

To be fair, we're making excellent progress on the medical front. Leaving aside for one minute the lack of vaccines to treat Third World diseases like malaria, hepatitis and AIDS, every day brings another thrilling announcement in the field of stem-cell research, cancer and Parkinson's. Tough patent laws have no doubt played a significant role in encouraging the pharmaceutical giants and the bio-science start-ups to invest aggressively, even if these same patents have limited the access of poorer countries to the generics.

Lessig's first point is worrying enough. We clearly haven't given much thought to the depletion aspect of rivalrous resources, like oxygen and the generosity of planet Earth. But that's another story.

It's the nonrivalrous resources that concern us here. As long as we lack the political will to address the issue we can clearly forget about another belle epoque in our lifetimes. On the other hand we could persuade ourselves, with what little imaginative power we have left, that a New Golden Age dawned the day we were able to download *Desperate Housewives* onto our phones, along with *Premiership Highlights* and clips from Anal Milf Parties; when we could trust *X-Factor* and *Pop Idol* and *Dragon's Den* to replenish the wells of creativity and innovation, and when *Mary Poppins* and *The Sound of Music* played to full houses and rapturous applause on Shaftesbury Avenue.

There's no use sitting back and pointing fingers at the copyright hoarders when the policy makers have been fast asleep in their cosy bureaucratic beds. The corporations simply did what came naturally to them, moving into the creative economy like settlers into the Wild West. And it's the policy makers, not the corporations, that need to take action, especially those who are concerned that our national cultures are now hawking their wares in the parking lot while the creative industries thrive in the mall. Which brings us back to Shalini Venturelli:

> Policy makers have worked from industrial assumptions to decide the fate of the information and creative marketplace, with scant intellectual or empirical grounds to assess how and in what manner the production and distribution of creative ideas and intellectual/cultural products are qualitatively different from the production and consumption of widgets, automobiles, appliances and other industrial products.

Venturelli, an associate professor at the School of International Service at American University, is trying to rouse legislators from their slumber. She argues that we should have become aware of the anomalous behaviour of cultural goods in an economic system designed around industrial products at least a century ago as the telegraph, the telephone, the cinema, photography, publishing and broadcasting began to change our consumption patterns to include nonrivalrous resource. It's a bit late now: 'As proprietary control over ideas spreads through the information network, the ability to work with existing ideas to innovate new forms becomes reduced, thus creating the economic and social irony of information scarcity coexisting within an environment of enlarged access to information technology.'

If there were any justice in the world that sentence would be tattooed on Rupert Murdoch's forehead in 15pt Franklin Gothic Extra Bold Condensed without the benefit of anaesthesia.

This is what it means in practice. Say your 12 year old daughter were to borrow your DV camera to make a five minute documentary of her life with a view to publishing it on MySpace, just for the fun of it. It's Boxing Day. She films her cat playing with a ping-pong ball in the study, her little brother fighting with her older sister about whether to watch *The Simpsons* or *America's Next Top Model*. She films you reading a newspaper. She films her sister miming to a Britney Spears song in the kitchen. The camera pans around the room revealing the remains of the turkey and the Christmas pudding. She films the neighbour mowing the lawn, the cars going past in the road outside. She ends with a shot of the Christmas tree, zooming in to a distorted self-portrait in a silver bauble. She uploads it in great excitement. And three minutes later it disappears.

What she doesn't realize is that she has committed no less than 17 copyright infringements.

'Home use' is exempt from this kind of restriction. So too, for the time being, are news programmes. Which is why you get to see that the man charged with the murder of five Ipswich prostitutes wears a Calloway cap. If Mexican drug smugglers wear Nike sneakers in real life they wouldn't be able to dress that way in a fictional movie about the subject, or certainly not without Nike's permission.

The point is that real life in the 20th century is inextricably linked to the way we use and consume brands, to the music and TV programmes that engulf us at home, in shops, at airports and in every kind of public space. We are assaulted by copyrighted images and sounds at every turn, and its increasingly difficult to imagine how life would be without them. Yet we are prohibited from using them in any account of our experience except under special circumstances. Since, as we have seen, these ephemera of our daily experience now constitute our central engagement with culture, we have been effectively robbed of our right to recreate for public consumption an accurate picture of the way we actually live. This is the equivalent of an anthropologist going to Papua New Guinea and discovering that she is allowed to film everything except the traditions, culture, taboos, sexual practices and life-styles of the people because they have all been copyrighted by Papua New Guinea Inc. George Orwell thought Big Brother would arrive in the form of a fascist dictatorship. If the future turned out to be more hospitable than he imagined it's only because we are numb to the freedoms we lost without noticing.

*

Not very long ago, when the wall was coming down and Nelson Mandela was being freed from Robben Island, we thought it was an unreservedly good thing that Levi's and McDonald's and Rock 'n' Roll were helping to unite the nations of the world in a global version of our Liberal Democratic Shangri La. Now, to add insult to the injury of trade barriers and immigration control, we can anticipate with some certainty that the developing nations of the world will soon be stuck with a cultural poverty just as invidious as the physical one. Wealth creation in the creative economy is no longer derived from technological hardware and infra-structure. It is, in the words of Venturelli, '. . . dependent upon the capacity of a nation to continually create content, or new forms of widely distributed expression for which they will need to invest in creative human capital throughout the economy and not merely in gadgets and hardware'.

It is fairly obvious who is going to suck the hind tit.

In retrospect we can see that those countries that tried so hard to protect their own cultures were undoubtedly right, though probably for the wrong reasons. Spain still insists that all non-Spanish films are dubbed into the local language. France is continually trying to eradicate Angloisms from French. These efforts have proven to be fruitless and trivial. Nothing can stop the tide of English blogs and American DVDs from overwhelming national cultures. What they should have been doing, instead of trying to reverse the inevitable, was investing massively in content creation of their own. It is no longer enough to have your culture gathering dust in museums and libraries. Your only hope is to fight back with

an educational system that places emphasis on creative freedom and on incentives for independent thinking, state and private sector investment in research and development of new ideas and technology, and low levels of risk and high levels of reward for creative risk-taking in the workplace and the economy. Most of all, forging an environment of creative dynamism requires regulatory stimulation of creative enterprises.

Never mind that the UN's World Commission on Culture and Development has called for 'concerted action to address development challenges and to sustain cultural diversity in a global world', or that the EU's Charter of Fundamental Rights insists that, 'The Union contributes to the preservation and to the development of these common values while respecting the diversity of the cultures and traditions of the people's of Europe.' These are fine words, but one can't help thinking they were written by people who didn't understand that their definition of culture was made irrelevant before the ink dried.

Venturelli hopes to persuade supranational regulators like the World Trade Organization, the World Intellectual Property Organization and the World Bank that the monopolization of ideas is just as inimical to economic progress as the monopolization of physical resources. But the record shows that pretty much everything they have done so far has favoured the protection of the copyright monopolies and eroded even further the principle of 'fair use'.

If you've ever spent any time working in the creative industries – especially if you've ever had to think up ideas yourself – you will know just how important 'fair use' is to creativity. It's the principle that allows scientists to build on the work of other scientists without having to seek permission from a hundred lawyers. It's the principle that allowed Masaccio to build on the work of Giotto and Piero de la Francesca to build on the work of Masaccio and so on and so forth through Michelangelo to Rembrandt to Turner to Damien Hirst. But in domains where 'fair use' is not recognized, creative people like my 12 year old daughter have to have an army of copyright lawyers on their side before they can freely distribute their opinions of icons like Barbie, Lisa Simpson and Minnie Mouse.

'Fair use' allows me to quote from the work of other authors without inviting the wrath of their publishers as long as excerpts are not more than 300 words in length. That's true of books. Song lyrics, poems and other sources are a lot more complicated, and rights can be very expensive. Lack of funds at the time of writing prevented me from buying the words to 'Pin Ball Wizard'. I chose to spend them on W.H. Auden instead.

Creative expression is also being hampered in other less obvious ways. The bulk of magazines published today draw their editorial directly from commercial press releases. I recently counted the number of original, non-commercial articles in a popular woman's magazine. Out of more than two hundred pages only 30 were devoted to editorial of any kind. Of these 24 had been supplied by cosmetic or fashion houses or boutiques and other retailers. Four were syndicated, and two articles were generated by the magazine itself, one of which was the Letter from the Editor. There is nothing illegal or morally wrong about this practice, and it enables the magazine publishing business to satisfy the demand for this kind of information from millions of readers.

What you don't see, though, in anything other than those magazines written expressively for political or satirical purposes (like *The Spectator* and *Private Eye* in the UK) is any point of view critical of the advertisers who buy up the vast majority of the pages or the companies that supply the editorials. Most readers wouldn't notice and wouldn't care, but this is a form of commercial censorship that strikes at the heart of freedom of expression. And it's as subtle as it is pervasive.

There was a time when publishers who reproduced articles given to them by PR agencies were obliged to flag them with bold warnings saying 'advertisement, advertisement, advertisement'. Occasionally you will still see this in newspapers or magazines, but only in those instances where the publisher would be too ashamed to admit they had written the stuff. Contemporary practice for PR agencies, and for advertising agencies in some cases, is to write these articles as though they were written by independent sources. These are called advertorials that, like infomercials, blur the line between editorial independence and overt advertising. I have written many of these myself, and it's easy enough to do with a little practice. Every now and again you want to throw in a sentence that sounds as though it's critical just for the sake of the illusion.

As with the internet we must rely on the intelligence of readers and viewers to discriminate between genuine opinion and 'paid-for puffery', which is as it should be. People are much smarter than PR companies think they are, and they will get even smarter as long as open forums on the internet enable them to find alternative views. But the issue affecting magazines and newspapers today is that they simply can't say anything critical of the advertisers to whom they are beholden for the money that keeps them going. This is just as true of commercial radio and television. Even with 'fair use' and regulatory practices that enhance the free flow of ideas, this kind of subtle censorship will continue to encroach upon the liberty of writers and artists.

Critics of this view might argue that Michelangelo was not at liberty to design the Sistine Chapel outside of the constraints of the commercial sponsorship of the Church, or that Velasquez was not free to interpret the brief he received from the Spanish monarchy. But it's hardly the same point. The difference between patronage and commercial constraint is crucial. Michelangelo's portrayal of the creation of man is as glorious as it is, not because it depicts the vision of Pope Julius II, but because it celebrates the sublime nature of man. And the works of Velasquez are a running criticism of the vanity of the Spanish court. There's a real risk in this debate of confusing 'the freedom of a tight brief' with limits to freedom imposed by other kinds of constraint, a subject we will explore in more detail. There is a monumental difference between the discipline imposed by the form of a sonnet and the constraint imposed by commercial interest or political ideology.

The 'Creative Economy' is a myth of its own making. It's certainly an economy; but let's not get too excited about how creative it is. Not just yet.

*

It was only when a bevy of bare-breasted female students occupied the podium of his lecture hall in 1969 that Theodor Adorno, the German sociologist, realized that his life-long critique of popular culture had ended up creating a popular counter-culture that was determined to get rid of him. He died a few months later, but not before leaving us with the most pessimistic view of the commercialization of culture ever committed to paper.

It's difficult to read Adorno. And it's especially difficult to read him without coming to the conclusion that he was a paranoid conspiracy theorist who imagined that the mass media and the people who owned it were deliberately dumbing down books and movies and magazines to make people docile and content so they wouldn't start another Marxist revolution. He was the first person to talk about the 'culture industry', and one of the first fully to understand the role that marketing played in defining people's needs, preferences and tastes. He coined the word 'pseudo-individualism' to describe the way we continue to believe we all have such unique identities while buying and consuming exactly the same things.

But what makes Adorno truly extraordinary is that he wrote and said all of this long before *I'm a Celebrity, Get Me Out of Here!*, globalization and Martin Sorrel.

As early as 1944, in *Dialectic of Enlightenment*, he was fuming against the way advertising was taking over the streets, debasing language and blurring the distinction between editorial comment and bare-faced salesmanship:

> Advertising becomes art and nothing else, just as Goebbels – with foresight – combines them: *l'art pour l'art*, advertising for its own sake, a pure representation of social power. In the most influential American magazines, Life and Fortune, a quick glance can now scarcely distinguish advertising from editorial picture and text . . .
>
> The assembly-line character of the culture industry, the synthetic, planned method of turning out its products (factory-like not only in the studio but, more or less, in the compilation of cheap biographies, pseudo-documentary novels, and hit songs) is very suited to advertising: the important individual points, by becoming detachable, interchangeable, and even technically alienated from any connected meaning, lend themselves to ends external to the work . . .
>
> Advertising and the culture industry merge technically as well as economically. In both cases the same thing can be seen in innumerable places, and the mechanical repetition of the same culture product has come to be the same as that of the propaganda slogan. In both cases the insistent demand for effectiveness makes technology into psycho-technology, into a procedure for manipulating men. In both cases the standards are the striking yet familiar, the easy yet catchy, the skilful yet simple; the object is to overpower the customer, who is conceived as absent-minded or resistant.

Adorno had the slogans of the Third Reich ringing in his ears, and he saw little distinction between the tone of their appeals and the slogans of advertising that were beginning to make their presence felt across Europe at the time. So it was only natural that he should equate capitalism with a new kind of fascism.

If most commentators now believe that Adorno was short-sighted or simply wrong, one can hardly look around at the cultural landscape of today without admiring his perspicacity and sharing some of his fears. Even in his lifetime the poor man got it from both sides. The Marxists said he wasn't a proper Marxist, and the student activists who had taken up the struggle against the imperialism of popular culture shouted him down as a reactionary for trying to keep order on the campus.

It's difficult to know what he would have made of Times Square, the Ginza, or text messages on your phone telling you to watch the latest episode of *Lost*. Just like Vance Packard, whose book *The Hidden Persuaders* became a best seller in the early 1960s, Adorno ascribed far too much power and cunning to the ad agencies. Both of them, from very different points of view, foolishly imagined that the people who came up with advertising campaigns were part of a military/ industrial conspiracy to manipulate ordinary people to buy things that they didn't want or need by using sophisticated psychological techniques including things like subliminal advertising and photographs of ice in whisky glasses subtly arranged to look like an underwater orgy.

As anyone who has worked in an advertising agency can tell you, they could hardly have got it more wrong. Far from being the considered consequence of a process of clinical dissection of consumer behaviour based on cutting edge techniques of psychological persuasion, most good ads are written at three o'clock in the morning, the night before presentation to the client, by two very tired and half drunk creatives whose own lives are a shamble of broken marriages and persistent neurosis.

Adorno and Packard, and other writers who have followed in their footsteps, also make the mistake of imagining the recipients of advertising as being passive, gullible or bloody minded idiots who either cannot or will not tell the difference between an ad for Coca-Cola and a documentary about Eskimos.

The problem isn't that popular culture, the culture industry, or the creative economy – or the people that own and manage the constituents of these – are masterminding a complex programme of bread and circuses to numb us into a defenceless acceptance of their evil capitalist agenda. The problem is that popular culture has redefined all other kinds of culture as 'unpopular', and that without a substantial effort to support the variety of creative skills nurtured by these less popular disciplines we are watering down the gene pool of talent and the diversity of ideas that popular culture needs for enduring growth.

CHAPTER 11

Poison in the water-cooler

> The number of controls and systems for controlling and predicting the behaviour of the members of our work organisations is mind-boggling. There are selection systems, induction systems, training systems, performance-measurement systems, reward systems, career-planning systems, promotion systems, discipline systems, human-resource-planning systems, industrial-relations systems and redundancy and retirement systems.
>
> John W. Hunt, *Managing People at Work*

Companies that cease to have a central purpose become abstractions. Cut loose from the moorings that connected them to the lives of real people in the real world, they float off into the ether on cushions of self-absorption. Now, like the fantastic airborne castles of Hayao Miyazaki, or like Swift's floating island of Laputa, their inhabitants drift free of the distractions of everyday life, their minds 'so taken up with intense speculations, that they neither can speak, nor attend to the discourses of others, without being roused by some external taction upon the organs of speech and hearing . . .'.

When their founders are still alive and active, and when the ideas that led to their initial successes still inform the manner of their daily operations, the corporate purpose remains self-evident. Sometimes it will be embodied in charismatic leadership. Sometimes it will be manifest in the passionate commitment of the employees to the original *raison d'être* of the company.

It sounds unfashionable and even a little improbable in today's climate but Johnson & Johnson once believed, 'The company exists to alleviate pain and disease.' 3M once had the following writ large as a corporate commandment: 'Though shalt not kill a new product idea.' In 1950 George Merck II said, 'We try never to forget that medicine is for people. It is not for profits. The profits follow and if we have remembered that, they have never failed to appear.' Akio Morita, founder of Sony, said in 1986, 'Our plan is to lead the market with new products, rather than ask them what kind of products they want.' And Apple famously described their mission as, 'To extend the boundaries of human freedom.'

This is rousing stuff. These are sentiments well worth getting out of bed for in the morning. And the simple reason why they are so rousing and so motivating is that they describe what these companies stand for – the values, in other words, against which their actions can be judged.

The great orators and the greatest leaders have always put values before strategies. And great companies continue to do so. Values are critical, according to the London Business School, because, 'they are a yardstick against which to measure behaviour, they guide decisions, they help to maintain the external reputation of the organisation, and they humanise the organisation and generate trust'.

When companies are bought or sold and become part of larger conglomerates they often lose touch with their founding inspiration. New managers and new recruits regard all that as history, the dusty and boring stuff that old-timers can't let go of. The new mission statements invariably open with, 'To increase shareholder value by . . . (insert company activity here).'

And then, not long after the lobby has been redesigned to look like a nightclub, anomie sets in.

It's one thing leashing yourself to a dream. It's quite another leashing yourself to a Laputa.

It's notoriously difficult to motivate workers in the knowledge-based industries, of which the creative sectors make up a substantial slice. There are two reasons for this. The first is what has come to be known as 'The White Collar Sweatshop', first coined by Jill Andresky Fraser, and the second is what is known as 'invisible work'.

We used to think that the unhappiest people in the world were those who were trapped in the repetitive misery of life on the production line. Today we envy them. When the bell rings and they pack up their lunch-boxes, grab their coats and head for the train home to their families, they leave their work behind at the factory. White-collar workers with laptops and mobile phones and Blackberries can't do that. Work haunts them wherever they are and whatever they're doing. It follows them home on the train. It sits in the passenger seat of their SUVs. When they're reading their children to sleep they can hear it panting and scratching restlessly in the passage outside, like a dog demanding a walk.

Their work is invisible. It surrounds them like a shimmering mirage. They no longer know where it starts or where it ends.

Look out the window of your gleaming tower. You see that man on the yellow bulldozer shifting earth from the pile on the left to the pile on the right? Zoom in close enough and you'll see a slight smile. It isn't there because he is listening to The Black-Eyed Peas on his iPod Nano, though that probably helps. It's there because he is thinking about going home to the loving arms of his wife, to bangers and mash and mushy peas, to playing ball with his kids in the park before the sun sets, to tinkering with the outboard motor in the garden shed, to prepping the fishing lines for Saturday, to the dreamless sleep of the man who knows the difference between work and life.

If you could ask him how he felt about his work he would simply shrug.

> O lurcher-loving collier, black as night,
> Follow your love across the smokeless hill;
> Your lamp is out, the cages all are still;
> Course for her heart and do not miss,
> For Sunday soon is past and, Kate, fly not so fast,
> For Monday comes when none may kiss:
> Be marble to his soot, and to his black be white.
> Better go now. The phone is ringing behind you.

> W.H. Auden

Invisible work is the curse of the modern world. It gets into your system like cancer. And unless you are one of the few who are lucky enough to be able to say, I go to work to alleviate pain and disease, or I go to work to extend the boundaries of human freedom, it will grow there, in the churning pit of your acidic gut.

You console yourself with Maalox and the fond thoughts of the day when your stock options are valuable enough to buy you your freedom.

*

In an interview with Fast Company, the controversial human resources guru Jeffrey Pfeffer describes some of the symptoms of the 'toxic workplace'.

Refuting the popular view that employees are to blame for the demise of organizational loyalty, Pfeffer is adamant that 'companies killed loyalty – by becoming toxic places to work!' He quotes the example of employment contracts that give the company the right to fire the employee at any time and for any reason: 'Think about it: It's your first day on the job, and I've already told you that you don't have a permanent employment relationship with me, that your job is based on a contractual relationship – and then I wonder why, on your second day, you're not approaching me with a long-term perspective and a feeling of trust!'

He described the enticement of stock options as:

> an operational definition of the toxic workplace: It's a place where people come to work so they can make enough money so they can leave.
>
> Another sign that a company is toxic: It requires people to choose between having a life and having a career. A toxic company says to people, 'We want to own you.' There's an old joke that they used to tell about working for Microsoft: 'We offer flexible time – you can work any 18 hours you want.'

Many companies talk a good game:

> It's easy for a company to say, 'We invest in people. We believe in training. We believe in mutual commitments between managers and the workforce. We believe in sharing information widely with people.
>
> Many organisations say those things – but in their heart of hearts, they don't believe them. Most managers, if they're being honest with themselves, will admit it: When they look at their people, they see costs, they see salaries, they see benefits, they see overheads. Very few companies look at their people and see assets.

In part, it's because of the financial-reporting systems that we've got. The fact is, your salary is an expense. If I buy a computer to replace you, I can capitalise the computer and then depreciate its useful life over many years. If I hire you, I take on an expense.

*

I suspect we will one day look back at the period between the mid-1960s and the mid-1980s as a golden age of entrepreneurial creativity. It dawned about the time the first baby-boomers, inspired by 'The Times They Are A-Changin'' and 'My Generation', realized that the world was going to be very different from the one they inherited from their parents. Intoxicated with optimism they succeeded in putting a man on the moon using only a fraction of the computing power of a modern calculator. Richard Branson founded Virgin, joining HP Labs, Toyota, Intel, Apple Records, Apple Computers and a legion of others who believed that business didn't have to be business as usual.

The hopes and dreams of that astonishing time were exemplified in the Governor of California, Jerry Brown, who managed not only to balance the budget, but to bring environmental issues, women's rights, immigrants' rights, arts funding and scores of other naïvely liberal concerns into the mainstream politics.

The era ended in the three or four years it took to get a personal computer on the desk of every white-collar worker in the western world.

When you only have a hammer, everything looks like a nail. Management by email, which had become the default means of communication by the time Windows replaced MS-DOS, spawned a breed of consultants that made Frederick Taylor look like the affable amateur he really was.

They first appeared in the innocuous form of technicians who burrowed under your desk with cables in their teeth and drills and screwdrivers in their back pockets. The next time you saw them they were in suits and ties addressing bewildered groups of employees, including you and your colleagues, on subjects like 'The Information Super-Highway' and 'You and Lotus Notes' as your office manager stood beaming in the background, the beneficent patron of this splendid new age.

Later, as the seminars became less frequent, you would catch a glimpse of them every now and then, through the half-opened door of your manager's office, huddled together over spreadsheets with the finance guy and a big cheese you vaguely recognized from photos in the new company magazine called *Wired for the Future*. You used to be able to call them in by their first names and ask them how you went about emailing more than one person at a time, or what to do when the words 'Runtime error: 277' appeared on your screen. You soon learned that those days were over, and that your petty IT anxieties and technical clumsiness were distracting the experts from the vitally important business of leading your company to glorious new levels of knowledge proficiency.

Knowledge, which once upon a time you foolishly believed was a word used to describe the stuff you knew, became something best left to the experts. Henceforth no discussion about company strategy would have any merit unless it was blessed by the superior intelligence of an IT guru. The way in which knowledge was shared in a company became more important than the knowledge itself, and pundits who had got in at the ground floor of information networking went on to become the high priests of management consultancy. You need only to look at someone like Thomas Davenport and his prolific series of books on the productivity of knowledge workers to appreciate just how cabalistic the field has become.

Email is a brilliant way of communicating. It's quick, it's efficient, it's cheap and it's extraordinarily powerful. It has become the indispensable tool of modern business and it is almost certainly the single technology most responsible for enabling the globalization of commerce and industry over the past two decades.

It's so good we can't remember what we used to do without it. That isn't just a rhetorical emphasis. We quite literally cannot remember how on earth we filled the time between nine and five without checking the inbox first thing in the morning and spending the rest of the day replying to correspondents in strict order of most politically important all the way down to those you can safely delete without dire consequence.

Before email arrived it was virtually impossible to tell if someone was working or not. It is now commonly understood that when someone is reading emails, writing emails or replying to emails he or she is working. On the other hand, if he or she is not reading emails, writing emails or replying to emails, it is commonly understood that he or she is not working. Unless, of course, he or she is in a meeting. This leaves workers with a real dilemma. Given the times we live in, most of them are unlikely to want to advertise the fact that they're not working. Which means that when they actually, truly and honestly run out of things to do they must either (a) arrange a meeting, (b) stare at their computers as though they are reading an email, (c) walk very slowly to and from the water-cooler or (d) think of entirely spurious reasons to write more emails.

When Apple famously announced at the Superbowl of January 1984 that 1984 was not going to be like *1984* they were quite right. Big Brother was not going to be watching us. We were going to be gazing into our screens hoping to catch glimpses of Him.

Email is the closest we can get to making invisible work visible. Often it is all we have to show for what we did today: the number we receive is the measure of our worth to the corporation, the number we send is the measure of our productivity. Because we have no way of knowing with any degree of certainty whether our emails are received with respect or indifference, or with appreciation or scorn, or whether the responses we get are sincere or just politically appropriate. In this sense the company intranet is a cyber version of the Truman Show, a fictional world created to sustain the illusion of our place in reality.

This is probably less true in companies that produce physical things for real people, at least among those employees engaged in doing something or managing something with a physical consequence. Then email becomes what it was designed to be in the first place, a quick and easy alternative to correspondence by mail. Before we had email we must have spoken to each other on the phone or in the flesh. We must also have written letters or sent faxes. But there could hardly have been enough trees in all the rain forests of the world to put on paper the amount of written words we now commit to electronic correspondence.

But if the only side effect of email were anomie we could learn to live with it. Unfortunately there are other much more dangerous consequences of believing that writing an email is the same as doing something important.

The technology that enables us to share information and to drink from a common pool of corporate knowledge has the effect of mediating our experience, screening us in the most literal sense from the direct impact of that information in the real world. The computer interface numbs our faculties, just as TV images of the carnage in Baghdad numb us to the reality of the suffering there. Work becomes a video game. We type in certain sentences and wait to see what happens.

At the same time it encourages us to believe that everyone else knows what we know, and that the collective brain which resides in the company server somewhere down in the basement is smart enough to fill in the gaps of our collective wisdom. We begin to think that the company knows everything, that it is invulnerable and – worse still – that it is inherently moral and wise.

The system that connects us, which is no more than an insensible tangle of wires and code and pixels, takes on a life and an identity of its own. No longer a passive conveyor of the collective spirit, it actively embodies it. It's the way that walls of bricks and clay turn into places of worship, transformed by consecration into the embodiment of the sacred, not the vessel of it. And in the act of consecration the worshippers give over their power and responsibility to the guardians of the church, and the men and women in ritualistic fancy dress who keep the keys to the door become the mediators of faith. Now the church knows more than the worshippers, and they are forever after cut off from direct communion with the highest power. They begin to censor their behaviour in the hope of ingratiating themselves with the priesthood. They see other worshippers being excommunicated for refusing to toe the ecclesiastical line.

*

Seventy-three seconds after blasting off from the Kennedy Space Center in Florida on 28th January 1986, the space shuttle Challenger disintegrated in an explosion watched live on television by millions of people around the world.

The investigation that followed revealed that there were NASA engineers who knew that the launch might be risky. But according to Irving Janis, the Yale social psychologist, their concerns evaporated in the cauldron of 'groupthink', the organizational phenomenon that Janis describes as, 'a mode of thinking that people engage in when they are deeply involved in a cohesive in-group, when the members' strivings for unanimity override their motivation to realistically appraise alternative courses of action'.

Janis blamed groupthink for Roosevelt's complacency before Pearl Harbor, for Truman's invasion of North Korea, for the Bay of Pigs fiasco, and for Johnson's escalation of the Vietnam War.

Groupthink makes groups of very clever people do very stupid things. It was almost certainly responsible for the apocryphal 'weapons of mass destruction' that led to the invasion of Iraq. It's written all over Enron and most other corporate disasters. And it is clearly responsible for increasingly high levels of toxicity in the contemporary workplace. Groupthink kills collective creativity in the same way, and for the same reasons, that brainstorming kills creativity in groups. It censors diversity of opinion, it mutes the aberrant voice, and it favours the opinion of the concurrence-seeking majority.

The typical knowledge company – wired by IBM and Microsoft, cursed by the stresses of invisible work, devoid of loyalty and corporate purpose – suffers from many of the symptoms of groupthink as listed by Janis: the illusion of invulnerability, a belief in the inherent morality of a group, collective rationalization, self-censorship, the illusion of unanimity, self-appointed 'mind-guards' and direct pressure on dissenters to keep their mouths shut.

Put all of this together and you get the 'white collar sweatshop', the 21st century version of the cotton mill. The difference today is that the only way to ensure that management notes your productivity is to get to work earlier and leave later than the rest of your colleagues. It is an exquisite form of social insanity played out day after day in office buildings of machine-like rationality, the torture chambers of the post-industrial epoch. The pinball table, the espresso machine and the casual work clothes only serve to pile on the pain by reminding us how much of life we're missing.

In manufacturing or service companies the results of innovation are clearly apparent. And the time line from concept to prototyping to testing to in-market trials to rollout will be familiar, if not always predictable. In knowledge companies, one good idea by one employee in one minute can revolutionize the entire business model. Which makes it all the more bizarre that knowledge companies expect their employees to work to schedules based on industrial practices. The five-day working week is, after all, a convenient fiction invented during the industrial revolution to ensure an optimal volume of steel or textile output. The nine-hour working day is just as absurd when all the evidence points to the fact the most people don't have good ideas at work.

Knowledge companies have squared this circle by routinizing the tasks of employees, effectively ruling out the possibility of idea-producing behaviour by insisting that productivity is a function of turnover and man-hours and nothing else. For all their talk of creativity, it is the random nature of idea production that worries them the most.

*

They say there are two kinds of people, those that divide the world into two kinds of people and those that don't, a statement that contains both the mischief of Dionysus and the sublime logic of Apollo. And that's the kind of pat resolution you get from unifying false dichotomies.

H.G. Wells knew better. When evolution divided the world into the beautiful Eloi and the savage Morlocks, resolution didn't come from a happy marriage between the beautiful but sensitive Eloi heroine and the savage but sensitive Morlock hero as it would have in the Hollywood version. Resolution came when the Morlocks ate all the Eloi.

Pareto, the 19th century economist and sociologist, divided the world into 'speculators' and 'rentiers'. The former are the entrepreneurs, the visionaries and the creative types who want to change the world. The latter are the conservative, steady types who are quite content with their unimaginative lot. Essentially it's a rewrite of Marx but with the capitalists as the good guys.

This division isn't all that helpful except for one thing: a distinguishing characteristic of the 'speculator' as noted by James Webb Young: '. . . according to Pareto . . . he is *constantly preoccupied with the possibilities of new combinations*'. (His italics.) Which reminds us once again of Steiner's 'men addicted to the drug of absolute thought' and Lumsden's 'people who, when given a measure of free rein, spend significant amounts of time engaged in the creative process'.

Creativity is not an occupation, it's a preoccupation.

It would be specious to equate creativity with the Dionysian spirit and a lack of creativity with the Apollonian one. Apollo, remember, represents culture, poetry and music just as much as he represents reason and harmony. To deny the creativity of the Apollonian spirit would be to deny the extraordinary achievements of western liberal democracies, to contemn most of the legacy of western art and philosophy, and to denigrate the life of comfort and material well-being that is the envy of all who do not have it.

As Camille Paglia says, 'Capitalism is an art form, an Apollonian fabrication to rival nature. It is hypocritical for feminists and intellectuals to enjoy the pleasures and conveniences of capitalism while sneering at it. Everyone born into capitalism has incurred a debt to it. Give Caesar his due.'

The beauty that some of us find in mathematics is essentially Apollonian, the way differential calculus describes a perfect curve, the way prime numbers create a perfect spiral when you zoom out of the number circle. This is the rational, formal beauty of the golden mean, the architecture of the Acropolis, the dome of St Paul's. And because the aesthetics of classical western music are so deeply entwined with the mathematics of harmony and rhythm it's easy to see why the Greeks included music among Apollo's divine gifts.

There's probably a good game to be had in contrasting Apollonian composers with Dionysian ones. Someone once said that listening to Bach was like listening to 'a pure mind at work', so he would probably go into the former camp without much difficulty. So too would all of those composers inspired by the serene beauty of musical architecture, as opposed to the romantics, the moderns, and Nirvana.

But this very quickly becomes academic. The same sort of creative impulse is at work in all musical composition, flavoured only by the formality of the Apollonian or the expressiveness of the Dionysian. The same thing applies to art, poetry, drama, film, fashion and all the other forms of creative expression. Because Blake is clearly more pagan than Milton doesn't mean that the former is less masculine or the latter less feminine. The Apollonian impulse can be just as bold and assertive as the Dionysian. Nor is one tonality better or worse than another as long as people find it significant, as Lumsden has pointed out.

This distinguishing principle has less to do with the nature or structure of any creative work than with the way it engages us. At its best the Apollonian spirit urges us to reflection, and we give ourselves up to the pure aesthetics of the intellect. The Dionysian, by contrast, challenges all our senses in a tumult of sensual chaos, subverting our cosy assumptions and shattering our illusions of a rational universe.

At its worst the Apollonian becomes self-obsessed, trivial, effete and narcissistic. It becomes celebrity for celebrity's sake, the supermodel circus of so much contemporary television programming. It becomes the vanity of wealth that can buy itself personality. Today Apollo drives a Porsche Cayenne, makes millions in the City, has rock stars for dinner and movie stars for lunch, with a diet of organic yoghurt in between.

As for Dionysus, look no further than Abu Ghraib.

What we find significant is defined as much by the age we live in as by the merits of the work itself. Among presocratic pagans the formal beauty of a perfect circle would have been truly astonishing. In the formal didacticism of medieval

Europe the naturalism of a Giotto portrait would have been cause for astonishment. The flowering of the Dionysian spirit in the 1960s was notable mostly for what it was reacting *against*. Context is as powerful as content, and it is only the long view of history that can make out the shining stars in the dust of the ephemeral.

As we begin to examine the creative products of our own time these reflections will serve as a useful vocabulary for what's working and what isn't. The way we manage creative talent to the best advantage of our commercial and cultural interests will be informed by our understanding of these concepts, and by our sensitivity to the aesthetic climate of the various environments in which creativity is obliged to operate.

Right now, as globalization continues apace to divide the world even more sharply between the corporate and institutional haves and the increasingly desperate have-nots who shiver in the cold winds of the passing train of progress, Apollo is clearly in the ascendancy.

Apollo bombed Baghdad, not Dionysus. Those F-22s were arrows straight from Apollo's bow. The suicide bomber sacrifices himself on Apollo's altar, for the sake of the abstract perfection of an ideology he knows as Islam. We must not be ambiguous about this. Poverty is not charmingly pagan; it is a consequence of Apollonian neglect. And so is crime that is caused by poverty. But the young hoodies on the streets of Bradford who wear their ASBOs as badges of honour are different. They're the disciples of Dionysus with nothing to do and nowhere to go since the Garden of Eden was turned into a strip mall. Their graffiti is in praise of Lucifer before the Fall.

*

Of all of Apollo's many brilliant manifestations, and the one that best exemplifies his love of reason, culture, harmony and restraint, is the modern corporation. The corporate world is exquisitely civilized, its structure exquisitely rational, and its relationship with the contingent world exquisitely restrained. The gleaming skyscrapers of Shanghai, New York and Canary Wharf are shrines to Apollonian perfection. And every gleaming computer screen on every gleaming desk glows with the exegesis of his Word.

In return for the manifold blessings of the corporate embrace, servants of Apollo must leave their messy emotions at home with their messy children, their messy dogs and cats, and their messy Dionysian dreams. The corporation requires of them only the enthusiastic application and dedication of their rational beings, eight hours a day, five days a week, 11 months of the year.

Many company buildings are set these days in so-called 'business parks', with beautifully mown lawns and manicured gardens, situated as far as possible away from the messy hustle and bustle of urban life. Some provide their employees with gyms and grocery stores on the premises, further insulating their staff from possible infection from the real world. Gyms are particularly good places for Apollo worship since the perfectly sculptured body is the most cherished expression of the Apollonian aesthetic.

David Whyte, the English poet, has made a valiant attempt to persuade corporate America that too much of this Apollonian stuff is not necessarily a good thing for creativity. The blurb to his celebrated book, *The Heart Aroused – Poetry and the Preservation of Soul in Corporate America*, describes his mission as, 'The best way to respond to the current call for creativity in organisational life is to overcome our habitual fear and reticence and bring our full passionate, creative human souls with all their urgencies and unnamed longings, right inside the office with us.' And, 'Whyte uses poetry to bring to life the experience of change itself. When he retells the story of Beowulf he shows us how to face the nightmares that intrude into even the most organised workplace, nightmares we face in the demands, conversations and relationships that make up our work life.'

You have to applaud him for the courage it must have taken to get IBM executives to sit down in a circle and read Blake to each other, or to get other corporate executives to appreciate the sensitivity of Rilke.

The Heart Aroused is indeed a telling indictment of a corporate world that has lost touch with the Dionysian spirit, and one suspects that it's going to take a lot more than Whyte's impassioned oratory to get it back. One of the problems is that Whyte's poetry is itself written in a style that is more Apollonian than Dionysian, as if, once admitted into the corporate fold, he didn't quite have the courage to follow through with a wholehearted Dionysian slap in the face.

Nevertheless, *The Heart Aroused* is rich in entertaining references to Greek mythology, T.S. Eliot and Chaos Theory, and an indispensable guide to the depth of the creative crisis we are currently experiencing. He is particularly good on Grendel and other monsters of the unconsciousness, and you keep wishing he'd use some of that raw, irrational power to pull down the pillars of corporate complacency.

Whyte quotes John Sculley, the former executive of Apple Computer, as saying, 'The new corporate contract is that we'll offer you an opportunity to express yourself and grow, if you promise to leash yourself to our dream, at least for a while.' Whyte's response is dead on the money:

> Loyalty in an organisation is now based on two ends of the creative spectrum – security in the form of money, power, and benefits; and creative engagement by way of excitement and innovation. The balance point on the scale between security and creativity is very different for each of us, but whatever our personal balance point, there is no doubt that the postmodern corporation is demanding more movement and adaptation to the insecure and mutable end of experience. It wants vitality and fire, not because it likes the dangerous beauty of these qualities, but because it will not survive without them. The hard news is that the corporate world wants us around while we are useful, but it offers no security based on how likeable or impassioned we are.

I hope Whyte makes a difference, and I wish him well. But I fear the worst. No amount of Jung or Joseph Campbell or James Gleick or Blake or Rilke or Auden will so much as disturb a gleaming hair on the head of any one of the corporate technocrats.

They have inherited these perfect worlds, sufficient unto themselves. Why on earth would they want to risk everything they have worked so hard to achieve for the sake of a soul when they've managed to get along quite nicely without one for so long?

If corporate America really does want 'vitality and fire' – for which read creativity and innovation – and if it does understand that it won't survive without them (and I agree with Whyte that it almost certainly does), it will do what it has always done, that is, employ creative people 'while they are useful' and then dump them when they're not.

The idea that corporate managers should open their hearts or minds and bring 'their urgencies and unnamed longings' into the workplace in the hope of accelerating the innovation process down at the canning plant is more than faintly ridiculous. An image comes into my head of David Brent acting out Beowulf's battle with Grendel as his assembled staff look on with glassy eyes.

*

The new Apollonians who run the great global empires of the Fortune 500 will deal with Dionysus on their own terms, at the time and place and in the manner of their own choosing. And they don't need David Whyte or Arthur Koestler or me to act as intermediaries. They've done tougher deals than this before. If they want Dionysus in to work his weird and crazy stuff they have contracts pre-prepared expressly for that. And they'll keep him waiting in reception just as long as they deem fit. If he can't sit still let him play on the pinball machine. Just don't break anything. And get someone to clean up that mess.

They are pragmatists, remember, and they want pragmatic solutions. If they want vitality and fire they'll Google it.

*

There is, in the end, no point trying the souls of the new Apollos by getting them to drink from the Dionysian cup. It might have worked when companies belonged to individual people in whom the flames of the entrepreneurial spirit still burned bright. But now that corporations no longer belong to anyone in particular, and are run and managed by functionaries as faceless and anonymous as the sharehold-ers themselves, they have taken on a life and purpose entirely separated from the ambitions of their founding fathers, and have become entirely immune to human weakness. In these gleaming abstractions there is therefore no place for the fren-zied excess of the Dionysian spirit to take hold, although there's a moment in *The Smartest Guys in the Room* when Jeffrey Skilling of Enron appears to have grown giddy by the smell of it.

It is naïve to think that individuation is possible for the corporate entity, that the unification of the masculine and the feminine, or the light and the shadow, or the conscious and the unconscious, or the Apollonian and the Dionysian, or the left-brain and the right-brain will somehow unleash new torrents of creativity through the company organogram.

The best we must hope for is an accommodation, a mutually satisfying arrangement that serves the interests of corporate ambition without emasculating the creative impulse by 'leashing it to the dream'. This will not be an arrangement of master and servant, or pimp and prostitute, or husband and wife, or mother and child. Nor will it be a compromise between conflicting interests, or a finely tuned balance of power.

Such an arrangement is possible. It exists. It does not need to be invented.

It simply needs to be grasped, understood, and implemented. Like now.

CHAPTER 12

Podsnaps and ponytails

If Botticelli were alive today, he'd be working for *Vogue*.

Peter Ustinov

If you're the manager of a business that relies on creative people to produce the goods or services you need to generate revenue, here's some very straightforward advice:

1.   Hire the best talent you can afford.
2.   Let them get on with it.

Judging from the paucity of startling new ideas in the marketplace most of your colleagues in the creative industries haven't the faintest notion of where or how to begin. Or, even more dangerously, they think they do. In the peculiar arena of creativity management a little bit of knowledge is a dangerous thing, and a lot of it is completely catastrophic.

Taking the most generous possible view, we could just about forgive the major film, TV and music companies for producing such a consistent stream of unmitigated *kak* during the past five or six years. Struggling with distribution issues, new technologies, internet piracy and declining profits it seems churlish to blame them for neglecting their core business, producing content that people want to see, read or hear. But blame them we shall.

As long ago as January 2003 *The Economist*, in a cover article entitled 'Lights! Camera! No profits!' took the entertainment industry to task for favouring 'instant commercial returns' over 'long-term investment in creativity'. But the public's appetite for new media content is as voracious as ever, despite these long years of being fed such indigestible schlock, or possibly because of it. *The Economist* quoted Veronis Suhler as forecasting a 6% annual increase in consumer spending on entertainment, a boom that the industry was clearly ill equipped to capitalize on. 'Yet the best companies,' said *The Economist*, without telling us who they were, '. . . are also those that successfully manage the tension between creative freedom and operational control.'

The article ended with the following paragraph, no less true for its unusually sloppy sententiousness:

> It sounds simple enough, but in a world of ample ego and capricious sentiment, it is a maddeningly difficult balance to get right. That the industry tends over time to swing too far in favour of the ponytails, only to swerve back too far in favour of the suits, shows how hard it is to find a middle way. Devising a habitat in which creativity can flourish, yet within tight operational constraints: there lies a sequel for the entertainment industry worthy of a Hollywood blockbuster.

The entertainment industry is the most obvious example of creative mismanagement because its failures are so excruciatingly public. We don't blame consumer goods companies, for example, for failing to innovate because their failed innovations seldom make it to the marketplace. But when the product itself is a shiny new exemplar of creativity – a much-hyped movie, a TV show, a new album – there is no escaping the wretchedness of a failure to entertain, like England against Croatia, or a train crash in slow motion, as the critics like to say.

Likewise with advertising – when it is stupid and patronizing it is visibly and acutely stupid and patronizing.

There's something particularly poignant about seeing talent being crushed to death in front of your eyes. All those wonderful skills, those brilliant special effects, the genius of the digital suites, the extraordinary photography, the wardrobe so perfect, so beautifully researched, the camera angles so masterfully arranged, the editing, the music, the design, the art direction, the sheer effort of it all – the acting so accomplished, the premise so full of promise – then the invisible, inexorable, inevitable intervention of the dead hand of management, the clumsy cynicism of commercial interest, cruel and careless, the awful end of it, stinking of stale sandwiches at the end of the focus group, the squirming writhing despair of it, stuck on the point of the strategic stick, the head on the stake, hopeless and hapless, ambition to ashes, trust to dust.

Here is the unedifying sight of ITV rummaging through the bottom drawer. Here is the fourth remake of *King Kong*, the eighth or ninth season of *Big Brother*, the sixth season of *Who Wants to be a Millionaire?* and seventeenth remake of *Robin Hood*. Here is *Doctor Who* disinterred. Here is *Love Island, Celebrity Island, Celebrity Love Island*, Celebrity Survival and Love Island Celebrity Survival. Here is another *Pop Idol* with another name.

As horrible as they are, these visible implosions of the imagination, they are merely a trope for the rampant disregard of the creative spirit that has spread like cancer through the institutions of corporate and governmental life. Hardly a sphere of organizational endeavour is immune to its corrosive presence. Here are newspapers obliged to reflect the political views of their owners, and obliged to self-censor articles unfavourable to their advertisers. Magazines stripped of original content in favour of so-called advertorials, PR articles about products or services written in the style of objective journalism. TV stations cowering to control by corporate memo. Music companies staggered with the realization that people want to listen to music. Car manufacturers frozen in the business paradigms of the 1960s, oil companies claiming that carbon dioxide is life, [governments privatizing water and the electromagnetic spectrum and oxygen itself any one of these days in the belief that greed will do a better job than the collective imagination.] Here is Microsoft telling me where to put my commas.

Let me say at once that there are still wonderful things out there. The ability of the internet utopians to resist the advance of the digital strip-mall. The way internet users are rallying to the defence of the internet commons. The renaissance of journalism, the war on mumbo-jumbo, the beauty of the blog. Brilliant writing, scathing satire. Independent film-making, superb documentary, inspired curation in galleries and museums around the world. The rediscovery of singer-songwriters. They shine like diamonds in the dross, like unexpected rays of warmth on a gloomy November day, precious and surprising, their value beyond rarity.

The Economist casts it as 'tension between creative freedom and operational control', the dialectics of suits and ponytails, as though there is something healthy and natural about it, something quaint and charming, like the cycle of frog-spawn, or the inevitability of spring. But it isn't at all like that; and if it ever was like that it won't be again. The plates have shifted, the continents are rearranged, the weather is damaged. It's not a cycle, and it's not a war. It's not even a series of skirmishes. It's a condition.

There was a time, before the end of history, when we thought that creativity and the arts stood in opposition to the establishment. It was the daisy in the barrel of the rifle. It was Picasso in his studio in Paris in 1941, the Nazi officer suspecting him of sheltering Jews, printed postcards of Guernica scattered on the studio table. The officer picks one up and asks Picasso, 'Did you do this?' And Picasso replies, 'No, you did.'

And it is generally true that the creative spirit has bravely resisted the suffocating constraints of oppressive ideologies whenever they have sought to shackle it. But the spectacles through which we look back on history are tinted with the rosy colours of the romantic legacy. Even today, well into the 21st century, our assumptions about the relationship between art and society remain firmly rooted in the revolutionary, pre-Freudian worldview of the 1800s. Beneath the meretricious sheen of our post-modern wit there's a warm and mushy place in our hearts where the sensibilities of Rousseau, Blake and Coleridge run as naked and free as Nature intended. The artist is man in touch with his feelings, the passionate rebel, the rugged individualist; Gothic, Faustian, Promethean.

We forget too easily how many great artists flourished within the constraints of the oppressive ideology of the Vatican, or in the claustrophobic confines of the European courts. Artists are not obliged to champion a political cause, though it goes against the romantic grain to say so. Art, in this tradition, is supposed to have some sort of uplifting moral or redemptive purpose, and artists are therefore duty bound to report back from their explorations of the human condition with the latest news on truth, justice and destiny. So it disappoints us to learn that Holbein had little to say about Henry VIII, or that Michelangelo was quite happy to work with the pope who established the Holy Inquisition.

The same sensibilities lead us to expect rock stars to rid the planet of poverty and injustice – not the Church, note, and not the world's governments. Bono must do it, and Bob Geldof and Sting. Or actors like George Clooney. An entire generation of hippies felt betrayed when Bob Dylan picked up an electric guitar in Manchester in 1971. The famous cry of 'Judas!' from someone in the audience summed up the feeling of the age. Dylan was supposed to be a protest singer with a folk guitar. He had written the anthems of the changing times, and they expected him to lead them to the Promised Land. But all Dylan wanted to do was to move on to the next thing, in whatever shape or form that happened to arrive.

Artists become political when their freedom to express themselves is constrained. Invariably that happens in circumstances of ideological oppression, in apartheid South Africa, in Spain under Franco, in Ireland under British rule, in

Stalinist Russia, in America under Nixon. And freedom of speech is often the fuse that lights the political fire, but there are others. 'Mad Ireland hurt you into poetry . . .' wrote Auden of Yeats. But the overtly political work of poets and writers and painters and film-makers is usually the least interesting and the most ephemeral.

If art is not the natural enemy of the state, it is certainly the natural enemy of the status quo. Clearly I am not talking about the decorative arts, the kind that is used to make fascism look pretty or capitalism seem jolly. I am talking about the kind of art that challenges the way we see things or hear things or feel things; the kind of art that creates gods and monsters, and monstrous gods; that sends chills down your spine and makes your hair stand on end; that makes you squirm or vomit, or dream and reflect; that reminds us how weak we are or how strong we are; that damages the retina, warps the anvil, turns your stomach inside out or takes your breath away.

The ideas we find significant.

The creative spirit stands in opposition to the narrow-minded, the picayune, the lifeless, the repetitive and the shallow. If that is political, then it is profoundly political. It stands in opposition to predictability and control, but it has no agenda beyond its need for expression. Which is to say, most importantly of all, that it has a Sphinx-like disregard for results.

The purpose of art is affect, not effect. Or, in the words of Frank Zappa, 'I dislike commercial pop because I cannot accept the intention behind it – I don't get those vibrations from Stravinsky.'

*

To cast the tension between 'creative freedom' and 'operational control' as the consequence of a struggle for power between the so-called ponytails and the so-called suits is to demean both and to understand neither. It's like saying that the sea is a struggle for power between water and fish. It's a false dichotomy and, worse yet, it reinforces the stereotypes that stand in the way of a mutually bene-ficial accommodation.

The tension, though, is real enough. Walk into any situation where creative people and business people are engaged in a critical project and you can cut the atmosphere with a knife. Disagreements between clients and creative people are the stuff of advertising legend, though obscenity and libel laws prevent most of them from making it into print.

Since the 1983 publication of her *Creativity in Context* the distinction Teresa Amabile makes between intrinsic and extrinsic motivation has been universally embraced by creative theorists as vital to our understanding of the creative process. But very oddly, despite the widespread publicity her findings have received, the implications of her work have yet to make any impact at all on the principles or practice of creative management. Why?

There are three possible explanations. It may be that the people who manage creative businesses are simply not interested in the esoteric speculations of academic research. They may have been too busy with the pressing concerns of the quarterly budget proposals to have got round to reading her 1998 article 'How to Kill Creativity' in the *Harvard Business Review*, or her follow-up, 'Creativity Under the Gun', in the same publication in 2002.

It may be that they did indeed come across her work, either in the HBR or elsewhere, and rejected it out of hand because it did not accord with their received views of scientific management, or simply ignored it because they didn't know what to do with it, which comes to the same thing.

And it may be that the business of creative productivity has been so effectively and so completely hijacked by the disciples of Osborn, de Bono and van Oech that creative managers cannot even conceive of the possibility of an alternative view.

All three are plausible, but only the first is forgivable. Time is more precious than ever before, work pressures are more intense, and very few people, especially in the fraught environments of the creative industries, can afford the luxury of reflection.

It is equally true that companies and institutions that are *not* directly involved in producing creative work – those for whom it is not a core competence – are much more interested in creativity than those who for whom creativity is a matter of survival. This isn't as paradoxical as it seems. Creative practitioners, like advertising agencies, film producers, dance companies and the rest of them, especially if they are successful, simply don't need to open the Pandora's Box of creative theory. The fact that they continue to exist, whether profitably or not, is proof enough that they know all they need to know about managing creativity. And the best of them will, in any event, be run by people who are themselves highly creative, or by managers who have a deep intuitive sense of how to get the best out of their available talent.

It's the rest of them we should be worrying about, that is, those creative businesses who suddenly find themselves unable to produce the kind of stonkingly good work that used to bring them fame and fortune, and those companies not directly involved in the production of creative goods (let's call them non-creative companies, but not pejoratively) who, for one reason or another, decide that they need to be more creative.

Chances are they won't turn to Sternberg or Torrance or Amabile or Martindale. They won't be looking for a theory, they'll be looking for a process. Or a quick fix.

In 2003 Proctor & Gamble, the notoriously conservative American packaged goods giant, sent a delegation of executives to attend the Cannes Advertising Festival in the south of France. The news was greeted with amused astonishment by the advertising fraternity and with some horror by their aligned ad agencies. Apart from the weather, the topless beaches, the free drinks, the cheap cocaine and the opportunity to rub shoulders with potential future employers, one of the most alluring thrills of spending a week at Cannes is being a long, long way from your clients. But P&G was serious about the mission. The company's top marketing executive, James R. Stengel, told the *New York Times*, 'We're going to Cannes to learn.'

That was the year that Extrinsic Motivation and Intrinsic Motivation bumped into each other in the lobby of the Carlton Hotel. The exchange of pleasantries was cordial enough. EM invited IM to a drink at the bar, a suggestion greeted enthusiastically by IM. Eyewitness accounts differ from this point on. Some say IM simply leaned forward to see what EM was writing in his journal and the rest was an accident. Others claim IM was hostile and drunk from the outset, and 'looking for a fight'. Cannes police admitted later it was a mistake to lock them up in the same cell. Late night revellers on the Croisette barely noticed the two ambulances heading out of Cannes in opposite directions, sirens blaring and lights flashing like neon under the fireworks.

Three years later, clients were heading for Cannes in droves. And it wasn't just because they discovered they were missing a good party. P&G's exploratory trip had yielded a startling insight that they were already incorporating into their consumer pre-tests of advertising spots. It was an additional question that read: 'Would you like to see this commercial again?'

Quick fixes like this don't always work as well as they did for P&G. Less daring companies would look for ways of embedding creativity into the organization as part of a long-term strategy, the way they have done with innovation processes.

There is a growing awareness in business today that creativity and innovation are two different things – that creativity is about coming up with ideas and that innovation is about the implementation of them in the real world. It's a vital distinction, but has proved difficult to implement in practice. Most businesses are prepared to settle for innovation on its own, without the bothersome complexities of the creativity bit, on the assumption that (a) anyone can come up with ideas, (b) innovation can be managed, and (c) that innovation is a direct route to increased profitablity through new product development.

Hardly a day goes by without the CEO of a large multinational company mentioning the pressing need for new ideas, and underlining, with heartfelt encomiums to the gods of Risk and Courage, the importance of innovation as the only viable strategy for growth and/or survival. Unsurprisingly, this has led to an explosion in the innovation consultancy business – books about innovation, seminars on innovation, case studies of successful innovations, the training of innovation, and more innovation processes than you can shake a stick at.

They will follow, almost without exception, five or six simple stages, almost identical to the CPS formula. But they will also include a multitude of complex interactions and protocols specifically relevant to the business of the company. I have come across these many times with former clients. They involve lengthy descriptions about the mechanics of each stage, what level of executive in the company can approve progress to the next stage, and who (in lengthy footnotes) are the 'stakeholders' of the innovation chain. What they all have in common, most notably, is an unassailable logic and an ingenuous assumption of guaranteed success. And since it is all so expressly and self-evidently manageable, with responsibilities so clearly defined, with checks and balances so ingeniously arranged, there is surely little room for either error or doubt.

What they have in common, most fundamentally, is that they gloss very quickly over the 'idea generation' part. It is the equivalent of a recipe that starts off by saying, 'After carefully removing the scales, the tongue and the tail, chop the dragon into small cubes.' Find yourself a dragon and the rest is dead simple.

*

Creativity without innovation, at least in the commercial context, is a self-indulgent waste of time. Innovation without creativity is absurd.

But the plain and simple truth is that it's that much easier to legislate for the control, elaboration and implementation of ideas than it is to legislate for a constant stream of good ones.

The 3M company is widely admired for adopting a radical and highly successful approach to this problem. Employees are encouraged to spend a significant part of their time working on ideas that are of particular interest to them and that are not directly related to their day-to-day projects. The famous '15% rule' is reputed to have led to the creation of the Post-It note and many other highly inventive new products. The brilliance of the 3M approach to innovation is that it explicitly acknowledges the role of intrinsic motivation. Workers can not only choose to pursue any ideas that take their fancy, they can also develop them on their own or with colleagues of their choice. By a stroke of sheer unadulterated genius, the 15% rule neatly side-steps three of the most serious obstacles to creative expression during the critical conceptual phase – the curse of the brainstorm, the curse of process, and the curse of having to work with a designated team.

If every other company in the world does not follow 3M's example it can only be for one of two reasons. Because the particular nature of the product category, that is, messing around with paper, plastic and the world's biggest chemistry set, lends itself exceptionally well to the rapid development of new product opportunities. Or because, for the technocrats who run most corporate enterprises, 15% of the workforce's time devoted to the unregulated search for ideas equates to a 15% loss of productivity.

For a large-scale manufacturer with thousands of SKUs, some sort of management control of innovation is obviously essential. During the elaboration phase, when resources are needed to experiment with prototypes, or when interdisciplinary teams are needed for additional skills and advice, the support of management is crucial. And if that requires a formal process, well and good. It could even be immensely helpful if it obliges management, in the form of funding and political backing, to get the rest of the organization to pay attention.

It's when the process blithely assumes that management control over the idea generation phase will be equally helpful that it becomes counterproductive. In the words of Davis and Scase:

... for creativity to flourish such that organisations produce a constant stream of innovative products and services, it is almost a structural imperative to have work processes that allow autonomy, nonconformity and indeterminacy. Without these, those with intellectual capital will be reluctant to exploit their own personal creativity for the overall goals of their employing organisations.

People who are naturally inventive don't mind giving their ideas to the companies they work for just as long as those companies, in return, give them the freedom to play with their favourite toys. When management intervenes in any way, by taking away the toys, or by deciding who can play with them where and when and how, the naturally inventive people will pretty soon begin looking around for other sandpits.

In a world that demands results, and that measures achievement in increments of growth, it is almost impossible for the technocratic temperament to make sense of the behaviour of people who are motivated entirely by the pleasure of doing something for its own sake.

As modern as we think we are, our notion of progress has yet to evolve beyond the narrow Victorian conception of gleaming locomotives thrusting forward on the shining rails of human ingenuity. Progress is linear, rational and manageable. Progress is practical, sensible and good. Progress does not stop to think.

It is enormously irritating, therefore, to discover that the ideas we need to fuel the gleaming locomotive of progress cannot be dug out of the earth like coal; that the requirements for their conception are so stubbornly irrational, so awkwardly non-linear, and so brazenly defiant of right and proper management.

There is no struggle for power between the creative spirit and those who wish to employ its magical powers for the advance of the great capitalist enterprise. Creative people are happy enough for the technocrats to drive the train, although, for the sheer thrill of it, they wouldn't mind having a go every now and then. Creative people are content to leave the management of the furnace and the logistics of power to more capable others. Creative people don't even mind going along for the ride. But if, one sunny day, rushing through green meadows, snow-capped mountains in the distance, the wind in their hair, they decide – quite arbitrarily – to stop right here beside the wooden barn, implements of a long-forgotten agricultural past rusting in the shadows, to dismantle the train and reassemble it in the shape of the cuneiform alphabet, just for the hell of it, they don't want to have to ask permission, or to be told that they're hindering the advance of progress.

Yoking the creative spirit to the coalscuttle will crush it of hope and imagination, and make of it a reluctant and dangerous slave.

Attaching idea generation to the innovation process amounts to the same thing. And makes Podsnaps of us all:

> . . . Elsewise, the world got up at eight, shaved close at a quarter-past, breakfasted at nine, went to the City at ten, came home at half-past-five, and dined at seven. Mr Podsnap's notion of the Arts in their integrity might have been stated thus. Literature; large print, respectively descriptive of getting up at eight, shaving close at a quarter-past, breakfasting at nine, going to the City at ten, coming home at half-past five, and dining at seven. Painting and Sculpture; models and portraits representing Professors of getting up at eight, shaving close at a quarter-past, breakfasting at nine, going to the City at ten, coming home at half-past-five, and dining at seven. Music; a respectable performance (without variation) on stringed and wind instruments, sedately expressive of getting up at eight, shaving close at a quarter-past, breakfasting at nine, going to the City at ten, coming home at half-past-five, and dining at seven. Nothing else to be permitted to those same vagrants, the Arts, on pain of excommunication. Nothing else To Be – anywhere! (From *Our Mutual Friend*, Charles Dickens.)

*

Without the bold and terrifying ideas that would emerge from a truly creative culture, the managers of these innovation processes become Podsnaps themselves. Nothing gets through the gate unless it looks like an innovation that has proved successful in the past. The process that was designed to liberate the imagination and produce fresh and profitable new streams of revenue becomes a bureaucratic enforcer of the status quo. The innovations that manage to get through the system are incremental versions of existing ideas – the razor with four blades based on the razor with three, the soap with aloe vera, the detergent with aloe vera, the hand-cream with aloe vera, the toilet paper with aloe vera. With consumer goods there is a further obstacle to real innovation in the form of retailer power, the horrendous cost of listings, and the strong resistance of retailers to place on their precious shelves anything that doesn't look like something with a past history of sales success.

The tendency towards homeostasis in any living system is never to be underestimated. Constituencies in favour of the status quo far outnumber those inclined to dabble with the occasional mutation, virus or novel idea. The same Podsnappian impulse operates just as forcefully within the so-called creative industries.

*

As the raging torrents of the imagination dwindle to a soodling thread, the wells of incremental growth begin inevitably to dry. That's when the cry goes out for more creativity. Companies and institutions that have been able to manipulate the profitability of these diminishing returns by squeezing supplier prices, cutting internal costs down to the bone, and ruthlessly weeding out any remaining inefficiencies in their systems and processes, will suddenly embrace the rhetoric of risk-taking, courage and experiment. The Podsnaps who have given the best of their working lives to enforcing the status quo will be swept aside to make way for a younger generation of functionaries prepared to recite the new litany of creativity without choking on their organic cereal bars. They will wear T-shirts emblazoned with slogans that would have been heretical only a few weeks ago, phrases such as 'Think for Yourself', 'Risk Everything' and 'Ask Why'.

Desperate times call for desperate measures. The new CEO will make a Rubicon speech. The new financial director will send memos to his colleagues with lengthy quotes from *Fast Company* and Nelson Mandela. The new marketing director will respond with case studies from Nike, Ideo and Amazon. And the new director of human resources will begin discussing culture change.

There will be a flurry of meetings. Brand consultants will be called in to reposition the company. A design firm will be hired to update the logo and design new letterheads, business cards, email banners, invoices and truck signage.

Along with the new mission statement and the redesigned lobby (gone is that three-quarter size model of a Spitfire so beloved by the previous chairman) come team building exercises, diversity training sessions, personal growth encounters and, yes, obligatory creativity immersion workshops.

*

There is no shortage of companies standing by to provide assistance, all of them promising the same sort of thing, that is, everything. Here's the blurb from a company called Creative Knowledge:

> As margins in business become tighter and tighter, organisations need to diversify their behaviours and processes to differentiate themselves from the competition and provide exceptional client services. Experiencing how artists think and see unlocks creative capability in a powerful way, releasing that extra bit of imagination and talent that can make the vital difference for business success. Creative Knowledge in association with the Royal Academy of Arts, London, uses the visual arts as a unique and effective tool to empower businesses with the creative edge, transforming individual and team performance and reinventing corporate culture.

As proof of the transforming power of the experiential immersion of a Creative Knowledge workshop, the brochure quotes one Mike Munroe, Vice President of Oral Care for Quest International: 'It was extraordinary to see one of my team developing a new toothpaste flavour from an intense engagement with Monet's paintings.'

But if Monet doesn't do it for you there are plenty of alternatives. You and your company can get in touch with your primal creative spirits by experiential immersion in African drumming round a bonfire on the beach near Brighton. You could get in touch with the musician inside you by experiential immersion in Mozart, or Vivaldi, or Wagner, or jazz, or opera, or theatre, or rock 'n' roll.

Arts-based training, as it has come to be known, is now so diversified in its offerings that there is almost no limit to the ways in which you could spend your training budgets. You could sculpt your way to an enhanced understanding of your company ethos. You could paint your way out of an innovation crisis. You could draw yourself a successful future. You could sketch new possibilities for growth. You could model competitive scenarios, compose a new culture, drum up new business, or harmonize your way to more efficient knowledge sharing.

There is no questioning the sincerity or the integrity of art-based trainers. If the companies that employ them believe they have a beneficial effect on their operations, well and good. Any day out of the office is clearly a good day. And if it involves splashing paint on canvas or having a go at being Mick Jagger, so much the better. The collective buzz of doing something different and interesting can only be helpful for morale, at least in the short term. A heady dose of creativity, administered with the blessing of company management, will undoubtedly have a stimulating placebo effect on a company's collective enthusiasm for a bolder and freer approach to the affairs of the working day.

But to attribute to these interventions miraculous changes in corporate culture by unlocking 'creative ability in a powerful way' is both disingenuous and misleading. Disregarding the anecdotal hallelujahs of participants who count them among life's most cherished and meaningful experiences, there is not a single shred of evidence to indicate that these kinds of programmes have any measurable effect on corporate creativity in the longer term. Nor is there any reason to suppose that the short-term effect would be less powerful if they had all been sent white-water rafting down the Zambezi, or to the Cannes Advertising Festival.

Organizational creativity has everything to do with the accommodation of creative talent within specific organizational structures, and nothing at all to do with teaching staff how to think 'outside the box', even if that were possible.

Arts-based workshops are by no means the most damaging of exercises you could inflict upon gullible believers in the redemptive power of creativity training. By far the most dangerous are those that purvey creativity as a process, a procedure of simple steps to be followed like a recipe, or a set of instructions for building a kite – an ABC reader for the imaginatively illiterate.

Creativity workshops won't unblock the innovation pipeline, and nor will process. The pipes themselves are the problem, configured in structures that defy both gravity and logic. It's time to call in the plumbers.

CHAPTER 13

Structures and strictures

Serious corporate persons can, with self-respect intact, confidently put a case to their board for sponsoring experimental laboratories, investing in a lot more R&D and hiring another six postgraduate chemists. They feel a great deal less manly when asking their boards to contemplate the astonishing commercial potential of an untried animated vampire duck.

> Jeremy Bullmore from 'Wanted: a new kind of incubator for hatching Harry Potters'

Of the three great plagues that beset the imaginative capacity of our public and private institutions, only one appears amenable to rapid redress.

Market forces will continue to erode vast tracts of the intellectual commons as long as national governments and supranational regulators lack the foresight or the will to intervene. Vested interests and political sensitivity will make it difficult for dissenting voices to be heard.

The Taylorist agenda, with its sights now firmly set on the productivity of knowledge workers, will continue to erode the discretionary powers of middle management. That toxic concoction of increasing responsibility with diminishing authority will serve to intensify their aversion to risk in all its forms.

It's in the third area, where the dysfunctional relationship between management and creative workers has been falsely framed as a struggle for dominance or control, that a cool assessment of the issues and opportunities can pave the way to immediate progress.

The first two problems are steeped in politics: this one is purely commercial. If it is possible to prove that a radical new approach to managing creativity will produce ideas that benefit the bottom line, the tide could still be turned in favour of a creative economy that merits the appellation.

There are several myths that need to be knocked on the head before we get there. I have dealt with the first one – that everyone has a sacred right to be as creative as the next person – at some length because it is fundamental to an appreciation of how the creative process can best be managed. The second myth – that competition and the forces of supply and demand combine to produce the best possible creative outcomes – should by now be staggering to the ground in the last throes of its miserable life. Against the third myth – that the principles of scientific management are as appropriate to the production of ideas as they are to the production of baked beans – we have yet to deliver the mortal blow.

Arthur Koestler never got round to addressing it as a specific issue, which is a real shame since he was one of the few commentators writing about creativity who had ever done anything creative. John Howkins devotes a chapter to managing creativity in *The Creative Economy* but he is so enthused by the sheer scale of the numbers to do anything more than reiterate the sort of 'ten steps to becoming a creative millionaire' advice that you'd get from *Fast Company* or *Cosmopolitan*. Apart from Amabile, whose research is seminal, we are left with Howard Davis and Richard Scase to fill in some of the yawning gaps in our knowledge of the subject.

Davis and Scase recognize that there is a problem, which is a very good place to start.

> To manage and to organise the work processes of those who constitute intellectual and creative labour it is necessary to apply different assumptions, methodologies and principles of organisational behaviour to those used when monitoring the tasks of factory workers, concentrated in large, single locations. Hence the management of creativity becomes a key organizational issue.

And they recognize, as a fundamental premise, that ' "management" and "creativity" are often seen as contradictory terms'. If, in the end, they are long on explanations and short on answers it's not for lack of diligence. They have interviewed creatives and managers working in most of the sectors of interest, and they have done a very good job of imposing order on some very chaotic data.

They identify three types of creative organization – the commercial, the licence fee model, and the state subsidy model. Though the categorizations vary from country to country, most of the 15 creative sectors fall squarely into the first of these, the commercial type. They would invariably include advertising, archi-tecture, fashion, publishing, games and video games, film, popular music, software development and R&D. TV and radio broadcasting, especially outside of the US, tend to operate on a licence fee basis, or what Davis and Scase call 'indirect public support'. Theatres, orchestras, museums and galleries, together with opera and dance companies, are usually supported by some form of state subsidy, though commercial sponsorships are increasingly being sought to make up the numbers.

The divisions between these three types of organization are by no means clear cut, as the authors acknowledge. In some countries film production, for example, is directly or indirectly supported by state subsidies. Certain R&D sectors are state funded in some countries – nuclear technology in Iran, for instance. As a rule of thumb, the more fascist the inclination of the individual government, the more likely it is to want a stake in sectors like publishing and broadcasting, and at its most extreme, even in architecture.

Each of the three organizational types gives rise to a unique set of manage-ment challenges, but each of these sets – in turn – is complicated by the type of creative sector in which it falls:

> If the paradox of creativity and control could be resolved with a single set of organisational principles or a standard formula it would be a simple matter to identify the tasks and apply the optimal solu-tion. In practice, the paradox is a genuine one and what looks like a solution from one perspective creates a new set of problems from another.

If they sound surprised, and even a little disheartened, it doesn't deter them from pressing ahead with a searching analysis of the strategies that organizations are using to maximize both control and creativity. They identify the four most signifi-cant of them, all of which cut across the three organizational types and the 15 creative sectors and none of which come without problems of their own making. If you've spent any significant time working in a creative organization you'll be able to pick out your personal favourite without too much difficulty.

The first strategy is characterized by 'a line of demarcation between "creatives" and others through job titles, responsibilities and working practices which attempt to show clearly where creative work ends and management begins'.

All advertising agencies work this way. So too do most design agencies, big architectural practices, fashion houses, and companies with R&D departments. You know you're in one of these organizations when people around you frequently use the words 'us' and 'them' and you know exactly whom they're talking about. Usually, but not always, the creative people in these organizations will dress differently from the rest to make sure that they are instantly recognized as a class of their own. Often the creative people will refer to everyone else in the organization as 'suits', a term which is not always derogatory. Often they will work in departments or office clusters physically separated from the rest of the business, and even if they don't they will usually want to.

This kind of strategy is 'based on the notion that the best way to maximise the potential of creative people is to set the task and then extend to them the necessary autonomy for its execution'. In other words, the managers trust the creative people to get on with it, treating them as professionals who understand what is required from them.

This is how the BBC was organized in the 1960s and 1970s, a time regarded by many as the golden age of British television broadcasting 'because of the high quality of output and sustained record of innovation'.

On the down side, especially during times of transition or financial crisis, the division between the creatives and the rest can explode into bloody wars of blame and retribution.

The 'demarcation' strategy is increasingly under attack from managers who believe it is clumsy, divisive and inefficient. In the case of the BBC the lines of division between managers and creatives has been deliberately blurred by recent restructuring aimed at reducing costs and at making the corporation more competitive. Which leads nicely on to the second strategy.

Davis and Scase call the second strategy 'incorporation' because it co-opts creative people into managerial roles, breaking down the physical and professional divisions between the creative tasks and administrative ones: 'The process does not necessarily involve a change of titles but the producer, editor, creative or A&R director actually becomes an executive, and is thereby engaged directly and formally in managerial tasks which previously would have been carried out by a former creative or specialist manager.'

Incorporation works well when the company's revenues derive mainly from standardized media outputs, like managing a back catalogue of music or publishing standardized text books or manuals. Software development, web design and other IT applications also fall into this category since the creative work required is usually incremental rather than radical. Skype 1.0 was a radical idea. Skype 2.0, 2.1 and 2.2 are glosses of the same thing.

It doesn't take an enormous amount of imagination to repackage 'The Eagles Greatest Hits' for the 97th time. Or to slap together an album called 'The Best Ever Country Love Songs' by looking through your list of copyright titles. As Davis and Scase point out with po-faced academic neutrality, 'Incorporation implies a loss of autonomy and a restriction on the freedom to invent new solutions to the creative process. At the same time, indeterminacy is minimised. This is likely to have an impact on moral and motivation as creative workers find that managerial priorities erode their autonomous professional identity.'

Or to put it in plain English, if you have any respect at all for your credentials as a bona fide creative person you will avoid such companies like the plague.

The good thing about incorporation, on the other hand, is that your performance will no longer be judged by people who don't understand what you actually do. As long as you stick with the procedures and deliver your quotas you know you're doing just fine.

When there is no distinction between creatives and management it's impossible to make a distinction between the idea and the stuff that gets to go around it. The project manager can have no objective opinion about the merits of the idea since the idea is never presented as something distinct and central to the process. The very idea of having an idea is lost in the business of pulling the project together.

The third approach, which Davis and Scase call 'clustering', is less of an organizational strategy than it is a natural response to a certain set of business conditions. Calling it 'the sub-contractor model' might have been more useful since it replicates almost exactly the kind of small, specialized businesses that cluster around the building industry – draughtsmen, electricians, plumbers, tiling companies and the like. Davis and Scase provide the example of the small independent television companies that sprang up in the UK when Channel 4 was established and independent production quotas were imposed on the broadcast sector. Often they were formed by creatives from the BBC disaffected by the erosion of autonomy that went hand in hand with the so-called modernization programme. Typically they would consist of one man and his dog specializing in a certain type of production, like gardening shows. Others would set up camera hire, post-production or lighting facilities, together with all the other kinds of peripheral supply companies that surround the film business: catering, wardrobe, casting agencies, limousine hire and so on.

This type of clustering occurs in several other creative sectors, especially in those like publishing, music and advertising where there is a heavy reliance on outside suppliers to provide services which are too cumbersome or expensive to maintain in house.

Eco-systems like these, with sub-contractors competing to provide the most efficient and cost-effective services to the core companies, are an indispensable part of any business sector. They provide all of the things that the market is good at providing – a wider variety of choice from cheap and cheerful to expensive and expert, niche skills, just-in-time resources, and optimal flexibility. They are particularly crucial for projects like movie productions that need quick turnarounds, a wide range of skills and talents, and highly adaptable pricing structures.

But it is questionable whether these outside suppliers are any good at all at providing ideas beyond the incremental. The niche producer who makes gardening programmes will clearly attempt to innovate within her particular domain if she is to remain a fresh, current and attractive supply source to her commissioning editor. But it is the very nature of such specialization that imposes constraining limits to her ability to innovate beyond her domain or across domains.

Far from providing a platform for creative diversity and experimentation, the outsourcing of programmes to independent producers has had the contradictory effect of demoting these contributors from creative partners to creative suppliers, obliging them to focus on the quality of their service rather than on the quality of their conceptual talents. Somewhat mysteriously, no one seems to have noticed that the quota system has turned the golden age of broadcasting into the golden age of cooking programmes.

It is painfully transparent, once again, that the same market forces that are so good at enhancing the quality and ambition of service businesses are so indubitably bad at enhancing the quality and ambition of creative businesses – I mean those, in the strict sense of the term creative, whose core value resides in their ability to conceive highly imaginative ideas, stripped of all other considerations of service and supply.

And finally, 'The fourth strategy represents the most radical way of resolving the organisational control/creativity paradox. It is a strategy of *segregating* the two elements, and is in fact the normal method of organising the "most" creative cultural workers such as novelists, scriptwriters, fine artists, actors, composers and musicians.'

Again, this isn't so much a strategy as a network, and a very loosely connected one at that. This is largely self-explanatory, not only because we are so familiar with the stereotype of cold and hungry artists working alone in their sheds with nothing but a 10 kilowatt heater to warm their knees, but also because it is the most historically enduring. J.K. Rowling worked like this, as did most of the writers and artists who either couldn't or wouldn't hold down a job in a creative sector organization.

Segregation of this kind gives maximum autonomy to the creative person, but it is clearly fraught with the possibility of financial and emotional distress. 'The disadvantages of the segregation of functions are the vulnerability of creative workers to market fluctuations on the one hand, and, for contractors, the difficulty of monitoring, controlling and assuring the outcome of the creative work process.'

*

I have taken the liberty of plundering large bits of *Managing Creativity* not only because Davis and Scase have done such an admirable job of making sense of creative organizations, but also because Davis and Scase are the only people who have ever attempted it. Before we leave them behind it's worth devoting a couple of paragraphs to the trends that they believe will shape creative organizations in the future, and the kind of challenges that creative workers are likely to face as a consequence.

The first and most significant is the decline of organizations, particularly the publicly funded ones such as the BBC, which have demarcated creative departments in-house.

The prevailing view is that these kinds of organizations are inefficient and uncompetitive, that they are sheltered from the real world of local and international market forces, and that their time has come and gone. In their place, Davis and Scase predict a rapid rise in what they call 'commercial bureaucracies', the vertically integrated creative and media giants such as Sony, Disney, Time Warner and The News Corporation, the powerful distributors like Universal, and the publishing giants that are snapping up independent book stores and publishing houses.

Increasingly these commercial bureaucracies will adopt the incorporation strategy, obliging creative workers to be directly responsible for managerial functions such as business forecasting, setting budgets and delivering results. Within these companies the trend will be to organize work processes around specific projects or clients, and employees will be given a limited amount of operational autonomy as long as they deliver to time and budget constraints.

Creative suppliers and subcontractors will continue to cluster around the commercial bureaucracies, but their survival will increasingly depend on the personal relationships and mutual favours that they can establish with the semi-autonomous managers or work groups inside the commercial bureaucracies. There will be an increasing emphasis on the efficiency of their service and their cost competitiveness. The shape of these new commercial structures will come increasingly to resemble the feudal system, in which the favours of the king are devolved to the barons, and the favours of the barons are devolved to the lords, and the favours of the lords are devolved to the villains.

The end game will leave us with gigantic towers of unlimited wealth and power, held together only by the glue of sycophancy. Those creative workers averse to the stench of the corporate fundament will find themselves shivering in sheds and attics and garrets along with the artists and writers and musicians who live on the fringes of the unemployable. When that finally happens, if it hasn't already, the paradox of creativity and control will finally have been resolved in favour of the latter, and the former will have been subsumed into a system of standardized outputs, as commoditized as Kalashnikovs or coconuts.

If you think that sounds a trifle alarmist, consider the following . . .

One of the most vital and competitive of all the creative sectors is the advertising industry. Globally, the business is worth around 50 billion dollars, and it's growing at an astonishing 7% a year. When lucrative media commissions once guaranteed whopping salaries to anyone who could survive a life of long lunches and the occasional late night, it was famously described as 'the most fun you can have with your clothes on'. In the early 1990s, as companies like WPP, Omnicom and IPG began to buy up independent network and local agencies, most of the fun and the loose cash was sucked out of the business by armies of accountants specially trained to sniff out receipts for Moet et Chandon. Things got worse when agencies' in-house media departments were parcelled off into global media buying networks owned by the same conglomerates, and agency managers were obliged to justify their exorbitant fees for the very first time.

Lunch was cancelled until further notice. Late nights followed more late nights. Soon the brand managers were driving fancier cars than the art directors, little luxuries like pensions and medical insurance went out the window and, with a sleight of hand as clever as anything achieved by Arthur Andersen, agency workers found that 100% of their time had been billed out to three separate clients.

Yet none of this diminished the eagerness of art school graduates and ambitious young MBA's to join the queue of hopefuls desperate to lay down their lives to enhance the shareholder value of the oligopolies. For all of the nastiness and the stress and the fickleness that consolidation had wrought upon the industry, advertising had lost nothing of its allure as a glamorous playground of unconstrained self-expression and creative opportunity.

If most of the advertising that you get to see around the world does precious little to palliate George Orwell's description of it as nothing more than the 'rattle of a stick in a swill bucket' it isn't for lack of ambition on the part of the agencies. While all advertising agencies know that they are paid to get as many pigs as possible to the feeding trough as quickly as they can, very few will admit that there is no more to it than that.

All of the creative industries, with the possible exception of software design and R&D, will be engaged in a constant struggle to reconcile the avowedly commercial side of their businesses with the siren call of aesthetics. Perhaps I am doing software designers a grave injustice. For all I know they too may be enraged by a manager's reluctance to spend a little more time and a little more money on a particularly elegant piece of code when the manager is convinced that a crude shortcut will work just as well. Perhaps there are chemists and microbiologists who still go to work entranced by the pure aesthetics of molecular configurations that have nothing to do with the pressing commercial demands of the project at hand. But it's difficult to imagine a creative industry in which the paradox of commercial constraint and aesthetic expression is quite as vivid as it is in advertising.

We expect people in the fashion business to be concerned with producing aesthetically pleasing fashions. We expect architects to design buildings in a way that is mindful of both form and function. We expect film-makers to make entertaining films, and musicians to make music that engages us and gratifies us in some mysterious way. But we don't expect advertising agencies to do anything more than grease the wheel of enterprise. We are pleased when they entertain us.

We are delighted when they charm us or amuse us. And when, every now and then, they manage to produce something that is so unexpectedly compelling or shocking or uplifting that it changes the way we think or feel about the world, we are inclined to forgive them for the countless times they barge into our living rooms with a bucket of slop and a clanging stick.

The more sophisticated and experienced clients understand, of course, that advertising is more powerful when it is likeable and insightful. Big advertisers like Procter & Gamble and Unilever spend a lot of time and money encouraging their agencies and their research partners to get under the skin of consumers, digging into their secret fears and desires, sifting through their attitudes, their likes and dislikes, their media consumption patterns, and even their pantries and their trash in search of the shiny golden keys that will unlock the door to their brand affinities and their wallets. And if, in the process, they discover that a certain group of consumers is susceptible to persuasion by a certain type of humour or a certain set of anxieties, they will brief their agencies to produce campaigns that press those appropriately hilarious or frightening buttons. Ingratiation, they have learned, is more effective than self-congratulation. This sounds every bit as Machiavellian as Vance Packard suggested it was, but thankfully it isn't. No matter how sophisticated the research, or how brilliant the final document that emerges from its agonizing passage through the agency's strategic planning department, it is still just a brief, a set of instructions, a job number, a springboard, a place to begin, a wish, a hope.

At this precise moment, as the brief is passed from the planning phase to the creative phase, everything changes. It is transformed, in the blink of an eye, into a pristine white canvas of infinite possibilities. The considerations of the brief are the colours on the palette and the brushes in the bottle. The constraints of the media might determine the shape and the size of the canvas, the information about the consumer might suggest a subject or a style. The product may or may not have to be in there somewhere. The values of the brand will have to be accommodated somehow, though these can often be translated as a guide to mood or metaphor, or to tint or texture. From now on such constraints as are mandated by the brief, whether they're technical or commercial, will serve only to contain the creative possibilities in the way a haiku contains an infinite variety of expressions within the severe restrictions of its form. The instrumental purpose of the project now recedes into the background, taking a distant second place to creative ambition, to *art pour l'art*.

A bad brief – a brief that is muddled, ill-conceived, overly prescriptive or constraining, and especially a brief that attempts to achieve more than one clear objective – if it is not rejected out of hand by the creatives and sent back for reworking by the client or the brand planners, will turn that same canvas into a barrier of impenetrable opacity. Nothing will stick to it. The paints will be useless, and the brushes will writhe and coil in your hand like spitting cobras.

The extraordinary thing about advertising, as illustrated by the process described above, is that it still clings tenaciously to the 'demarcation' strategy. The creative people are designated as 'creatives' and they work in well-demarcated creative departments, separated from the rest of the agency as much by culture as by demarcations of space.

Which raises two very big questions: how have advertising agencies managed to preserve this structure in the face of the overwhelming tide of opinion and precedent in favour of the incorporation strategy? And why would they want to?

*

Contrary to the obstinate belief among industry luminaries like Sir Martin Sorrel that traditional agencies – his own included – are organizational dinosaurs that must adapt or die in the swiftly changing environment of media fragmentation and new media technologies, advertising companies have always experimented freely with different structures and different ways of meeting their clients' expectations. And they will clearly continue to do so. Because they come and go so rapidly, splitting and intermarrying and spawning new ones with such a dizzying rate of churn, ad agencies are to observers of the creative sectors as fruit flies are to the evolutionary sciences. It doesn't take long to get a fix on what works in their favour and what doesn't.

Adaptations that have proved useful, like pairing art directors and writers into creative teams, or like the addition of a strategic function in the form of brand planning, have survived and replicated. Other mutations, like 'hot-desking' and experiments with multidisciplinary creative groups, have failed quickly and miserably. Neither new technology, which has transformed so many of the functional aspects of the agency with such dazzling alacrity, nor even the drastic surgical removal of the in-house media departments with its disastrous effect of lobotomizing the market intelligence of the entire advertising profession, has done anything to change the fundamental organizational shape.

It has survived the shift from commission-based remuneration to fees. It has survived transplantation to markets as different and as far apart as New Zealand and Nigeria, Mozambique and Macedonia, Peru and Pakistan. It has survived attempts by clients to control the creative function in other ways, by co-opting it into the client organization, or ring-fencing creative people for exclusive client use. Most notably, it has survived the most deliberate, aggressive and vitriolic attempts to dismantle it from inside the agencies themselves, always by the same bloodless technocrats infuriated by their inability to control the process once the brief has crossed the great divide into the creative department.

More powerful than their natural inclination to despise creative people for their messy, unmanageable lives, more powerful even than their undisguised contempt for the mumbo-jumbo of the creative process, it is this lack of control that fuels the technocrat's rage against the demarcation of creative and non-creative territories. It is an insult to his omnipotence, a reproach to her professionalism, a slur on his competence, a stain on her vanity.

They must destroy it at any cost. They must dismantle it physically by breaking down the walls and obliging the creatives to work in the Dilbert-like hell of open plan. They dismantle it culturally by distributing the creatives among the rest of the staff, copywriters next to secretaries, art directors next to junior account people, all of them at workstations of equal blandness and equal measure. They must dismantle it emotionally by removing their Helmut Krone books, their Helmut Newton posters and their silly signs saying, 'Helmut Was Here'. No pictures allowed, no music allowed (except on headphones), no internet allowed (except to pre-approved sites), no cynicism allowed. All emails monitored, all entries and exits noted by the card-swipe machine. No more mess, no more madness, no more puerile pranks.

But inevitably, like weeds growing through tarmac, the creatives regroup. They build walls of U-matic tapes. They regroup in pubs and coffee shops outside the office. They get fired. They regroup again. They make free-standing sculptures out of staplers and sellotape. They invent code words to communicate, like prisoners on Robben Island. They reassert their creative identities with ever more idiotic attempts at corporate subversion. Soon it's an uprising, a rebellion, a full-scale revolution.

There will be compliant ones who toe the line. They will be co-opted into management meetings, they will volunteer for unlikely administrative tasks, they will be incorporated. Then they will fail.

The separation of the creative function from the other agency disciplines has survived for the simple reason that it works. It is resilient, immutable, tenacious and indestructible. Which explains how it survives, but not why.

Here we can say with some certainty that those creative sectors that are vulnerable to incorporation are those in which the line between service and idea-creation is easily blurred. Architecture, for example, except among those practices notable for a highly distinctive creative style, can quite easily find themselves in the service business, planning and re-planning buildings according to the whims of their clients. Design becomes a service once the primacy of the design idea takes second place to the delivery of letterheads, new packaging and shop fronts. Music becomes a service when session musicians are pulled together in a studio to cover yet another compilation of chart toppers. Broadcasting becomes a service when programmes are shaped by a focus group of cereal shoppers in Basingstoke. Magazines become a service when car manufacturers or a hairdressing franchise commission them as an extension of their marketing campaigns. You can see the pattern. As soon as the idea no longer matters, or as soon as the idea is no longer central to the exchange between the client and the creative business, service takes over.

There are several creative sectors that have proved to be as resilient to incorporation as advertising. Clearly they include those that have always been segregated, or networked, such as the fine arts, literature, dance, the opera and others. But they are structurally different anyway, and are subject to a different set of pressures and expectations. Unlike publishing, media and music, they are very unlikely to cluster into commercial bureaucracies.

The exception is research and development, by far the biggest both in terms of number of employees and financial investment. The R&D departments of large corporations are almost always clearly demarcated as separate functional arms. By their very nature they are made up of professionals with specialized skills, such as chemists, engineers or electronics experts as the case may be. The companies that employ them clearly recognize that it is not in their interests to get these highly paid professionals to do anything beyond the application of their professional skills. Which is not to say, of course, that highly qualified people who demonstrate managerial talent cannot or will not migrate to managerial, supervisory or administrative roles. But, by and large, they will stick to their designated functions within designated departments where their skills can best be utilized. Companies invest heavily in R&D in the hope of inventing valuable patents. The idea is the thing. Indeed, the idea is everything. So the line between service and idea-creation is as clear as it is in advertising, and made even clearer by the professional status of these employees, their professional qualifications and their titles.

In this way R&D departments are the perfect crucible for theories of creativity management, and it is unsurprising that most of the serious research in the field, most notably by Amabile and her colleagues, has been devoted to this sector.

*

We have seen from the work of Davis and Scase that there is a clear trend among the high-value creative sectors for the consolidation of 'demarcated' creative companies and creative business 'clusters' into 'commercial bureaucracies'. These are most likely to emerge in those sectors where creative tasks can be deskilled and routinized by replicable processes, and especially where creative skills can be deployed to the *service* of client needs. The incorporation of creative talent into managerial or quasi-managerial roles is also more likely to occur in these instances, and *much less likely to occur when the creative task cannot be deskilled.*

The boom and bust of the dot.coms is a spectacular demonstration of this theory in action. The generation that grew up playing with computers and the internet in the 1980s and early 1990s developed a set of skills that marked them out as an entirely new species of creative practitioners. For a period of five or six years, as their skills matured and they began to put them to commercial use, they were the only people on the planet who could design websites and make them work in ways that astonished and amazed the business community. They were a creative elite, a golden generation of digital angels with the keys to unimaginable wealth.

Initially they worked as independents, following the pattern of a network strategy that kept them well away from the controlling and limiting influence of their sponsors. But very rapidly, as they began to realize the extent of their potential worth, they set up their own companies with suitably sexy cyber names and started to cluster in those regions and cities most amenable to their talents and ambitions. And many of them were enticed into media and advertising companies, or into corporations with the vision to appreciate what an on-line future could hold.

During that brief window of fame and fortune that preceded the dot.com crash of 2001 they were graced with all the blessings the creative spirit desires, complete autonomy to experiment, unconditional financial support, all the resources money could buy, and the demarcation of space and title that designated them as untouchables within their corporate environments.

Three organizational strategies evolved spontaneously – the network, the cluster and the demarcated – each one designed, albeit unconsciously, to insulate the creative endeavours of the digital geniuses from exposure to the potentially harmful constraints of normal business practice.

This is fascinating. Right here, at the end of the century that had made the scientific management of production the universally dominant model of operational control, a belle époque of creativity germinated and flourished under the precise conditions that characterized the blossoming of creativity in 15th century Florence. The Medicis were bankers. The patrons of the dot.com boom were the venture capitalists of New York, London and Tokyo.

The crash came the moment it dawned on the managerial community that the creative expertise required to design a website could be taught to an IT idiot in three or four hours. In the time it takes to debone a large trout, digital creativity was deskilled.

Within a few months the creative tasks required to set up and manage a digital business had been routinized and integrated into the normal operations of those companies who could see beyond the dust and debris of the dot.com implosion. The most skilled of the website wizards were incorporated into management. And those independent digital companies that survived the crash, their creative haloes tarnished irretrievably by the fallout, were humbled into offering their services to an oversaturated market at prices they would have scorned only a year or two prior.

The digital enterprises that emerged from the dot.com disaster and went on to make the promised fortune – like Amazon, Google, eBay, Yahoo! and others – were based, somewhat unsurprisingly, on good ideas. What the venture capitalists had failed so dismally to recognize was the critical distinction between creative talent and conceptual talent, between the skill of craft and the skill of idea-creation.

They had fallen for the delusion of creative homogeneity, the first and most dangerous of all the myths of innovation.

The dot.com story turns out to be the perfect parable of the catastrophes that attend the misconceptions surrounding creativity in the modern age. It reminds us of the crucial difference between talent that can be learned and talent that is bred in the bone. The early dot.commers had a talent for the medium. The ones who survived had a passion for something that the medium could do, for content not form.

Talents that can be learned are useful and necessary. But they change nothing. A talent for ideas is fundamental. It can change everything.

It reminds us that good ideas don't sell themselves. The really good ideas were buried under the meretricious surface of the dot.com phenomenon. Most people bought the phenomenon. Those who were prepared to dig a little deeper bought the good ideas that lay buried beneath the wave. Time and faith made the difference.

It reminds us that ideas are things, as concrete as concrete. Some people recognize them long before they get their names. Ideas change the domains in which they occur.

In the creative sectors, commercial bureaucracies grow out of talents that can be replicated and turned into processes. Commercial bureaucracies will end up owning everything except the possibility of greatness.

But the dot.com story is more than a cautionary tale. At its brilliant ephemeral best, when the world was at its feet, it illuminated the conditions under which creativity thrives.

CHAPTER 14

Place matters

> Every creative deed . . . issues from one's most authentic, innermost, nethermost regions.
>
> Nietzsche

As it is in the brain so it is in the community. The more variables there are at play the higher the probability that novelty will be generated.

The demographics of creativity have recently attracted widespread attention thanks largely to the work of Richard Florida. Though social commentators had been bandying around phrases like 'the knowledge economy' since the early 1990s it wasn't until the publication of *The Rise of the Creative Class* in 2002 that the world and his dog woke up to the sea change that had taken place in the last two or three decades of the 20th century.

The thing that had them rubbing their sleepy eyes in disbelief wasn't the fact that the so-called creative class now constituted nearly 30% of the US workforce, it was Florida's extraordinary assertion that creative people were more likely to want to live and work in cities that were cool rather than in cities that weren't cool.

This might sound self-evident to you and me but apparently it came as a massive surprise to the city fathers and the corporate managers who had spent so much time and money transforming their urban workplaces into so many Stepfords. By cleaning out the gays and the blacks and the immigrants, and by replacing the speakeasies and stripjoints with Burger Kings and Wal-Marts, they had unwittingly condemned their local economies to creative death. And here was Florida with the evidence to prove it.

As much as he would prefer it otherwise Florida is best known for his so-called Gay Index, which reveals a remarkable correlation between concentrations of gay people and measures of hi-tech growth. He stumbled upon this while researching the underlying factors driving regional economic development, and the rest is history.

Florida's basic premise is this: in post-industrial societies such as the US, Japan and most of Europe economic growth is increasingly being driven by creative and hi-tech businesses that rely on the intellectual talent and imaginative skills of an entirely new class of white-collar workers. 'Access to talented and creative people is to modern business what access to coal and iron ore was to steel-making,' says Florida, echoing Jeremy Bullmore's assertion that, 'the exploitation of the imagination' will be as important to business in the 21st century as the exploitation of coal once was for the industrial economies of the past. But unlike those earlier eras when workers used to migrate to where the jobs were, *businesses must now move to where the talent is.*

This is a radical reversal of previous assumptions, with dramatic implications for the way we think about urban design, infrastructure development and the whole broad sweep of capital deployment. Florida quotes Hewlett-Packard CEO Carley Fiorina as saying, 'Keep your tax incentives and highway interchanges; we will go where the highly skilled people are.'

The highly skilled people – especially the creative ones – are drawn (surprise, surprise) to places that feed their curiosity, delight their senses and reciprocate their compulsions.

From classical Athens and Rome, to the Florence of the Medici and Elizabethan London, to Greenwich Village and the San Francisco Bay Area, creativity has always gravitated to specific locations. As the great urbanist Jane Jacobs pointed out long ago, successful places are multidimensional and diverse – they don't just cater to a single industry or a single demographic group; they are full of stimulation and creativity interplay.

By digging into the available data on the demographics of hi-tech industries, innovation centres, population diversity and a bunch of other measures, Florida pieced together his celebrated Creativity Index, a ranking of US cities from the most to the least creative. There are few surprises. San Francisco, Austin, San Diego, Boston, Seattle, Raleigh-Durham, Houston, Washington-Baltimore, New York, Dallas and Minneapolis-St Paul make up the top 10. The least creative, from 39th to 49th, are Detroit, Providence (RI), Greensboro (NC), Oklahoma City, New Orleans, Grand Rapids (MI), Louisville, Buffalo, Las Vegas, Norfolk (VA) and Memphis. Los Angeles comes in at 12, Chicago at 15, Philadelphia at 17, Kansas City at 25 and Miami at 29.

This is well and good as far as it goes. It has got a lot of people recognizing, possibly for the very first time, that the price of creativity is the chaos of diversity. Without a vibrant mix of students, immigrants, gays, ethnic minorities and assorted weirdos rubbing shoulders in a milieu that celebrates self-expression and tolerates eccentricity the chances of new ideas bubbling to the surface in the form of economic or artistic vibrancy are severely handicapped. It has helped to identify, for example in the case of Detroit, how incompatible the principles of scientific management are with the conditions required for creativity and innovation. And it has earned Florida the lucrative patrimony of company CEOs who were thinking of moving their corporate headquarters to Buffalo.

Unfortunately, and I'm sorry to have to say this because I'm a great admirer of his passionate espousal of the creative power of diversity, *The Rise of the Creative Class* has muddied the waters of creative management so badly that it's going to take some serious effort to distil the shinola from the rest of it.

There are a couple of serious problems. The first is his understanding of creativity and, hence, his classification of creative people. The second is his apparent ignorance of Peter Hall's definitive study of creativity and the urban environment in *Cities in Civilization*.

We should deal with the latter first because it helps to flesh out the historical context into which Florida should surely have placed his analysis.

Like Florida and Johansson, Hall wants to understand why certain places, at certain times in history, have produced a sudden efflorescence of cultural and innovative achievement, a 'great burst of creativity' that fades almost as rapidly as it arrives.

Cities in Civilization is an epic tour of Periclean Athens, quattrocento Florence, 16th century London, the two great periods of Viennese creativity in the 18th and 19th centuries, and Paris at the end of the 19th century. But it isn't all art, music and Shakespeare. Hall looks at Manchester during the industrial revolution, Detroit in the early 20th century, Los Angeles and the San Francisco Bay Area, the roots of rock 'n' roll from the Mississippi Delta to 1960s London, Berlin in the 1930s, the rise of Tokyo as a centre of global innovation and the urban utopia of contemporary Stockholm.

This is how he sets out his stall:

So there is a nagging question: why should great cities have such golden ages, these *belles epoques*? How do these golden ages come about? Why should the creative flame burn so especially, so uniquely, in cities and not in the countryside? What makes a particular city, at a particular time, suddenly become immensely creative, exceptionally innovative?

Then follow a thousand pages of brilliant analysis and dazzling detail in which Hall gets as near as anyone has ever got to answering, in a way that makes sense to ordinary mortals, his own 'nagging question'.

Hall's thesis is at least as salient to contemporary business practice as Florida's, probably even more so since it digs much deeper beneath the demographic epidermis. And he too has his eye on the main chance – how to predict with any degree of certainty when and where the next great boom in innovation is likely to occur, whether there is anything we can do to accelerate its arrival, how we might harness its energy, and what kinds of business are most likely to benefit from it:

> . . . the so-called real world of industrialists and economists and politicians is now obsessed by the topic of innovation. It is, they incessantly tell us, the key to economic survival: in a dynamic capitalist system, every day more frenetic and invaded by global forces, the nation or the city that fails to innovate is destined to join the ranks of the economic has-beens, its old industries condemned to hopeless competition with the new plants and the cheap labour of the newly industrialising world. And, we are reminded, industry need not mean industry any more: as the new countries take over manufacturing and do it more cheaply and more efficiently than the old ones, so the old ones will and must shift out of manufacturing and goods-handling into the service sector and the processing of information.

I daresay that if Peter Hall had ended *Cities in Civilization* with a handy list entitled 'Ten Ways to Create a Golden Age of Innovation in Your Community' he would also have ended up on the front page of *Marketing Week* and with several corporate contracts just as juicy as Florida's. But he didn't, and I fear that the thousand-and-something pages he takes to get from Athens to Silicon Valley may represent too much hard work for a sub-editor of a media magazine looking for a zippy sound-byte.

*

Broadly speaking, the great creative epochs had the following in common. Almost invariably there would have been a wealthy upper class with time and leisure on their hands. They would have been well educated and aware of their place in history, profoundly conscious of the cultural legacy they had inherited from the prior generations. They might have been aristocrats, royalty or simply a wealthy bourgeoisie; the form itself hardly matters. The city or urban conurbation would be experiencing rapid economic growth and development, attracting a new generation of migrants in search of fame or fortune. They would be bringing with them a diversity of perspectives, expectations and cultures. Often they would speak different languages and have a variety of different skills and talents. In all of these ways, the societies bear the hallmarks of early global cities, trafficking in global products and global labour.

Critically, as Hall points out, it is this army of resident aliens 'who maintained the real economy and were responsible for a disproportionate part of all the real advances, whether in commerce or in art or philosophy'. That was the case in Athens, Florence and Elizabethan London just as it is the case in today's San Francisco, 'where a city benefits from a class that is half inside the mainstream society, half outside it, chafing at the ambiguity of its status but gaining additional energy from it'.

These three conditions – the wealthy, leisured class, the booming economy and a transient population of global migrants – seem to require one additional, overarching element to create the recipe for a cultural and innovative explosion, that is, a sense of transition between two ways of thinking. This could be political crisis, a shift in the moral or philosophical order, or a sense of unpredictable change in the deepest foundations of the social order. Often this last ingredient will manifest itself as an awareness that everything is up for grabs, and that the old order is becoming irrelevant. With this realization comes a sense of individual empowerment, a new order in which people become masters of their own destiny.

This would have been a good place to quote a few verses of 'The Times They Are a-Changin''.

When all four of these variables exist on a significant scale, because size does seem to matter in these cases, the wealthy class begins to put money and effort into patronage. Now that so many multinational companies have populations of employees larger than the cities we're talking about, this last point will reveal itself to be highly significant.

Both Florida and Johansson are right about the importance of diversity. In every single case, and in every single city that has demonstrated any degree of cultural or scientific achievement, the presence of a sizeable population of economic migrants is a necessary condition for success. Clearly the intersection of skills and perspectives is a departure point for novelty. So too, as Florida points out, is tolerance and self-expression.

The societies that might have all the other ingredients but that are not prepared to embrace eccentricity have very little hope of progress. Apartheid South Africa is a classic example. Here was a wealthy class of white people with time and money on their hands, thanks to an underclass at least as oppressed as the slaves of Athens. It attracted immigrants from all over Europe, particularly after the Second World War. But because of its lack of tolerance is was quite unable to produce anything more edifying than the Voortrekker Monument in 48 years of government. It was only after the release of Nelson Mandela in 1990, and the sudden awareness that the political structures were crumbling around them, that South Africans began to express themselves once again in a vibrant, renaissance of music, art, innovation and entreprenurship.

Today both Cape Town and Johannesburg, to the extent that they can become truly global cities, and to the extent that they can attract enough economic migrants to propel rapid economic growth, have the potential to become centres of creative and innovative excellence. If advertising is any measure at all of a country's capacity for creative achievement, the signs are particularly good. The South African advertising industry punches well above its weight in those festivals such as Cannes and others that celebrate world class originality. With nine official languages, a substantial population of Indian, Portuguese, Greek and Chinese immigrants, it boasts diversity in spades. But two questions remain. The first is whether the emerging black middle class grows rapidly enough to blur the racial demarcation that still exists between rich and poor, and succeeds thereby in depoliticizing the largesse of the bourgeoisie. And the second is simply a question of critical mass or, more crudely, whether the country will reach a point where there are enough people with enough money to reach a cultural consensus on what is worth investing in:

Both fifteenth century Florence and sixteenth century London were societies in profound transition from the medieval to the modern. In both societies, the best of the art reflects the resulting tensions between older traditional values, of the justly ordered society and of social responsibilities, and the newer values of individual self-advancement. In both, artists were kicking over the traces, reacting against an older order they found constraining, but not certain what to do with their new freedom or even how much they wanted of it. This is the permanent precondition of all great art. It can come about only in a very special kind of city, a city at the forefront of economic advance, which acts as a magnet to the in-migration of talent, and which is venturing into a new and unknown social arrangement. It is an unusual kind of city; but, in their time, Athens, Florence, and London were all such cities.

(Hall, 1999)

The really big question, of course, is whether it is possible to replicate Athens or Florence in today's global cities, whether it can happen again in a Barcelona, a New York, a Johannesburg, a Sydney or a Shanghai. Hall is not so sure. His chapter on the creation of Stockholm, surely the most perfect of all urban utopias, suggests that no amount of planning and investment can ignite the spark of creativity unless some additional magic ingredient is present as a catalyst. He can't tell us what that magic ingredient might be but there are sufficient clues to suggest that planning for creativity is deeply paradoxical. Stockholm has everything that one could wish from an ordered city environment, excellent public transport, beautiful garden suburbs, a vibrant city centre and a keen awareness and interest in public arts, architecture and culture. But in the end all the planning and all the capital expenditure hasn't been able to deliver anything more than a nice place to live: 'Overseas visitors to Sweden are first struck by the extraordinary level of good taste and high-quality design in everything, from the biggest building to the smallest detail of the table setting of an ordinary cafeteria. Only later do they come to notice an extraordinary uniformity, a certain deadness, in the overall effect.'

It seems that the more you plan the less you get. Singapore proves the point. Spotless and gleaming, it is a monument to urban design without a soul.

Florida believes that one can plan for urban creativity at least at the level of immigration. Cities that consciously set out to attract immigrants tend to benefit economically, especially in high-tech industries. Interestingly, though, immigration is not strongly associated with innovation according to his so-called Melting Pot Index.

A much better indicator of innovation comes from the distribution of the gay population. This is telling. Florida also found, when digging into this peculiar phenomenon, that big public amenities like opera houses, theatres and sports stadia were much less likely to attract gay people than 'vibrant street life, readily available outdoor recreation and a cutting-edge music scene'. Good places for cruising, in other words.

Think of 1964 and a grubby industrial city in the north west of England. Derek Taylor, in *It Was Twenty Years Ago Today*, tells us:

> In Liverpool there was a drifting together of people of like mind which had in it something of pubs, something of poetry and folk-song, something of art school. It was pure Melting Pot, as it would be everywhere. In that kingdom of the brave only the unwilling were unwelcome. The Beatles were a catalyst and levellers, bringing everyone together on one 'we're all one and life flows within you and without you' trip, captivating and capturing all hearts save the stony. The Beatles' detractors were and are a mean minority maddened by impotence – immovable, rocklike in their hostility. It was well that it were so. Had they had not pricks to kick against, they would not have been the Beatles, notable freedom fighters.

It's almost impossible to imagine that happening now, in health-and-safety Britain with its malls and Starbucks and political correctness.

Planning for creativity on any kind of scale appears to be a contradiction in terms. Planning by its very nature suggests a limit to the kind of street-level spontaneity that made *fin de siecle* Paris and Weimar Berlin such hives of inventiveness. And most people, when given the choice, would like their urban environments to be free of the crime and the dirt and the decadence that must apparently accompany creative expression on such a popular scale.

This is the circle that must be squared. How does one reconcile the need that ordinary decent people have for public order and nice, clean public amenities with the need that creativity has for the dark, the dangerous and the desperate? If it were a trade-off between an absence of personal security and a life of boredom who would not choose the latter? Except, of course, that the choice is an artificial one, given only to those with the means and wit to make it. It is easy to forget, in the world of broadband, satellite TV and cheap travel, that geography still exists out there, and that for most people geography is the only thing that counts. How far to the nearest clean water? How much for a bag of mielies or a couple of yams? How close to the nearest factory, and how long the queue outside the gate?

The great urban experiments, the planned cities like Brazilia, Canberra and Milton Keynes, are creative vacuums. Ideas tend not to thrive under fascism, and there's something inescapably fascist about places like Canary Wharf in London and the Renaissance Center in Detroit. The magic of Paris isn't in the glorious boulevards and the grand squares, as beautiful as they are, it's in the higgledy-piggledy café culture of the Left Bank. The chaos of Hamburg is a lot more exciting than the imposed order of Frankfurt. Barcelona is much more interesting than Madrid for exactly the same reason. Since Giuliani turned New York into a theme park it's not nearly as attractive as it once was, at least not to the visitor who used to thrive on the anonymity afforded by the decadent bustle of the dubious streets. The plans for Ground Zero originally proposed by Liebeskind have been compromised out of all recognition by the sweaty palms of the corporate greed. Whatever monument finally emerges from the ashes and the dust you can be sure its value will be measured in dollars per square metre of office space, not in the aesthetics of sacrifice and freedom.

*

The parallels with the Davis and Scase analysis of the organizational strategies for creativity are clear.

The planned cities like Stockholm, Singapore or Canary Wharf represent the commercial bureaucracies, lovely places to work, with gyms and cafeterias and pension plans and plenty of parking, but utterly devoid of the ingredients required for the spontaneous combustion of ideas.

The cluster strategy, with its emphasis on service, finds concrete expression in the modern industrial park or, better still, in the vast and soulless conurbation that surrounds an international airport like Heathrow.

The network organization is now completely virtual, entirely independent of space and time, divorced by the wizardry of mobile phones and Microsoft from culture, geography and language itself.

The demarcated organization, to the extent that it survives at all, is paralleled most closely by those cities that do or did divide the vibrancy of inner city chaos from the sleepy suburbs of bourgeois reflection. They were cities demarcated by wealth or class, fragmented by the faultlines of domesticity and decadence, yet whole enough to constitute a community, a place where Apollo and Dionysus frequented the same bars and clubs, in mutual suspicion, as always, but not without a recognition of the enrichment that each provided the other. Athens, Florence, Paris, London, Vienna: each in their time and in their manner.

*

For authentic city life we must now look to Latin America where the grand designs of the city planners have consistently been thwarted by an obdurate citizenry, corrupt institutions and a less than transparent approach to public finance.

The creative energy of Brazil is shown off to best advantage in two domains: there is the football, and there is the advertising.

Brazilian taxi drivers are as familiar with the names of the creative directors of the top ad agencies as they are with their football heroes. This is bizarre because the advertising you see on the popular TV channels is irredeemably awful. But the Brazilian public knows what it takes an advertising insider to know – that Brazilian agencies dominate international advertising festivals through a peculiar subculture of the business known as 'ghost' advertising.

The rules regarding the submission of advertising to awards festivals are constantly under scrutiny because it is so difficult to prove whether any individual piece of work was commissioned by a genuine client for genuine advertising exposure. It is quite possible, for example, to write and shoot a commercial for your local hairdresser, get her to promise that she paid for at least one flighting of it in a local cinema, and win a large gold statue at Cannes.

Technically this doesn't break the rules, though of course it makes a complete mockery of everything these festivals are supposed to celebrate. All advertising agencies in every country of the world are aware of this loophole and constantly try to exploit it. But no one exploits it as successfully as the Brazilians do. Often creative directors will be employed to do nothing other than 'ghost' ads while the hacks get on in the basement with producing the stuff that makes the money.

The same thing happens in Argentina and most of the other Latin markets, though the Mexicans don't seem to be able to do it no matter how hard they try. But it's by no means an exclusively Latin phenomenon. You'll find the same thing happening in Singapore, Hong Kong, Shanghai, Budapest, Riga, Milan, Hamburg, Johannesburg, Jakarta, Lisbon, Madrid, Sydney and occasionally in London where the chances are high that you will get found out and exposed as a fraud in *Campaign* magazine. The Americans are either too honest or too naïve to play this game with any degree of success.

But it's the Latins who do it as a national pastime, and it's the Brazilians and the Argentines who do it with most aplomb.

It's clearly schizophrenic, but it's not without justification. Particularly in those countries that lack other means of public creative expression, where the visual arts suffer from lack of funding, where theatre is withering on the vine, where the film industry struggles for support and literature struggles to find a readership, advertising has become an art form in its own right. The money that's made from the commercial side of the business is then used to sponsor ideas that can get produced without commercial restraint, and festivals like Cannes become the equivalent of the Oscars or the Nobel Prizes.

It's notable that the self-same ALMAP BBDO sponsored the acclaimed Brazilian film *City of God* directed by Katia Lund and Fernanado Meirelles, which was nominated for four Oscars in 2002.

This isn't just a lengthy aside. Creativity must out. Cultures that make no effort to support the traditional creative domains will find it expressed in a multitude of other ways. Sometimes it will be as eccentric and harmless as the advertising 'truchas' of Brazil. Sometimes they will be in graffiti or pornography or serious crime. Though she was making a very different point, Camille Paglia's observation that 'the reason why there is no female Mozart is that same reason there is no female Jack the Ripper' precisely describes how the creative impulse finds a way to assert itself without much regard for legitimacy or consequence.

*

The Rise of the Creative Class is unapologetic about lumping all species of knowledge workers into the same large pot and calling them creative. Indeed, Florida brands as creative every US worker other than those in the agricultural sector, the industrial sector or the service sector, as though by default.

Let's take a closer look at his definitions.

He divides his creative class into two sections. The first is called the 'Super-Creative Core' which consists of the 'computer and mathematical occupations', 'architecture and engineering occupations', 'life, physical and social science occupations', 'education, training and library occupations' and 'arts, design, entertainment, sports and media occupations'. The other class he calls 'Creative Professionals'. These include 'management occupations', 'business and financial operations', 'legal occupations', 'healthcare practitioners and technical occupations' and 'high-end sales and sales management'. All of this is hidden in the appendix on page 328.

If all of these people are creative one has to ask the question – who isn't? They turn out to be working class people engaged in construction, maintenance, production and transportation, as well as food preparation and food-service-related occupations – such as everyone who works at McDonald's except for the manager – and people who work in low-level administrative, sales and security jobs. Farmers, fisherman and foresters are also not creative.

The Rise of the Creative Class talks a lot about artists and other kinds of bohemians, but the generalizations that Florida makes are based on a broad sweep of workers very few of whom can truly be called creative in any real sense. This is supremely unhelpful, more so because business in general has been so quick to embrace his conclusions and recommendations. By failing to make a distinction between creative people and those who manage them, Florida's thesis becomes downright misleading. If the book had been called *The Rise of the Knowledge Worker* it would have been much more accurate, but clearly much less appealing to both the publisher and its expectant readers.

In my experience creative people are philosophically much closer to farmers and fishermen than they are to, say, the librarians that Florida includes in his 'Super-Creative Core'.

While it is clearly true that highly affluent American knowledge workers will gravitate to those cities that are most likely to satisfy their lifestyle needs, we clearly have to question whether this has anything at all to do with creativity in the strictest sense.

Mexico provides us with a much clearer perspective.

The young and mobile Mexican who wishes to carve out a career as a knowledge worker will naturally gravitate towards the US along with the strawberry pickers and everyone else who simply wants a better job and a better life. Mexican creative people, on the other hand, will tend to stay at home where the surrounding culture is more appreciative of the arts, and possibly even more rewarding.

An estimated 24 million people live in the vast polluted metropolis of 'El DF', as the chilangos of Mexico City call their capital, a sprawling mass of

Volkswagen Beetles and restless humanity that makes Istanbul look like Copenhagen. Unless you've lived there it's hard to believe that the city can work. Somehow it does, with water in the taps, an efficient Metro system, good public amenities, at least one decent park and roads that get repaired in the middle of the night.

As ugly as it is on the outside, an extraordinary elegance is to be found behind the high walls and the grubby exteriors. Restaurants, art galleries, private salons, art studios, theatres and hotels, most of them exquisitely appointed in a unique contemporary Mexican style, are just a knock on a door or a push on a bell away from the throat-clenching dust and pollution of the chaotic streets.

Every Mexican is an artist, and not just with a paint brush. It's hard to find a single Mexican who cannot sing or sculpt or carve or embroider or weave or cook or turn his or her hand to some form of creative expression.

There are public squares, like the Sullivan where canvasses and paints are sold to the eager masses. There's the Bazaar Sabado where hundreds of artists gather each week to sell oil paintings of arum lilies and watermelons. There are acres of retail space devoted exclusively to the sale of papier mâché sculptures. It is craft heaven gone mad, with every conceivable material that can be manipulated or painted or both and is a medium for the Mexican impulse to combine garish colours and weird shapes in surreal expressions of the Aztec psyche.

The Mexicans love installations. If you're part of the social elite hardly a day will go by without an invitation to attend the opening of a new one. They will be made of cardboard boxes, engine parts, Rottweiler puppies, agave plants, AK-47s, polystyrene slabs and all of the above. They will be held in the foyers of five star hotels, in magnificent haciendas, replete with Talavera tiling and the waft of good havanas, in the embassies with in-door swimming pools and the so-called industrial clubs where the richest Mexicans get together to drink tequila and play dominoes every Thursday from noon to midnight. The installations will be deeply symbolic, requiring you to wonder whether the whole thing should be blamed on Cortez or on Monctezuma.

If its not an installation it will be an art opening or the launch of a new coffee table book by the son or daughter of a rich socialite from Lomas de Chapultepec and San Angel. You will meet professors of surrealism and cousins of Octavio Paz. You will be told stories of human sacrifice that will make your hair stand on end. If you're lucky you will be invited to play golf on Sunday in

Acapulco or Los Cabos where the caddies place the ball on your tee for you, each nine will have a fully stocked member's bar, and a buggy will come around with tequila and cigars just in case you can't wait that long.

When I first arrived in Mexico I couldn't understand why the advertising was so bad and why the creative people at my agency were so unlike the creative people I had met at agencies in other parts of the world. Unlike the eager young whipper-snappers with their restless ambition and their hostile arrogance that I'd been used to working with, the Mexicans seemed half-hearted, hangdog and hopelessly demotivated. I knew, of course, that Mexican advertising was in poor shape. Not a single ad of any description had ever won at Cannes despite the fact that Mexico was the 10th biggest advertising market in the world.

It wasn't as though opportunities did not abound. With a department of only a dozen teams we were producing upwards of 400 spots a year, admittedly many of them cut-downs of ads from the US, Peru and the Philippines. The multinational clients were just as reasonable or unreasonable as they were elsewhere in the world, but the Mexican clients were clearly a problem. Advertising was something they did with grudging reluctance. They treated the agencies as suppliers whose job it was to execute, for a peso-pinching fee, the kind of monkey-see-monkey-do approach that typifies Hispanic advertising in the US, a bronze version of the white ads with the jokes and the intelligence excised.

So why, in this land of creative plenty, was there such an apparent dearth of advertising talent?

It took me four or five months to discover the truth. You could make more money writing poems in Mexico than you could as a copywriter in a Mexican agency. You could make more money designing corporate calendars than you could as an art director. All the young talent of Mexico, it turned out, was working for corporate patrons and the great families of the Mexican oligarchs, designing installations, decorating restaurants, painting murals in corporate headquarters and playing in bands at private Mexican parties. Why on earth would anyone want to work in an ad agency when their uncle's best friend would pay them double for editing a coffee table book on the splendours of Mexican artisania?

The lost art of patronage is alive and well and living in Polanco.

This is as close as you'll ever get to experiencing Elizabethan London or Paris in the 1920s. This is Weimar Berlin and post-Hapsburg Vienna fuelled by mescal and the visions of Carlos Castenada. This is Hall's cultural city about to bubble over.

So the border between Mexico and the US acts as a kind of filter, straining out those in search of financial security from those dedicated to creative expression. This results in a higher concentration of creatives in the Mexican mix, which in turn provides an even better reason for creative people to stay. We come back to the point that Hall makes in *Cities in Civilization*, that is, that those societies that care about creative expression are more likely to see it flourish.

The Mexican determination to translate the most banal events and objects into aesthetic experiences of one kind or another extends from food and the daily ritual of the *comida* through arts and crafts to superb architecture and interior design. Texture is central, at the literal level of wood and iron and concrete and clay, as well as at the experiential level of taking time to appreciate the sensual blends of music, drink, food, and conversation that accompany an evening out at the theatre or a leisurely lunch with friends. If the Mexican aesthetic does not export as well as it deserves to it is perhaps because it relies so much for its success on the context of location, language and leisure.

It is easy to romanticize all this while conveniently forgetting the violent crime, the dire poverty and the endemic corruption of a country teetering on the brink of anarchy. There is nothing charming about the begging in the streets, the petty theft, the pollution or the politics. But Mexico stands as a reminder of how little time and effort the rest of us devote to living fully and living well, or to creating the conditions necessary for a cultural life rich in the imaginative expression of the widest possible community.

*

In the case of Latin America in general it is possible to pick out from the chaos and confusion a certain worldview that is highly conducive to creative expression – a relaxed approach to work and life, a high tolerance of ambiguity, a notable appreciation of sensual pleasure, and a widespread cultural affinity for the arts.

It is significant that Chile, the most Americanized and business-friendly country in South America, is also by some margin the least creatively expressive. Santiago is blessed with the natural majesty of the surrounding Cordilleras, and a wonderful legacy of colonial architecture. On a good day it can be as breathtakingly beautiful as Cape Town or Vancouver. The people are busy and polite, and there's a certain earnest efficiency about the way they live their lives. But it's a miserable cultural backwater so depressing it makes Bloemfontein seem vibrant and sexy.

Unfortunately, to generalize wildly for Latin America as a whole, there's a serious downside. The superstitions of the Catholic Church continue to impose suffocating constraints on the imaginative life of all but the most intellectually liberated classes. Centuries of religious oppression have left the broad mass of Latins susceptible to ideological manipulation and highly vulnerable to attacks of occasional idiocy. This kind of gullibility is clearly inimical to one of our key criteria for creative achievement – the sense of individual empowerment and mastery of one's own destiny which is the ultimate aphrodisiac for imaginative expression.

The Church has been especially damaging in Mexico where syncretism has blended the horrors of heaven and hell with the terrors of Aztec ritual, still fresh in the collective memory, producing a population of fatalists who believe their only salvation is in numbers. When pressed for answers to the thorny problems of endemic corruption, poor governance and dire social problems, many Mexicans will default to ant worship. The solutions, they say, will be found in working together in some vast collective hive, the way that ants do, thereby relinquishing all claims to a personal identity, let alone to a personal destiny.

It's the attitude of the eternal victim, summed up memorably by President Porfirio Diaz: 'Poor Mexico, so far from God, so close to the United States.' And it does seem like a cruel trick of history that the country with the world's worst inferiority complex should share its border with the world's most arrogant nation.

The culture clash between white America and the Mexican immigrant invasion is widely documented as a contentious political issue. Unlike previous waves of immigrants from Europe and elsewhere, who readily relinquished their home languages and national associations in return for a slice of apple pie, the Mexicans who now constitute as much as 20% of the population of California and sizeable percentages of the other southern states represent an entirely different challenge. With home and family just across the border, and with the reassurance of numbers, they can enjoy the economic and social benefits of the American lifestyle without giving up any of the familiar comforts and delights of their own.

So a reverse colonization is taking place, subverting the cultural status quo and threatening to undermine the complacent certainties of American homogeneity. If Hall and Florida are anything to go by, this will turn out to be a very good thing. For all its claims to diversity, ex pluribus unum has ended up doing exactly that, creating one uniform monoculture out of many. Ethnicity without a credible cultural legacy is diversity in name only. If anything is going to save the US from death by obesity, Fox News and barbecue sauce it will be a Mexican wave breaking through the levees of self-satisfaction.

*

Geography will continue to be the defining variable of cultural expression for some time to come, or at least as long as art needs audiences and innovation needs markets. But on this side of the digital divide – a chasm that deepens with each succeeding generation of Windows software – virtual communities of media production and media consumption are becoming increasingly evident. MySpace and Facebook are the obvious examples. As long as the internet remains a step ahead of governmental and commercial interference it will continue to provide the very best possible forum of creative exchange, if not of creative quality.

But long before the internet, film and music were finding mass audiences around the planet, uniting people from many different countries in a virtual culture that overlaid their own. The world's first virtual creative revolution was the Enlightenment, made possible by the printing press and global travel, albeit in dodgy wooden boats. The second was the 1960s, made possible by vinyl and celluloid. Creativity and technology have been inseparable ever since the pyramids. And it doesn't require a Marxist analysis to see that the people who own the technology will be hugely influential in prescribing the nature of the creative output. If they're open-minded and adventurous, like the Jews who owned Hollywood, or like Sam Phillips of Sun Records, they will inevitably produce some great creative work among the lamentable dreck.

The cities and countries that produced great art and great ideas, and the cities and communities – corporate, institutional or virtual – that continue to produce great art and great ideas, seem in many ways to be mirror images of the kind of individual human brains that consistently produce great art and great ideas. In the same way that ontogeny recapitulates phylogeny, that is, that the growth of the individual in any species re-enacts the development of the species as a whole (e.g. from swimming in the womb, to crawling, to standing upright in the case of human beings), cities and communities apparently require the same conditions for creative success as the neurological conditions of the individual creative brain.

We have seen that highly creative individuals tend to have low levels of cortical inhibition, as though the policemen who are supposed to be patrolling the streets have gone awol, and the censors and administrators charged with maintaining public morals and social order are on holiday in the Bahamas or asleep at their desks. Which is more or less what happened in Athens, Florence, Paris and Berlin as the accepted order of things began to give way to uncertain futures. In every case, as Hall has pointed out, great bursts of creativity coincided with the sense of individual empowerment that rose as the authority of the polity declined.

The parallel between the city and the brain is even more apparent in the case of diversity. Creative people need to have a wide variety of very diverse experiences to draw from, just as cities benefit from a wide diversity of skills and cultures. During the critical phase of 'defocused attention' as the creative brain experiments with different combinations of mental material, '. . . creativity is favoured by an intellect that has been enriched with diverse experiences and perspectives' (Simonton). For 'defocused attention' we should imagine the streets of Elizabethan London alive with drunken revelry, the taverns bustling with the chatter and gossip of playwrights and prostitutes, as carriages of Spanish treasure roll through Southwark towards the Tower.

And then there are the 'innermost, nethermost regions', the shadows of the unconscious mind replicated in the parts of the city where decent people just don't go, the underworld of Jack the Ripper and the asylums of tortured souls. What else is the Gay Index measuring if it isn't a tolerance of deviation, of access to the streets, bars, cafés and clubs that celebrate decadence? Whenever these parts of the city are cut off from the squares and suburbs of respectable citizenry a kind of urban schizophrenia prevails, expressing itself in paroxysms of violence and repression. Creative brains have an ability to access the darkest parts of the psyche without lapsing into psychosis. It's when the constraints of the social code prevent this access that they finally go mad.

And the last condition is that cities or societies should care. More than that, they should obsess about collecting, inspiring and patronizing the artistic impulse the way the Jews did in Vienna and Hollywood, the way the merchants did in London, the way the bourgeoisie did in Paris and Berlin, and the way the Medicis did in Florence. At the level of the individual this parallels the compulsive condition of the creative spirit, the craving for novelty against all the odds of precedent and logic.

CHAPTER 15

The road to Exit Five

... organisations are political systems in which the politicians win.

John W. Hunt, *Managing People at Work*

We have learned that you can't bully creativity into being. It cannot be coerced by finance people or bureaucratic efficiency or even state-of-the-art market research. And because creativity is so hard to come by, many agencies base their success on other skills. For example, maintaining good personal rapport with the client. But, eventually, you can't cover a shortfall of imagination.

Phil Dusenberry, BBDO

Crafts are reactionary. Creativity is revolutionary. Crafts are inherently conservative. Creativity is inherently subversive. Crafts reinforce existing cultural values. Creativity undermines them. Crafts help to bond clans and communities together by reaffirming, in paints or pots or poetry, the traditions that unite them as a group. Creativity is iconoclastic: it disrupts the conventions of community in pursuit of a personal vision, a universal truth, or both.

The Ndebele people of Kwa-Ndebele, a region of South Africa north of Pretoria, are famous for painting their mud huts with arresting geometric patterns in a vibrant range of colours. The effect can be stunning, especially in the winter when the transparent light of the Transvaal etches these radiant hieroglyphs on a background of dun, dry veld. The aesthetic is purely abstract; the motifs are drawn from traditional Ndebele designs as well as from stylized versions of contemporary objects such as lightbulbs, razor blades and commercial packaging. But it is not symbolic: or not, at least, in the sense of standing for anything beyond the decorative.

The design, and the painting itself, is done exclusively by the women. They use whatever pigments come to hand, the browns, reds and ochres from clay and earth, the whites and blacks from lime and coal. When they can afford to, they buy commercial paints for greens, yellows, purples and blues. Kids will break open used batteries and use the mush of chemicals to add to the range of blacks and greys.

When asked why they do it they simply say they've always done it. They say, 'It's the law of the Ndebele.'

In the unfortunate history of southern Africa's indigenous people, cursed in turn by Zulu, British and Afrikaner imperialism, the Ndebele are perhaps the most unfortunate. They lost not only their land but also, quite exceptionally, their language, which obliged them to forsake almost all of their cultural traditions. The house paintings of the Ndebele are an extraordinary example of how embattled communities, stripped of everything that would normally bind them together, reassert their identities through art.

This is art as community; culture as glue. It is Morris dancing, Oaxacan woodcarving, Peruvian flute music, the tango, English football. With a few years of apprenticeship it is relatively easy to replicate, which is why so much of it is repetitive and mundane. Occasionally, in the hands of an exceptional talent, motivated by an extraordinary passion, it becomes sublime – it changes the rules, raises the bar, expands the domain. It's at the confluence of these variables that craft becomes creativity, when – by general agreement – we assign the word genius to the craftsman supreme.

Teresa Amabile has a model that puts all of this into a logical context. She calls it 'The Three Component Model of Creativity'.

Imagine a Venn diagram of three overlapping circles. At the top left is a circle called Expertise, at the top right a circle called Creative Skills and centre bottom a circle called Task Motivation. The area where all three circles overlap she calls Creativity. This isn't as technical as it sounds.

Expertise simply stands for the craft that is necessary to engage in the domain – in the case of Ndebele house painting these are the skills that get passed on from mother to daughter, how to mix the paint, how to apply it, and the rudiments of symmetry and geometric design. Of course, the daughter will already have a lot of this expertise in her head simply from growing up in this community of house painters and from watching her mother and grandmother.

Creative Skills should properly be called individual talent, because this describes the particular and personal level of aptitude that the creative person brings to the task, that array of brain and personality attributes discussed in

Part I. These are not skills the daughter could have learned; it's the aptitude that she is born with, the degree to which she will be able to interpret and apply the domain skills in a unique and imaginative way.

The third component of creativity, 'Task Motivation', has to do with the amount of passion she applies to designing and executing her house painting. If she loves doing it because she finds it enjoyable and challenging she will obviously produce something more beautiful and imaginative than if she feels resentful about doing it simply because it is a tradition she is obliged to uphold.

When a high level of expertise and a high level of individual talent overlap with a particularly passionate level of task motivation you get the most brilliant example of house painting ever seen in the community. It's the one that all the house painters admire the most, the one that becomes the new benchmark for excellence and the object of aspiration for all the other house painters.

Different creative domains have different kinds of apprenticeship. Composing classical music, for example, probably requires more years of training than learning to play the guitar in a rock band. Writing a novel, as J.K. Rowling has proved, requires little or no apprenticeship – just an enormous amount of individual talent and an extraordinary level of motivation.

Poetry used to require years of apprenticeship in the abstruse skills of rhyme and metre. These days it would probably take you 10 to 15 years to become a theoretical physicist. Einstein did it in about five. The painters and sculptors of the early renaissance usually spent their early years working as apprentices in the studios and foundries of their more established mentors, learning how to make paints, how to bind them, how to mix them, or how to cast bronze and how to work with silver and gold.

So all domains have their basis in one or another form of craft, a degree of competency that must be acquired before the artist or scientist can strike off on his or her own.

People who write about creativity make an enormous issue out of domain specificity, the implication being that creativity is entirely domain dependent. Perhaps it is true that Picasso would not have been a great musician, or that Einstein would not have been an exceptional painter. Finding the right domain at the right time obviously helps to steer genius in the right direction. But we know that creativity is not domain limited.

Extraordinary talent will find a way to express itself even if the domain to which it is most suited doesn't exist. Often this kind of talent will create entirely new domains, or find a way of blurring the boundaries between two or three different domains. You have only to look at recent achievements in the computer field to see how new domains can spring up like mushrooms as the boundaries between hardware and software, or mathematics and computer science, merge into radical new expressions and applications. And right now, on the brink of the convergence of television, computers and telephony, we wait with bated breath to see which players have the ingenuity to capture the Holy Grail. It could be the established companies like Microsoft or IBM. It could be handset manufacturers like Nokia or Motorola. It could be content owners like Time Warner or Sony. Or it could be entirely new players coming at the field from totally different angles, like Google or Skype or someone we've never heard of.

Howard Gardner warns that,

> As domains become increasingly technical, it becomes far more difficult to make a mark in the absence of training. Future scientists, who might have succeeded with a bachelor's degree eighty years ago, now need at least one postdoctoral stint. Aspiring performance artists must spend time at Juilliard, working with a master teacher for many years. Only in the newest areas – for example, creation of software – is there opportunity for an individual who lacks established credentials. And yet there is a risk for the individual who remains forever in training. At a certain moment, she must test her wings and risk flying solo in an often hostile environment.

This is certainly true if we choose to accept that the boundaries between domains are as clearly delineated as academic and artistic institutions would have us believe: that history is one thing and geography is another, or that music and the visual arts are mutually exclusive.

E.O. Wilson blames this kind of 'professional atomization' for ending the Enlightenment:

> The faculties of higher education around the world are a congeries of experts. To be an original scholar is to be a highly specialised world authority in a polyglot Calcutta of similarly focused world authorities. In 1797, when Jefferson took the president's chair at the American Philosophical Society, all American scientists could be

seated comfortably in the lecture room of the Philosophical Hall. Most could discourse reasonably well on the entire world of learning, which was still small enough to be seen whole. Their successors today, including 450000 holders of the doctorate in science and engineering alone, would overcrowd Philadelphia. Professional scholars in general have little choice but to dice up research expertise and research agendas among themselves. To be a successful scholar means spending a career on membrane biophysics, the Romantic poets, early American history, or some other such constricted area of formal study.

Clearly this demands much longer apprenticeships for those eager minds wishing to race to the frontiers of established domains in the hope of making discoveries of their own. And it is probably more of an issue in the sciences than in the arts. But creative people have a curious ability to find the cracks between domains, to build bridges from one to another, or to construct domains of their own.

This is what makes Amabile's distinction between domain skills and creative talent so useful and so important. It is the highly trained and the highly skilled individual working within the constraints of a particular domain that will extend its boundaries in increments of knowledge or innovation. These are the people who will give us the next application of stem cell research or the next generation of mobile technology. They will be very dedicated, highly specialized and extremely clever. But it is the very passionate, less specialized and probably very naïve creative person who connects a piece of one domain to a piece of another domain and ends up creating a new one.

We have seen that creative people are only moderately clever. And we have seen that too much education correlates negatively with creativity in the long run. So it makes very good sense to distinguish between domain skills that can be learned or acquired, and the natural inclination of the creative mind to subvert the fundamental premises of the domains in which they find themselves operating.

The first circle is the guild, the academic faculty, the goldsmith's studio, the cabal, the handshake of the Freemason, the secret meeting of the Rosicrucians, the Society of Jesus, the Marylebone Cricket Club. It is the tradition, the craft and the collective spirit of the Ndebele. It is the tradition, the craft and the collective spirit of companies that are still in touch with the founding vision.

It is the Bentley Museum at Crewe and the third generation of coach-builders who continue to make and fit the polished burr walnut interior fascias of the Bentley Arnage by hand. It is the people in the company who live and breathe the spirit of W.O. Bentley, including those from Volkswagen, the new owners, who have drunk deeply from the same well.

It is the boring old fart at the office party who tells you how great the company used to be. It is the granddaughter of the founder stuck in a corner office where she can't do any harm. It is the coffee table book commissioned on the 50th anniversary depicting the firm's legacy of innovation.

In ad agencies it is the showreel. 'The work, the work, the work,' to quote the BBDO mantra. If the showreel isn't all that good then it's, 'The network, the network, the network.' Or the PowerPoint presentation describing the matrix of cutting edge interdisciplinary media technologies including CRM, Digital, Interactive, Through-the-Line Planning™, Brand Vizioning™ and a bunch of other trade-marked processes they made up the day before yesterday. Most agencies are allergic to their own history. It's just too old and stuffy. Unless, like DDB, you're still working in the brilliant tradition of the founder.

*

If the first circle is the MCC, the second circle is Kerry Packer. If the first circle is 16th century Rome, then the second circle is Galileo. If the first circle represents the aesthetic sensibilities of France during the Second Empire then the second circle is Manet's shocking *Déjeuner sur l'herbe*. It's the iconic piece of work that breaks the mould, the iconic individual who breaks the paradigm. It's all the usual suspects. Gandhi, Virginia Woolf, Freud, Dylan, Bonnie, Disney, Le Corbusier, Herriman, Kubrick, Mozart, Pynchon, Kahlo, Groenig.

The second circle is always, and very specifically, individual. It is an unforgettable voice, a peculiarly memorable taste, a mood, a sensation, an icon. It is the rare combination of molecules that makes up the scent of your first girlfriend's skin. It's the shuffle of the genetic pack that ends up with Dostoyevsky or David Abbott.

It is not a theory. It is passion in practice.

It is particular, discrete, idiosyncratic, special, original, quirky, distinctive, unique, precise, explicit, remarkable. It is singular. Warhol's Brillo pack is a real, physical, tangible object. It is the idea of mundane replicability made concrete in one specific magnificent physical thing. You have to see it to believe it. It is the interaction of the first and the second circle made manifest.

The second circle can become a movement or a revolution, like Surrealism. It thrives as long as we still recognize the individuals within it: Breton, Ernst, Aragon, Man Ray, Elouard, Bunuel. But as soon as it becomes a club it is all over. On 5th February 1934 the Surrealists, led by Breton, called Salvador Dali to account for not playing to the Surrealist rules. That was the end of it.

It becomes the first circle, a tradition, a guild, a collection of memories. It becomes a church.

The agents of the second circle need something to work within and to work against. They need to come up against the stifling traditions of the domain in order to subvert it. This thought has been reduced to the cliché of knowing the rules before you break them.

Companies that throw their history on the trash heap deny their employees the opportunity of reinventing it. There is nothing to push against, nothing to test, nothing to break. It's like trying to do Judo on your own.

In the contemporary commercial bureaucracy history is replaced by process and systems invented by management consultants who have no names or faces. The distinction between craft and creativity is lost as the two circles merge into one. Lost, too, is the distinction between the company and the individuals who comprise it. The mavericks are co-opted into managing the process. It is the Surrealist Club that will allow Dali to join only if he agrees to help them enforce the rules of surrealism.

In demarcated organizations, where the creative function is clearly separated from managerial considerations, a healthy and natural tension exists between those engaged in the production of ideas and those concerned with their commercial application. As the craft side of creative businesses diminishes in importance because of technology and the routinization of tasks, the conceptual function is thrown into stark relief as something clearly outside of the managerial ambit. The two circles begin to separate and the true nature of creativity is revealed for what it is. Ideas begin to separate from the stuff they're made of the way cultures separate from agar in a Petri dish. And it's the idea that counts after all. Just the pure idea.

The demarcated organization is Athens. The commercial bureaucracy is Rome.

*

Teresa Amabile takes a thoroughly pragmatic approach to the study of creativity. She is much less interested in why it happens than in how it happens, and possibly even less interested in how it happens than in when and where it happens. She disdains idle speculations into the nature of the creative process, treating it as a sealed black box inaccessible to empirical analysis. She focuses, instead, on the observable and measurable conditions that precede the creative process, and contrasts them with the observable and measurable results that emerge on the other side. It is input and output, as simple as that.

She began her career studying creativity in children, during which period she formulated her now-famous 'principle of intrinsic motivation'. More recently she has been engaged in several long-term studies observing the creativity of workers in research and development departments. Her book *Creativity in Context* is an essential primer for anyone interested in how to get the best out of creative people in commercial organizations.

For many years her work was known and recognized only by that elite group of academics working in creativity research. In 1998, with an article entitled 'How to Kill Creativity' published in the *Harvard Business Review*, she sprang to prominence as someone whose academic findings might be of relevance to the commercial world and, more specifically, to companies investing large sums in R&D.

Amabile arrived at her three component model long after she had discovered the importance of 'task motivation'. It is this last circle that is of most relevance to the management of creativity. If you can't mechanize craft skills at least you can teach them. There is nothing you can do about the second circle except hire the people you think are the most naturally gifted in your domain. There are some pointers that could help you make the right choice. The personality characteristics of creative people are a good place to start but they are by no means definitive, as we have seen.

Amabile herself advises us to seek out people who can look at things in different ways, who can live with complexity, who keep their response options open as long as possible – those who don't mind suspending judgement until the very last minute – people who pick up bits of information from a wide variety of categories and resist specialization, and those who are prepared to break the rules of a given domain. I would add to the list people who have recurring dreams of clouds bursting into flame in the middle of a summer's day.

But even if you don't pick a Mozart or a Miro there's an enormous amount you can do by manipulating the variables of task motivation. Without wishing to overstate Amabile's case I will venture to suggest that a sensitive and intuitive application of her principles of intrinsic motivation is the hallmark of good creativity management in every type of creative organization and in every creative sector, bar none.

She divides task motivation, the third circle, into two distinct and mutually exclusive types: extrinsic and intrinsic.

Intrinsic motivation, to put it in the simplest possible terms is the enjoyment you feel when you're doing something you like doing. Extrinsic motivation, by contrast, is doing stuff because you have to. Intrinsic and extrinsic motivation obviously affect every part of our day-to-day lives. There is nothing enjoyable about taking out the garbage but you have to. That is extrinsic motivation. A lot of people hate shopping – men, for example. But some people get a real kick out of it – women, for example. The mysterious joy that accompanies shopping for shoes is a good example of intrinsic motivation. We take all this for granted and we deal with it as it comes, for better or for worse. An alarm clock is the extrinsic motivation that it takes to get most of us up in the morning. The gnawing pressure to earn enough money to pay the mortgage and feed our children is the extrinsic motivation that gets us onto the train and through the traffic to the office. The thought of getting home on a Friday night to a blissful weekend peace and quiet, or to the reckless abandon of clubbing till dawn, is what gets us onto the train and home again.

We accomplish most of the tasks of everyday life because extrinsic factors require us to get them done. Usually they take the form of fears or anxieties or threats of disaster. We climb onto the roof in the rain armed with bitumen and a spatula to make sure that the rain doesn't seep through the ceiling and fry the computer. A sense of overwhelming responsibility obliges us to find precisely the right pair of football boots for our eight-year-old boy as the spectre of a childhood traumatized by insensitive parenting looms in the background.

Most of the things we do, as Tumin noted, we do to achieve some sort of result – to gain a reward for things well done, or to postpone the unimaginable horrors of things undone.

There are three things that we do for their own sake, without any thought of consequence. We play games, we have sex and we create things. You might say you read a book or watch TV or go to movies for their own sake, and that's true, of course, but these are passive activities, during which we allow the creativity of the author, the programme maker or the film-maker to entèrtain us. In that sense they are very different from making the effort required to cart your golf clubs from the shed to the car, the effort of seduction, or the effort of preparing a canvas. As adults we tend to lose the undiluted enjoyment of games. But you only have to watch children making up the spontaneous and arbitrary rules that turn a cardboard box and a straw hat into three hours of uninhibited mayhem to remind yourself of how games used to be. The result doesn't matter: the game is the thing.

What Amabile discovered was that the presence of intrinsic motivation and the absence of extrinsic motivation made a profound difference to creativity. Perhaps it shouldn't have been so surprising. Clearly when you enjoy doing something you are more likely to do it well. But Amabile was able to prove, in controlled experimental circumstances, that intrinsic motivation had an extraordinary affect on the quality of work produced in creative exercises.

Here's my favourite study. In 1985 Amabile got 72 creative writers from Brandeis University and Boston University to draw up a list of their reasons for writing. She took the best of the reasons and divided them into two different groups, seven that were clearly intrinsic, and seven that where clearly extrinsic.

The seven extrinsic reasons included thoughts such as, 'You want your writing teachers to be favourably impressed with your writing talent' and 'You have heard of cases where one best-selling novel or collection of poems has made the author financially secure'.

The seven intrinsic reasons were things like, 'You like to play with words' and 'You derive satisfaction from expressing yourself clearly and eloquently'.

The subjects were then divided into three groups, a control group, an intrinsic group and an extrinsic group, though, of course, they had no idea which group they were in. All of the students were first asked to write a Haiku poem on the subject of 'snow'. They were then given a short story to read. Students in the control group read the story for 15 minutes and were then asked to describe their impressions of the story and the author. The experimental group subjects read the story for only 10 minutes and were then asked to spend five minutes putting the lists of intrinsic or extrinsic reasons for writing into order of importance. The intrinsic group rank ordered the intrinsic list, and the extrinsic group rank ordered the extrinsic list. All three groups were then asked to write a Haiku on the theme of laughter and then complete a questionnaire on their reaction to the poem writing activity.

Twelve poetry experts rated the snow poems and the laughter poems on levels of creativity, achieving a high level of consensus.

As expected, the control group of students were just as creative with their Haikus on laughter as they were on their Haikus on snow. The Haikus of the students who rank ordered the list of extrinsic reasons for writing showed a marked decrease in creativity between snow and laughter, while the students who rank ordered the intrinsic list showed a remarkable and substantial jump in the quality of their second Haikus.

Considering that the two experimental groups spent only five minutes on the ranking exercise, the increase and decrease of creative quality associated with the mere awareness of intrinsic and extrinsic factors is astounding.

Since 1985 Amabile and her colleagues have confirmed the results of this early trial in a variety of experiments and, most importantly, in their observations of people at work in real world situations, especially among those working in research and development where continuously high levels of innovation are expected as a matter of course. The evidence that task motivation is the single most important factor in determining the quality of creative output is as substantial as it is incontrovertible.

The Ndebele woman who paints her house because she loves the art and craft of house painting will do a much better job of it than the Ndebele woman who paints her house because the headman says she has to. The laboratory biochemist who is intrigued by the effect of different doses of plutonium on the breeding patterns of white mice is more likely to discover a cure for infertility than the biochemist who hates his job. The musician who writes a song because it pops into her head while she is brooding about how much she hates her ex-boyfriend is more likely to produce a hit single than the same musician given two days of recording time, a blank piece of paper and a ticking clock. A creative team in an advertising agency is more likely to produce a breathtaking idea if they know they're not going to be fired for failing.

We define as *intrinsic* any motivation that arises from the individual's positive reaction to qualities of the task itself; this reaction can be experienced as interest, involvement, curiosity, satisfaction, or positive challenge. We define as *extrinsic* any motivation that arises from sources outside of the task itself; these sources include expected evaluation, contracted-for reward, external directives, or any of several similar sources.

We will look at the several factors that make up intrinsic and extrinsic motivation in the next few chapters, using 'How to Kill Creativity' as a handy guide. But first we should look back at the three overlapping circles and the ingredients they contribute to that sweet spot of creative brilliance at the centre.

For the sake of the thought experiment, let's see what happens when we play with some of the variables.

First, we'll remove circle two and leave circle one overlapping with high intrinsic motivation. This gives you craftspeople who really enjoy what they're doing – the amateur watercolourist painting scenes of Richmond Park in the early autumn, the clouds scudding over Pembroke Lodge, the thermos steaming with freshly brewed tea, and the red setter lolling at her feet. She does hundreds of wonderful watercolours that are admired by her wide circle of friends and family.

You get the session musician practising into the night in preparation for the gig at Abbey Road that will cover the Japanese re-release of *A Hard Day's Night*. In other words you get creative craftspeople loving what they do and doing what they love.

Now we'll remove the first circle and examine the overlap of creative individualism with intrinsic motivation. You get a passionate genius in search of a domain. You get unschooled brilliance or spectacular naïvete. You get 'The Natural'. You get Van Gogh, Henri Rousseau, J.K. Rowling, Kennedy O'Toole, Pete Doherty. You get children.

Switching the task motivation circle to extrinsic and keeping circle one out of the equation you get unhappy children, mad adolescents and frustrated monsters. You get serial killers, Hitler, Pol Pot.

With a high level of extrinsic motivation and a high level of craft skill you get most of the people working the creative industries, doing what they love in circumstances they hate, and producing to the minimum requirements of acceptability. You get toxic companies.

When everything comes together – a mastery of craft, the elemental force of genius, and the sheer uninhibited joy of doing the thing you love – you get Stravinsky, Donatello, *Sgt Pepper*, *Guernica*, Borges, *King Lear*, *Pan's Labyrinth*, the *Four Quartets*, Velcro. You get Cannes Lions that really work.

In reality, of course, the circles are not quite as neat as they look. Creative people bring a natural passion to their work. If it rages fiercely enough it can overcome the most damaging extrinsic factors. It can make up for a lack of schooling or a lack of skill. A conducive environment, rich in the kind of stimulation that gives succour to broken spirits, can reveal untold treasures in ordinary mortals. If you can't find a Miro for your graphics department and Matisse is too expensive, perhaps Mary and Mike will do – with sufficient training and lots of the factors that make for intrinsic motivation.

Assuming task motivation is more or less neutral, with intrinsic factors and extrinsic factors more or less cancelling each other out, craft and creativity struggle for dominance. Craft is naturally conservative, as we have seen. Creativity is naturally subversive. Without the intrinsic motivation needed to tip the balance in favour of the creative impulse, which thrives on freedom and the joy of exploration, the steady hand of craft can keep creativity under control. Craft can survive the constraining effects of extrinsic motivation better than creativity can because craft is essentially repetitive. With motivation in neutral, craft and creativity consume each other.

Craft represents continuity – the continuity of tradition, the passing down of skills from one generation to the next, the mentality of the guild, the obligations of apprenticeship and the preservation of culture. Creativity represents surprise and discontinuity – the sudden shock of novelty, the twisting of the rules, the corruption of tradition and the dissolution of history. As much as it aspires to novelty, management favours continuity; if it favours innovation, it prefers it to arrive in small and steady increments. With motivation in neutral, management will be strongly inclined to support the reliability of the craftspeople rather than the risk that discontinuity might bring.

The history of art and literature is an account of the struggle between craft and creativity, between continuity and surprise. It is impossible to appreciate just how radical and exciting the work of Giotto was to his contemporaries without seeing him in the context of the long and worthy tradition from which he emerged. His predecessors were craftsmen who for centuries had been painting in the flat Byzantine-style tradition acceptable to the church fathers. Giotto took the same subjects, such as the Madonna and Child and the Annunciation, and turned the central characters into real, three-dimensional people as though they were made of flesh and blood like you and me. That was the beginning of the Renaissance.

In his 1908 film, *After Many Years*, D.W. Griffith did something so shocking it had movie-goers hiding under their seats and running for the exits in terror. In the words of Lewis Jacobs, 'Going further than he had ventured before, in a scene showing Annie Lee brooding and waiting for her husband's return, Griffith daringly used a large close-up of her face . . .' Until that moment film-makers had been content to allow that action to unfold in a series of wide shots. In a single stroke Griffith changed the language of film forever – the continuity of the film-maker's craft was subverted by the discontinuity of genius.

Again and again in every creative and technological field it is the disconti-nuities that mark the intervention of true creativity.

This phenomenon is particularly evident in the fruit-fly laboratory of adver-tising. In the relentless quest to capture consumer attention, even for a fleeting moment, advertisers are driven by the pressure cooker of commerce to seek out and exploit novelty wherever they can find it. So every new TV commercial is an opportunity for discontinuity, for doing something new, fresh and radical, for exploring the limits of the medium in the hope of producing a new renaissance or a new close-up.

Thousands of TV commercials are produced everyday, each of them con-ceived in the hope of doing something that no one has ever done before, so the chances of doing something extraordinary are increasingly rare. The craft skills of advertising have been honed to perfection, so it takes an extraordinary effort for genius to impose itself on the genre.

The struggle between continuity and surprise is played out everyday between agencies and their clients in thousands of offices all over the world. In 99.9% of cases the conservatism of craft triumphs over the intent of originality. That's why we see so many commercials that look and feel just like the one we saw two minutes ago. But every now and then a rare mutation takes place, redefining the way in which advertisers communicate with their audiences. Every year at the Cannes Advertising Festival you will see a hundred examples of these, the surpris-ing and delightful discontinuities that subvert and refresh this notoriously mundane artform.

Usually these are the ones that slip through the net, the truchas, the ghost ads done for fictitious pro bono clients. And the reason for this is clear. The con-servative tendencies of the advertising craft are exacerbated by the risk aversion of most clients. There is probably no other form of creative endeavour in which the inhibiting factors of extrinsic motivation play such a powerful role. It is only when the shackles of extrinsic motivation are broken, when the restraints of risk aversion are lifted, and when the creative impulse is fuelled by the oxygen of intrinsic motivation, that the rules can be challenged and surprise can triumph over continuity. The fruit-flies are still fruit-flies, but they have golden wings.

At the micro level, within individual campaign ideas for specific brands, the same struggle is even more specific and even more evident. When advertisers have developed strong and salient brand properties that have a history of appealing to consumers, it is even more difficult for novelty to emerge. The conservatism of craft and the natural risk aversion of the marketing establishment is weighed down even more heavily by the considerable investment that has already been made in those brand properties. Every new iteration of the same ideas dilutes the gene pool.

It is usually out of sheer desperation that the clients will resort to the kind of mutations necessary to restore new life to the brand construct. Often, of course, they will find their new genetic material at another advertising agency.

*

The really fascinating thing about all of this is that task motivation is the easiest and the cheapest thing to manage. Training has become something of a luxury these days. Creative sector companies expect their new recruits to arrive for work primed and prepped for a productive day at the office. They can pick up additional skills along the way, in their own damn time. Proven creative talent can cost a fortune. Unproven creative talent is hard to find. And even when you find it, it's a huge risk.

But managing the variables that make for high levels of intrinsic motivation is relatively simple. You don't need a company gym, a ping-pong table, or even a causal dress code. These things are less than meaningless. All it requires is an attitude, a mindset, a commitment. Reducing the factors that contribute to an extrinsically motivated work environment can be done with the stroke of a manager's pen.

Management coaches like to say that performance equals potential minus interference. In the creative industries, thanks to Amabile, we now have a very good idea of what that interference looks like.

*

In the demarcated company, designated creative people can create a subculture that immunizes them, at least to some extent, from the inimical effects of extrinsic motivation. That was why the BBC was able to produce such a brilliant stream of innovative programming during its golden years. The same thing happens in agencies with strong creative departments, and in companies like 3M that have a cohesive subculture of creativity. These creative communities will go to great lengths to protect themselves, often at the risk of alienating management support. The more toxic the company, the higher the walls erected by the creative community. It takes an exceptional manager to understand why creative people behave this way.

Yet absurdly enough it is no different from the division of labour that characterized the manufacturing industries in the 20th century. The workers who produced the goods always thought of themselves as a species apart from the people who were managing them. And the managers themselves would have it no other way. It is only because creativity is regarded as a service rather than as a unit of production that we have arrived at this ludicrous point where we want to co-opt creative workers into management roles.

There are other benefits that come with isolating creative people from the rest of the company. The quality of the work becomes the focal point of the creative subculture. Inured from the politics of control and power, creative rivalries centre on the ambition and fame of the creative product. Status must be earned because it cannot be conferred. The subculture creates its own value system, and its own badges of honour. Such political in-fighting that will inevitably arise in closed organizations will be the politics of ideas and the politics of originality – who stole what from whom, what is derivative, what is authentic, what is good and what is exceptional.

They require diversity and challenge, of course, to prevent them from disintegrating into *Lord of the Flies*. And they need intermediaries skilled in the art of translating their work to management and translating management objectives to them.

They will observe each other, learn from each other and test each other. They will discuss the work of competing organizations in degrees of admiration and disdain. They will traffic in memes, old ones and new ones. The subculture will become a hothouse in which mutated memes can thrive and flourish and replicate and die their own natural deaths, or survive and grow strong enough to withstand the toxic atmosphere of the outside world.

Cluster companies, those that spring up around great creative enterprises, are de facto subcultures that feed off the same sort of energy. Typically they will be led by creative people who have outgrown or outlived the hothouse. They will tend to be charismatic, specialized and fiercely independent. Since the quality of their work will be the single measure of their success and survival they will defend the territory that demarcates the source of their inspiration – their zone of intrinsic motivation – with tigerish determination. They are not beholden to anyone or anything except their reputation, so they can shape their accommodation with the real world of extrinsic pressures in whatever way they wish. And usually they are small enough to avoid the kind of management hierarchies that breed the politics of power and control.

Many of these, however, will fall back on a particular craft skill and give up any claim to originality. They will become suppliers to the creative sector in which they operate, delivering replicable services that are necessary but peripheral.

Then there are those individuals working alone, the writers and painters and sculptors and photographers who comprise the network structure described by Davis and Scase. Typically they will have someone working as an intermediary to defend them from the extrinsic pressures that could undermine their motivation. It could be a parent or a partner, a friend or an agent: someone who is happy to send out the invoices, provide moral support and make the tea. 'Being the wife of a genius is work enough,' they say. Or they will slice up their time, devoting some hours to creativity and some hours to dealing with the exigencies of daily life.

These three together – the demarcated organization with its creative sub-culture, the creative cluster companies that provide additional skills and services, and the network of creative independents – form a loose federation ideally positioned to fend off the worst excesses of extrinsic constraint. Working together in the same geographical area they will form symbiotic connections that sharpen the creative edge and supplement the overall skill set of the community.

Athens, Florence, London, Paris, Vienna and Berlin worked this way. Early Hollywood worked this way. Greenwich Village worked this way in the 1960s. California worked this way in the 1970s: Palo Alto in the 1980s and 1990s.

In the incorporated creative organization, to use the terminology of Davis and Scase, extrinsic motivation is the default condition of creative production. This is inevitable as soon as creativity – not craft – becomes client facing. Time, money, competition and constraint are central issues of management discourse, all of them instantly deleterious to intrinsic motivation. Rigid hierarchies don't help. A creative person faced with the choice of putting her energies into the quality of the work or into defending her position from the aggrandizing instincts of lower and higher levels of management will usually opt for the latter. Self-preservation is a more powerful drive than ambition, except in the most zealous of creative martyrs.

We shall see that the nine or 10 factors most likely to kill creativity in organizations germinate and flourish best in the dank political soil of commercial bureaucracies. Yet despite all the evidence pointing to the decline of originality across all of the creative sectors, with the possible exception of the tech and biotech industries, the trend toward the bureaucratization of the creative process now appears unstoppable.

The prognosis is as murky as the language Davis and Scase use to describe it:

> . . . formalised management processes have incorporated the creative processes – as in commercial bureaucratic forms of organisation – such that the traditional divide between management and creativity (as found in cultural bureaucracies) no longer prevails. Indeed, the former is rapidly superseding the latter as publishing, television and other sectors of the creative industries find themselves increasingly in competition with each other in regional, national and international markets. At the same time, new manifestations of network organisation have been developing, with creative processes which take the form of highly concentrated sources of energy organised in clusters . . .

And then, comparing clusters with traditional networks:

> Traditional/charismatic forms of organisation are equally structured according to informal practices but, in contrast with network organisations, their hierarchically imposed cultures, emanating from founders or owners (or their successors), demand employee compliance and, thereby, inhibit the personal autonomy, indeterminacy of outcomes, and nonconformity which are intrinsic to creativity. Although these forms of organisation are continually reproduced, particularly as a result of business start-ups and various entrepreneurial ventures in different sectors of the creative industries, they probably represent

an organisational dynamic that is in decline. It is, then, the commercial bureaucracy and the network organisation that will, increasingly, constitute the paradigms according to which creative organisations will be structured in the years ahead.

It's a shame that this is such heavy going because it's a message that should be trumpeted to the four corners of the creative economy in clear and strident voice. It's also a shame that the authors are apparently unaware of the work of Amabile if only because they would have saved me the trouble of explaining the impact on intrinsic motivation in the case of each of their four organizational types. Yet it's clear that they understand the principle. The three words that they use to describe 'the dimensions of creativity as an organisational process' – *autonomy, nonconformity* and *indeterminacy* – are the bedrock of intrinsic motivation.

Autonomy is obvious enough. It gives creative people in organizations the freedom to experiment, to use their own judgement, and to decide for themselves how to achieve the aims and objectives of the organization. It's at the top of the list of Amabile's 'work environment's stimulants to creativity'.

Nonconformity is the cultural consequence of autonomy: 'By contrast with the formally prescribed features of the bureaucratic organisation that foster conformity and stifle innovation, creative work processes explicitly encourage employees to undertake their tasks and to pursue their goals in often different and unusual ways.' Somehow nonconformity got a bad name a couple of decades ago. It might have been the peculiarly unfortunate combination of Ronald Reagan, Margaret Thatcher, AIDS and the synthesizer arriving all at once, the four horseman of the spiritual apocalypse flying the banners of McDonald's, Starbucks and 'The Age of Ritalin'. By the mid-1990s conformity had become cool, and the nonconformists were those who didn't have cell-phones and Nike sneakers.

Indeterminacy is not just a requisite condition for creativity; it is the most salient feature of the creative process, so it goes to the heart of the organizational debate. Put it this way. If you could predict the outcome of any creative task you would hardly need to employ creative people to do it. You could routinize it or mechanize it and build a factory around it. But creativity is essentially, and by definition, unpredictable. So it clearly demands an organizational structure that not only allows for indeterminacy, but one that actively encourages it. More profoundly still, the indeterminacy of the creative process suggests that the company should be shaped around its results, and that such structure as is necessary should be flexible enough to account for the unpredictability of the ideas produced. It would be absurd for a film production company, for example, to gear up for the shoot before it knows what the script demands. How do you know how many books to print until you know how popular it's going to be? How do you budget or forecast for anything in the creative sector without guessing wildly? How do you budget for innovation when the whole point of innovation is to make your forecast redundant?

When you build a factory you design it around the specifications of the product you know you are going to produce. The point of a factory is to replicate the production of the same product over and over again to the highest possible standards at the lowest possible costs. The creative factory is the opposite. Everything it produces, must, by definition, be different. If any two products are the same it stops being a creative factory and becomes a regular production line. You might have some idea of the number of ideas you need to produce, or the amount of airtime those ideas have to fill, or the minimum number of records you have to sell to keep your shareholders happy. But clearly the creative factory presents a very different kind of management challenge to a factory that produces baked beans.

> Indeed, in many work settings, the goals of the organisation will be shaped by the creative work process, with senior managers having an almost entirely supportive or facilitative function. Many research institutes, software companies, medical establishments, and particularly, media companies operate in this way. The creative work process, which depends upon the interactions of relatively autonomous employees, determines the management process rather than vice versa.

The BBC provides an excellent parable for what happens when demarcated creative organizations are taken apart in the interests of greater efficiency. Readers in countries other than the UK, to whom the politics of BBC are of little or no consequence, might wish to substitute in place of those three letters the name of their favourite creative sector company – your ad agency, your design studio, your production house. It's a parable, after all, not a story.

In the golden days of the corporation, when it was acknowledged around the world for the consistent quality of its news, entertainment and educational programming, it operated with a demarcated structure, employing a hoard of producers, writers and technicians with clearly designated creative functions. There was a massive 'creative department' with a culture of its own clearly distinct from the management and administrative functions. These were the days before it regarded itself as a brand competing against other brands in the media marketplace.

People who worked at the BBC at that time recall that the creative culture served as a powerful stimulant for experimentation and originality, glued together by common values that took the goals of the organization to heart, that is, to inform, to entertain and to educate. Individual producers had a high degree of autonomy, and management was tolerant of the non-conformity that resulted. If many of the creative people were 'redundant' in the sense that not every creative person was accountable for the amount of work they generated during a given period, their redundancy was not just tolerated, it was deliberately ignored. We have seen before that redundancy is a key principle of autonomous creative systems: it is present in species development and survival, as well as in the human brain. The management of the BBC at that time, consciously or unconsciously, understood the indeterminate nature of the creative process and organized itself accordingly. We have approximately 100 billion cells in our brains. If some of them are not working all of the time it doesn't necessarily mean that we can do without them.

In the 1980s and 1990s a new generation of managers began to infiltrate the BBC. Their agenda was to make the Corporation more 'efficient' and 'market-led'. The first wave of them was interested in accountability and cost cutting, which was fair enough. But the second wave of technocrats was determined to go much further: they would stop at nothing short of a fundamental restructuring, breaking down the walls that surrounded the creative functions, and obliging those producers who had survived the first cut to share the burden of management and administration. As new technologies, and new entrants such as Sky, began to fracture the British TV audience into different subgroups with different entertainment preferences, the organization was encouraged to adopt the language and structure of traditional marketing companies. Someone decided that the BBC was a brand that needed to behave like a brand, so marketing – rather than creativity – became the core agenda.

This became clear in the 2006 restructuring by new director general Mark Thompson who decided to put 'Marketing, Communications and Audiences' at the centre of the management hub. He told the staff, 'We need a BBC ready for digital and for 360 degree multi-platform content creation, which brings different kinds of creativity together – in technology as well as content – to deliver what we need in this converging world.' This is familiar to anyone who has spent time chained to the leg of a boardroom table and forced to listen to a new marketing director's vision for the future. The implication is clear. If you're not hip enough to download a podcast perhaps you shouldn't be working here. Or in Mark Thompson's own words, '. . . if this doesn't sound like your kind of place, then it's time for you to decide if the BBC is right for you'.

The audience, who were duly paying their licence fees to sustain all this, were now described as clients, and the new management became obsessed with the things that traditional marketing companies obsess about – strategic planning, brand planning, brand visioning and the many and abstruse measures of consumer feedback, handing over the soul of the organization to the high priests of marketing, the brand consultants who read the future in the entrails of the chicken sandwiches left over from the focus groups.

Someone calling himself or herself JugHead captured the consequent displacement of creative purpose in this blog to *The Guardian's* 'Organgrinder' website:

> Marketing, Communications and Audiences at the centre of the creative process?? I'm sure this will go down great guns with the old school Beeb producers. They've been bringing in various audience insight and other such people (to predict the future) for a long time. The producers always sit politely through the meetings and then ignore it all and fly by their instinct.

The producers clearly know where their intrinsic motivation lies, and it's not in that room.

And a word about that '360 degree multi-platform content creation' thing for those of you wondering what kind of drugs Mr Thompson has been taking.

The '360 degree' part of it is a phrase that comes directly out of The New Age Marketer's Dictionary of Platitudes and Euphemisms. It derives from ad-agency-speak of the early 1990s when it became a fashionable way of claiming that your ad agency didn't just make ads, the salience of which needs some historical context.

You might have heard of the phrases 'above-the-line' and 'below-the-line'. In the old days of advertising, when agencies were paid a commission based on a percentage of the media bought on a client's behalf, agency accountants drew a line between revenues accruing from the commission and those revenues that came from other sources, such as designing a client's logo, helping her with a sales conference, her promotions, and any of the other services that did not fall into the commissionable area. Above-the-line referred to the advertising side, the work that had a media consequence. Below-the-line referred to all the other stuff that no one really wanted to do but you had to in order to keep the client happy. Above-the-line became the sexy side of the business, attracting the most ambitious creative talents because of the opportunities it offered for fame and fortune. The juniors were set to work on the below-the-line projects.

Sometime in the mid-1980s 'the line' became the focus of controversy among clients who wanted their agencies to take a more holistic view of their marketing programmes. They wanted their promotions and pack designs and sales conferences to be taken just as seriously as their advertising plans. This was about the time they began to talk about their agencies as 'communications partners'. If the creative people were less than enthusiastic about dirtying their hands with below-the-line work, the agency managers were quick to take advantage of these abundant new streams of potential revenue. Within two or three years they had set up direct mail departments, promotional departments, design and packaging departments, event marketing departments, new media departments and sales marketing departments, each with their own financials. Soon there was an agency department for every line item in the client's marketing budget. If all of them were manned by the same three people it still looked mightily impressive on the agency's operational flowchart.

Agency profits soared, but the clients soon smelled a rat. Far from getting rid of the distinction between above- and below-the-line, the new departmental structure had consolidated it. They began to apply even more pressure on their agencies to bring all marketing communications, or 'marcoms', to the centre of the agency business where it would get the attention of the best creatives, the best planners and the agency managers themselves. They wanted 'through-the-line' agencies, integrated marketing agencies, total communication agencies. As the agencies began to tear themselves apart in an effort to meet client expectations, some bright spark came up with the idea of '360 degrees service'. What it meant in theory, for the agencies that adopted this spankingly modern new positioning, was that they would deliver 'media neutral' recommendations to their clients, ideas that might or might not contain an advertising component. What it meant in practice was that business went on as usual except for a few additional MBAs who sat around the table talking about customer relationship models and alternative media proposals and guerilla marketing exercises that would all cost a great deal of money but were well worth it.

So when Mark Thompson was talking about '360 degrees' the phrase was loaded with the loathing that clients had for creative companies that believed their only job was to deliver brilliant and sexy new creative ideas that would bring them fame and fortune.

'Multi-platform content creation' was code for saying that the content didn't matter as long as it was delivered in really interesting Web 2.0 ways, another triumph of media over message, and another triumph of marketing over magic.

Slowly and inexorably the quality of the BBC's work began to decline, but since this was no longer the point of the organization it didn't really matter. A quota system was introduced to ensure that independent production companies got their fair share of budget and to create competition in the marketplace for independence. This didn't help. No one realized that competition had a negative effect on quality because the independent suppliers were now pitching only the most bankable ideas. The autonomy of the producers was curtailed, redundancy was excised, noncomformity was taboo, and indeterminacy was replaced by predictable controls and processes of the typical commercial bureaucracy.

In the space of less than 20 years the BBC was transformed from a demarcated organization into a commercial bureaucracy with all the features and elements of a commercial bureaucracy, except for one thing – it wasn't commercial. The cluster of suppliers and independents that sprang up to replace those parts of the Corporation that were no longer efficient or accountable became craven sycophants to a system that valued predictability over originality. The rest went home to their garrets and sheds and spare bedrooms and the hope of making a living from the occasional bits of freelance work that fell off the table.

In early 2007, the stupidity of successive restructuring made itself visibly manifest in the idiotic branding device that the BBC used as a filler before the news. It showed various news men and women in different parts of the world beaming images back home to west London via a series of red (because BBC One's brand colour is red) image streams bouncing off various satellite dishes all clearly branded with the BBC logo as though we needed to be reminded that

BBC reporters were responsible for beaming BBC news to the BBC. It tried so hard to be digitally hip, but it has the thumbprints of marketing's dead hand all over it.

A straw in the wind, maybe, but it said almost everything that needed to be said about the pseudo-commercial monster that the Corporation has become.

If the BBC is still recognized around the world as one of the most innovative and entertaining media producers it is thanks only to the fact that similar organizations in other countries were commercialized many years before. It is also, one must say, a tribute to the intelligence and the tenacity of the creative and production people that have refused to succumb to the commercial illusion. When Jeremy Paxman refused to read the newly introduced weather forecast on Newsnight beyond saying so memorably one April night in 2005, as a weather system of rain moved across the UK in the background, 'It's April – what do you expect?', he was drawing a line in the sand. But it's a line in retreat.

In 2006 the BBC was asked to budget for the amount it would need from licence fees to fund its operations for the next decade. Since no one at the BBC had either the gumption or the arguments needed to make out a strong enough case for the importance of public funding, future budgets were slashed. The principle of indirect public funding is still, thankfully, intact. But in the next few years, as diminishing revenues from licence fees oblige people like the current director general to make more and more 'hard choices' about where and how the money is to be deployed, the debilitating effects of two decades of poor decision making will be felt where it hurts the most, on the screen in your living room.

The BBC is only one example of how we ignore the new imperatives of creativity management at our peril. What makes it so particularly egregious is that it has inflicted upon itself all of the negative dynamics of a commercial bureaucracy without the excuse of having to do so in response to commercial pressures. Despite what the people who run the Corporation might think, the BBC is not a service. Of course it must bring us the news and the weather and the time. And it's wonderful that it is also prepared to bring us all that very informative stuff you'll find on its website. But anyone can do that, and many of them do. No, the BBC is there to make things. And those things are the ideas that inform us, the ideas that entertain us and the ideas that educate us.

*

In order to make ideas you need an organization that is structured around them – that is structured for them and because of them. You need management that understands the difference between craft and creativity, and that appreciates the vital role that intrinsic motivation plays in making the most of the latter. It needs to remind itself constantly that good ideas come from individuals, not groups. Those individuals need a culture of experimentation to feed off, and a management culture that is sensitive to their need for autonomy, and tolerant of their nonconformity. And all of this can happen only in an environment that honours and cherishes creativity as a resource that is different in kind and in capability from the other functions of the organization, a resource that is as redundant as most of the human brain – and just as unpredictable.

The creative economy consists of thousands and thousands of companies that differ vastly, in both scale and complexity, from a typical Ndebele village. Yet many of them are still unprepared to learn the simple lessons of creative management that the Ndebele tribe implements as naturally as bees finding honey.

And only a few of them have produced anything quite as memorable or remarkable as those colourful facades.

CHAPTER 16

The maze

'Salvation,' Mimi said, 'is a word denoting "Being led out of the space-time maze, where the servant has become the master."'

Philip K. Dick, *Valis*

There is a story told of a Genoese merchant who, by the mediation of Cosimo, prevailed upon Donatello to make a bronze head for him. When it was finished, the merchant coming to pay him thought that Donatello asked too much, so the matter was referred to Cosimo. He had it brought to the upper court of the palace and placed it on the wall overlooking the street, that it might be seen better. But when he tried to settle the difference, he found the merchant's offer very much below Donatello's demand, and turning to him he said it was too little. The merchant who thought it too much, answered that Donatello had worked upon it for a month, or a little more and that he would give him more than half a florin a day. Donatello upon that turned upon him in anger thinking these words too great an insult, and telling the merchant that he had found means in a hundredth part of an hour to destroy the work of a year, he gave the head a sudden blow and knocked it down into the street, where it was broken into many pieces, adding that it was evident that he was in the habit of bargaining about beans and not statues. The merchant repenting, offered to give him double as much if he would make it again, but neither his promises nor Cosimo's entreaties could make him consent.

Giorgio Vasari, *Lives of the Artists*

We are in the habit of bargaining about beans, not statues. So we have forgotten that creativity cannot be bought, it can only be paid for.

For all the talk of how creativity is the only thing that can save us from economic, political and social stagnation, we have yet to understand that it is not a commodity. It cannot be harvested like beans or manufactured like frying pans. It cannot be traded on the NASDAQ or bottled like 'Shhh . . .' or Chanel No. 5. It cannot be planned for except in the broadest and most forgiving sense. It cannot be predicted or floated on the stock exchange. Financial analysts on Bloomberg will refer to it as the engine of growth, but it has yet to appear on the scrolling ticker tape.

Creativity can only be seduced into existence. Wishing for it and hoping for it will help; appreciating it will help even more. But the only thing that will guarantee its appearance is an understanding of the conditions in which it thrives, and the removal of those factors inimical to its germination.

Teresa Amabile draws on the analogy of the maze to help us picture how ideas happen. One could equally imagine an enchanted forest, a featureless desert or a hall of mirrors. The premise of the analogy must simply be a place in which it is easy to get lost, that doesn't appear to have any easy escape route, that demands exploration and that is rich in the promise of buried treasure. Creative people have different ways of describing this strange, dreamlike realm of illumination. I have heard it compared to a rainbow, a roller coaster, a field of dreams, a house of leaves, a book of blank pages, an odyssey, Wonderland, Middle Earth and a monkey-puzzle tree. For Coleridge it was 'Kubla Khan'. For creative people growing up in the a 60s it was 'Lucy in the Sky with Diamonds', a boat on a river under marmalade skies.

Physiologically, we know, it is a journey into the alpha state, the sudden cessation of beta's insistent noise, a reduced heart rate and a lower galvanic skin response. Or, as Nietzsche says, 'For art to be possible at all – that is to say, in order that an aesthetic mode of action and of observation may exist, a certain preliminary physiological state is indispensable: ecstasy.'

Emotionally it is experienced as a deep and reassuring trance, a state of being that is at once tranquil and thrilling. It combines the excitement of the unknown with a Zen-like calm; it is a place that simultaneously urges you to stay in forever and to escape from immediately in fear of your sanity, a place in which you are both fully attentive and oddly numb. This is Auden's description:

> Sometimes we see astonishingly clearly
> The out-there when we are already in . . .

But Amabile is not known for her flights of fancy so we'll stay with the maze, the reductionist's version of the glade of the unicorns. It is almost culturally neutral, and it's easy to draw. Also, for those of you who have been following the Adventures of Exit Five with such unswerving devotion, it is familiar.

For the sake of simplicity Amabile gives her maze, which is shaped in a rigid rectangle, five clearly demarcated exits. Exit One is straight ahead. When you get into the maze, the light you see in the distance is Exit One promising you an easy way out. The path to Exit One bypasses the library, the playground and the cellar. Getting to Exit Two is a little trickier. The maze twists and turns and leads to several frustrating dead ends. You'll be forced to retreat through the library before you find the right path. The way to Exit Three is even more complicated, and ankle deep in unicorn dung. The library and the playground become more important. You will need luck, judgement and a large spade. Very few people ever get to Exit Four or Exit Five so accounts are sketchy. All I can say is that you'll know them when you see them.

Amabile's diagram is misleading, but we'll live with it. In reality, as anyone who has spent time in the maze will tell you, the borders of the maze are 'infinitely porous' like the borders of Afghanistan as described by Donald Rumsfeld. Though you will have some sort of vaguely defined goal when you enter, you have no idea when or where you'll come out. It could be at Exit Two-Point-Five-Seven-Five-Four. Or it could be under a thorn tree.

The maze is the part of the creative process variously described as 'illumination', 'inspiration', 'the Eureka moment' or, more mundanely, 'having an idea'. And since having an idea is the only part of the creative process that actually matters you would think it to be the chief subject of concern for those who write about these things. But that clearly hasn't been the case, as we have seen. There's a very simple reason for this striking omission from the literature – it's the only part of the creative process that can't be described as a process.

De Bono's pseudo-neurological description, in *The Mechanism of Mind*, provides a useful visual image of the rivulets of hot water that need to be connected if we are to make mental leaps across the cortical jelly. But it stops well short of explaining why some people can do this with ease and some people can't seem to do it at all. So it is no more useful than saying that ideas happen when unusual connections are made in our neural pathways, which in our present state of neurological knowledge is the equivalent of saying that it happens by magic.

William Calvin, who believes that ideas must fight to survive the journey from unconscious to conscious in the same way that spermatozoa must fight their way to the front of the queue has a framework for thinking about how certain ideas get selected in favour of others. His micro-Darwinian explanation is compelling, especially for those ideas that clearly have an adaptive purpose, such as being able to find a solution to the wobbly chair problem. But he wisely refrains from attempting to extend this theory to explain the inspiration behind Giorgione's *Tempest* or why Charlie Chaplin elected to wear that moustache.

Illumination remains the black box of creativity. You can't take the lid off without destroying everything inside, just as you can't pin down a subatomic particle without killing Schroedinger's cat. Scalpels won't work, and nor will Pandora's curiosity. The air is thick with the hideous flapping creatures unleashed by her direct descendants: Osborn, de Bono, van Oech, Vance and the industrious Mr Plsek.

The maze is a metaphor, not a description. Nor is it an analogy, like the hot water and the jelly – and it's certainly not a process. There is real danger here. For the past few years I have been talking about the maze to a wide variety of audiences around the world. I have seen the concupiscent delight on the faces of those to whom it appears a parting of the veils, a revelation of the flesh, an invitation to consummate the long-sought union of creativity and predictability. Amabile's linear schematic, the rectangular outline and the five exits, looks for all the world as though the lid of the black box has been lifted, and that the maze within is no more mysterious than a printed circuit, or an aerial view of Hampton Court. I have seen the eagerness with which they have translated it into a process that can be replicated, routinized and deskilled – Five Simple Steps to Creative Glory. I saw the maze become The Maze, and I recoiled in horror. Now it bears a massive disclaimer saying: THIS IS NOT A HUMAN BRAIN.

Amabile came up with the maze as a way of explaining the difference between extrinsic motivation and intrinsic motivation:

> One person might be motivated to make it through the maze as quickly and safely as possible in order to get a tangible reward, such as money – the same way a mouse would rush through for a piece of cheese. This person would look for the simplest, most straightforward path and then take it . . . This approach, based on extrinsic motivation, will indeed get him out of the maze. But the solution that arises from the process is likely to be unimaginative.

Another person might have a different approach to the maze. She might actually find the process of wandering around the different path – the challenge and exploration itself – fun and intriguing. No doubt, this journey will take longer and include mistakes, because any maze . . . has many more dead ends than exits. But when the intrinsically motivated person does find a way out of the maze . . . it very likely will be more interesting than the rote algorithm. It will be more creative.

That's the whole point of the maze, and the only point. Assuming you have the appropriate craft skills and a creative brain, the quality of the creativity you get out of the black box will depend almost exclusively on the nature of the motivation with which you approach the task. Extrinsic motivation will hurry you through the maze. You will seek out the nearest exits. Intrinsic motivation will encourage you to explore many more pathways, increasing the likelihood of you reaching the furthest exits and, hence, the most original and innovative results.

I suspect that everyone has been into the maze at one time or another, even if he or she has never shown any outward signs of hostility or psychosis. You know you're in there when the noise of your surroundings suddenly mutes, your vision blurs, you lose your sense of space and time, and you feel, when you suddenly snap out of it, that you've been in some sort of a trance. Sometimes it's just a daydream, but if you really were in the maze it will almost certainly have been a productive one. Sometimes you go into the maze and wander around for a little while and you come out the entrance again and you find yourself back where you started with nothing resolved and nothing gained.

Daydreams are good for us in all sorts of ways, just as real dreaming is. It refreshes us mentally and emotionally, freeing the mind, if only temporarily, from the concerns of the moment. But the feeling of entering the maze in an active search for something is slightly different. It's a managed daydream, a forced reverie, a deliberate embarkation.

The experience of solving a problem is both qualitatively and psychologically different from the experience of entering the maze. The maze is open-ended, non-linear and discontinuous. Solving a problem calls into play the heuristics of intelligence. When you want to solve the problem of your wobbly chair you use a specific set of algorithms. You consider replacing your chair with another one. You consider sawing off the bottom of the other three legs to make them equal in length to the one that's giving you a problem. You then consider putting something under the wobbly leg and you scan the room in the hope of finding an appropriate object. Paper will do nicely because you can fold it to the exact thickness required. That is not the maze – it is the intelligence you inherited from three million years of primate evolution. We are clever creatures, and we have been blessed with brains that are good at solving the problems that threaten our survival and our comfort.

The maze is an entirely different order of experience. It is not an engagement so much as a letting go.

Take the example of 30 kids in a classroom. In the years before the self-consciousness of adolescence destroys those last shreds of intrinsic motivation that haven't already been obliterated by an educational system intent on reducing all intellectual endeavour to the production of acceptable outcomes, children have a natural inclination towards the random and naïve imaginings so necessary for creativity. Let's imagine that the class of pre-adolescents – nine and 10 year olds, for instance – is asked to write a story that begins with the sentence, 'I woke up with a terrible fright.'

For all of them, assuming their imaginations are still intact, this is a wonderful opportunity to express themselves. It's an invitation to an open-ended fantasy that should have them scrambling for pen and ink. But it isn't quite as simple as that. The quality of the stories that come out of the exercise will vary wildly, from awful through indifferent to good or brilliant, all depending on one single variable – the balance of intrinsic and extrinsic motivation experienced by the individual child.

Some of them will see it as a problem to be solved, such as how to write the story in a way that will please the teacher. Some of them will have basic craft issues that dial up the extrinsic motivation, such as bad handwriting or a problem with spelling, things that they know or believe to be an irritation to the teacher. Some of them might love the idea of inventing the story but find the physical act of writing too tedious and too difficult as a means of communication. Some of them might remember how angry the teacher was with the bad punctuation of the boy at the back and be afraid to commit the same mistakes. Some of them, knowing that they are slow writers, might be worried about the time they will take to write their stories. Some of them will self-censor their ideas because they don't want the teacher to know what kind of weird stuff goes on in their heads. Even if she's the nicest teacher in the world there will be a thousand factors, perceived or real, that have the potential to choke the creative impulse.

Some of them will have confidence in their craft skills and plunge ahead. The clever ones will write clever stories with clever endings. One of them will know that you can fill up a lot of space by writing dialogue. One of them will have seen a movie just like this on a DVD the night before. And one of them, the problem child with the brooding eyes and the dirty fingernails, the girl who has long since stopped caring about spelling and punctuation and the difference between verbs and adjectives, will reach into a dream and write a dark and chilling tale that will make the teacher's hair stand on end when she gets round to marking it next Saturday just after midnight.

How do we legislate for a teaching environment that's more conducive to creativity? We could devote more classroom time to the kind of open-ended thinking skills of programmes recommended by Debby Evans and other experts in the field. We could make more time for play and art and music and games. And we could make a much clearer distinction between craft skills that need to be learned, like maths, science, spelling and vocabulary development, and those that are open to individual interpretation, like religious studies and history and creative writing.

Kids need to know which is which. They need to understand that learning the times tables and learning to write 'their' instead of 'there' is not optional. They are craft skills that are the foundations of all future progress. Certainly we can teach these things in interesting ways, but the children need to know that they are not part of a game. But when it comes to other subjects, those that cannot be taught without engaging the imagination of the child, we need to change the mood, the environment, the media, maybe even the teacher.

But the best thing we could do is train teachers to understand the difference between craft skills and creativity, and the difference between extrinsic and intrinsic motivation, so that they know when to apply the former and when to encourage the latter.

When you only have a carrot and a stick everyone looks like a donkey.

*

When I consider all the organizations I have studied and worked with over the past 22 years, there can be no doubt: creativity gets killed much more often that it gets supported. For the most part, this isn't because managers have a vendetta against creativity. On the contrary, most believe in the value of new and useful ideas. However, creativity is undermined unintentionally every day in work environments that were established – for entirely good reasons – to maximize business imperatives such as co-ordination, productivity and control.

That's how Teresa Amabile begins her *Harvard Business Review* article 'How to Kill Creativity'. It gets worse and worse, or better and better, depending on where you sit. It's worth bearing in mind, as we begin to look at the specific factors that kill creativity, that Amabile isn't talking about the way the Pharaohs got the slaves to build the pyramids. Her analysis is based on research into contemporary management practice in blue chip companies with sophisticated human resource departments and famous CEOs. So she measures her words very carefully indeed, abjures wild and irresponsible generalizations, and relates her findings with commendable academic restraint.

Of all the creativity killers the deadliest by far is constraint.

Constraint is the carbon monoxide of social and work organizations. It is silent, invisible and pervasive. It emanates from the culture itself; it surrounds you, deprives you of oxygen, and slowly but surely suffocates you to death. It's difficult to detect. You can't put your finger on the leaking pipe.

Sometimes you might be able to trace it coming from that corner office where the micro-managing technocrat is poring over plans for another corporate restructure. Sometimes you will be able to read its symptoms in the strained voice of a colleague, in the red eyes of a secretary, in the headaches that stiffen your neck and blur your vision. But usually it is much less obvious because it is built into the fabric of everything that surrounds you. When you touch your computer is permeates your skin and gets into your bloodstream.

Constraint is the accommodation we make with the people we choose to lead us, the contract that limits our freedom in exchange for comfort. This is no bad thing in a society that values human rights, the rule of law, individual liberty and freedom of expression. The politics of western liberal democracies, here at the end of history, concern themselves with the precise location of the line between liberty and licence. But there's no longer much of an argument about whether or not we need that line, except, of course, among religious extremists.

But not all societal constraints are as explicit as the laws governing crime, taxation and the use and misuse of bicycle paths. They can appear apparently from nowhere, like clouds in a blue sky. They cannot be legislated for or against; they are simply a consequence of the chaotic system we call society.

The best and most obvious example is political correctness, a particularly noxious form of constraint that has us dancing around the dictionary in search of safe stepping-stones. Clearly it has its origins in the good intentions of the laws protecting people from discrimination of all kinds. But it has taken on a life of its own, contaminating the everyday discourse of politicians, the media and the citizenry with an epidemic of constraints more pernicious than parking tickets precisely because there is no warning sign advertising the rules and regulations that govern them. The codes of political correctness are as inscrutable as the laws of Salem and enforced with commensurate vigour. The burning of witches no longer takes place in the village square – they are far more public than that. The audience that drooled through the immolation of Jade Goody in the Big Brother house was measured in millions.

Constraint is the voice that whispers in the back of your brain, like the famous ad for *The Independent*, reminding you not to raise your voice in public, not to disagree too vehemently with the people at the dinner party, not to embarrass yourself in front of strangers, not to let the children shriek so loudly, not to interrupt, not to bargain, not to question, not to stand still and not to move too fast. These are the magazines that tell you how to have sex, and the TV shows that tell you how to dress. These are the quiet and reasonable words of teachers and priests and politicians and bureaucrats that persuade you not to challenge, not to question and not to think too much. These are the constraints of living life second hand, an existence mediated by experts who know better, or celebrities who know best.

Like a low, incessant noise that eventually sounds like silence, this isn't something we're conscious of most of the time. And when we do become aware of it we often put it down to the voice of conscience, a comforting, regulating sort of creature that soothes and reassures with the liquid syllables of righteousness.

It's worse for Protestants than it is for Catholics, worse for Muslims than for Hindus, and worse for agnostics than for atheists. It's much worse for liberals than for conservatives. Buddhists and Baha'is get off lightly.

It's only when we enter the maze that we confront it for what it is. The whispers echo through the empty corridors, becoming louder and louder the further we go. We make out the voices of our mothers and fathers, brothers and sisters, husbands and wives, sons and lovers, advising, restraining, guiding, leading, admonishing, cross-fading into the babble of teachers and friends and neighbours and newsreaders, rising and falling, cautioning, calling in a chorus of shibboleths, this way not that way, that way not this. We find pathways closed with bans and embargoes, doorways curtained with taboos we dare not push aside. Our fears increase with every turn we take, fears of rejection, fears of abandonment, fears of crossing a line we never knew was there. There are areas of light and shade. We are attracted down the sunlit lanes of memory full of the promise of childhood innocence and the comfort of the familiar. But they take us back to where we began and we must set out anew, into the darkness of the unknown. There is nothing to guide us further, and the torch of courage begins to splutter. Think Harrison Ford in *Dante's Inferno*.

I was recently invited to speak at Hungary's premier advertising festival where I was treated to a showreel of the top 20 ads produced by that country's fledgling advertising industry. I wasn't expecting very much, which turned out to be just as well. There were one or two interesting parodies of life under communism, but the majority of the spots were anaemic attempts to mimic the advertising conventions of Western Europe. In discussions with the creative directors who had put the ads together I found them unanimously ashamed of the work that had been produced. They were angry and frustrated, despondent and desperate. Some of them blamed the clients for having no imagination. Some of them blamed a long history of oppression. One of them came to me afterwards and owned up to the truth.

We were standing outside in a light rain that speckled the paving stones on the veranda where we stood. In the distance we could see small, white sails scudding across the lake outside Tata. He pointed at his feet, the line between two paving stones separating one brown cowboy boot from the other. 'Whenever I am thinking of ideas,' he said, 'I feel as though I have one foot in advertising and the other foot in the church.'

During all those years under the communist jackboot, the church came to represent his only avenue for freedom of thought and expression. When the future arrived he was overwhelmed by its dazzling new liberties, boundless, endless and uncircumscribed. So he clung even more fiercely to the tenets of his faith, with its familiar boundaries and its comforting prescriptions. The Hungarians were suffering from the fear of freedom.

Religious faith is no more of a barrier to creativity than being an Arsenal fan. But blind religiosity, superstition and all forms of doctrinaire fanaticism will turn large tracts of the maze into no-go areas. Fear of any kind fuels extrinsic motivation – fear of failure, fear of offending, fear of authority, fear of doing something wrong, and fear of fear itself. Anything to do with making or losing money promotes fear unless, of course, you have lots and lots of it – 'fuck you money' as it is commonly called.

When creative sector companies become commercial bureaucracies they expose their creative people to all of the constraints and to all of the fears and anxieties associated with the management of time and money. The maze demands that you risk everything in the search for the highest exits. The responsibility of management demands that you risk the barest minimum in the search for higher productivity and profitability. These two styles of thinking are not only mutually incompatible, they are mutually exclusive.

Just as the greed of loggers and soya farmers continues to destroy massive tracts of rain forest with every passing year, the copyright hoarders are making vast tracts of the maze inaccessible to creative exploration. The constraint of copyright protection that now applies to so much of our knowledge and experience litters the maze with landmines that cannot be detected or defused without the help of expensive lawyers. With so much of the maze out of bounds to free intellectual enquiry, it's little wonder that the path to Exit Five becomes more dangerous and difficult by the day.

All kinds of constraint kill creativity, except one – the constraint of a tight brief. Clearly defined objectives for a creative task will usually enhance creativity simply because they define the boundaries of the maze. Without the clarity of a goal the maze has no boundaries and the area of exploration extends beyond the limits of the imagination. The possibilities may be endless but the exits are unreachable.

The maze needs a shape – a canvas, a sonnet, a sonata, a business objective, a ceiling of a chapel. In advertising they call it 'the freedom of a tight brief', or what Adrian Holmes calls 'thinking inside the box'. It doesn't matter if the shape of the maze is self-imposed or imposed by someone else, as long as all other constraints are left behind at the entrance. Rembrandt chose to use only three colours in all his paintings. The brief for Michelangelo's Pietà was precise and unequivocal:

Be it known that manifest to all who shall read this present writing that the Most Reverend Cardinal di San Dionisio has agreed that

Maestro Michelangelo, statuary of Florence, that the said Maestro shall at his own proper costs make a Pietà of marble: that is to say, a draped figure of the Virgin Mary with the dead Christ in her arms, the figures being life-size, for the sum of four hundred and fifty gold ducats in papal gold, to be finished within the term of one year from the beginning of the work.

Few advertising briefs are as tight as that.

The opposite of constraint is autonomy, the freedom to explore the maze in your own way and on your own terms. Of all the factors that contribute to intrinsic motivation none is more enabling, more stimulating, or more of an aphrodisiac than the freedom from constraint.

Because the brief itself delineates the outline of the maze, which should be the only constraint of any given creative task, it's a good thing to get the agreement of the creative people before work begins. Michelangelo would not have agreed to the brief to the Pietà if he hadn't considered the time frame reasonable and the project achievable.

Amabile describes two ways in which executives commonly mismanage creative freedom:

First, managers tend to change goals frequently or fail to define them clearly. Employees may have freedom around process, but if they don't know where they are headed, such freedom is pointless. And second, some managers fall short on this dimension by granting autonomy in name only. They claim that employees are 'empowered' to explore the maze as they search for solutions, but, in fact, the process is prescribed. Employees diverge at their own risk.

To use another Amabile metaphor, 'People will be more creative . . . if you give them freedom to decide how to climb a particular mountain. You needn't let them choose which mountain to climb.'

Creative people who work independently, such as authors and artists, will clearly choose the mountain and the way they want to climb it. In creative organizations it is the prerogative of management to define the objectives, as it is in all other commercial organizations. Creative people don't have a problem with that. It's when managers instruct them how to get to the top that intrinsic motivation gets annihilated.

We should be absolutely clear about what 'freedom of process' means. It means that in the period between the brief and the creative solution, complete autonomy needs to be granted to the creative people involved. This includes the freedom to work on it where they want to, when they want to and how they want to. It means that they must be trusted to use their time and available resources in the way that suits them, not in the way that suits the company. It means that their performance will be measured only on the quality of the result and not on the way in which they went about getting there. This requires total trust on the part of management, and complete responsibility on the part of the creatives. Any interference during the creative process can only be harmful.

It isn't easy to do this in a commercial bureaucracy. Managers like to know what their employees are doing and how they are doing it. They tend to get twitchy when they hear that the creatives are down at the club playing darts or that they have blown the budget on a trip to Morocco for no apparent reason. It's bad enough when managers catch them staring out of the window, feet on the desk, arms folded, computers switched off and silence prevailing. The modern office is probably the worst place in the world to come up with an idea, especially now that the open-plan system has robbed creative people of both silence and privacy. But even if they have their own space, they still breath the toxic air of office politics, read the toxic emails and take calls on the toxic telephone.

Or you can do it the other way around. The first time I visited SCPF in Barcelona, Spain's most consistently brilliant advertising agency, I was struck to see all the creative people working in one large open barn. The managers and the account people were locked away in separate offices with walls that sealed off the sound of their conversations and the ringing of their phones from the ears of the creatives. The message was very clear – creative people need to breathe creative air. The creative barn felt like sacred space, uncontaminated by anything other than the dedication to make new things. In the corner stood the Statue of Chaos made of Coke tins, rubber bands and a broken bicycle, arms raised in a gesture that blessed the madness. That was the first time I understood how freedom of process could operate in a commercial environment, and it laid the foundations for a project that came to be known as The Idea Hotel.

I began to wonder what an environment would look like if it were built around the principle of intrinsic motivation. How different would it have to look from a normal office? How different would it have to feel? How would projects be managed through the creative space? I knew it would need an elite group of creatives handpicked for their brilliant craft skills and their unrelenting passion to produce great work. I knew it would need some sort of management, some kind of interaction with the outside world, and a large and regular dose of diversity. It would have to accommodate complete autonomy and nonconformity, and be structured around the indeterminacy of the creative output.

But first I had to make sure that I could irradiate all of the creativity killers while simultaneously building into the structure and the operation all those factors conducive to intrinsic motivation.

*

After constraint, the second most dangerous obstacle to creativity is organizational disinterest. The organization must care about the results, and the creative people must know that it cares. This seems painfully obvious. Common sense would suggest that companies that depend for their existence of the quality of the creative work they produce would naturally be interested in the ideas emerging from the maze. But it is by no means always the case that the managers of creative sector companies are drawn to those positions by their passion for the creative product. They might be drawn to them because they seem sexy and cool. Or they might be drawn to them because of the rapid growth of the creative economy and they seem like a good financial bet.

The bigger creative organizations get, and the more global they become, the more likely they are to recruit managers from other business sectors. These would typically be people who are good at managing systems and processes; people who don't care whether the factory turns out movies or pork pies. In contrast to the serious and pressing concerns of managing large amounts of money, negotiating massive IT contracts and allocating parking spaces, the script for a new comedy slot or the pilot for a new video game will seem of trivial consequence.

The demotivating effect of this kind of management attitude is self-evident. But organizational disinterest in the creative product becomes even more devastating when you look at it in the context of the maze.

Take a project that has all the ingredients of spectacular success. The brief is clear and free of constraint. It is perfectly matched to the skills of the creative team and rich in the promise of mouth-watering gratification. Intrinsic motivation is at an all-time high.

The creatives enter the maze and begin their exploration. They very quickly get through the easy options, bypassing Exit One and Exit Two. Driven on by determination and a passion for adventure they explore the cul-de-sacs around Exit Three, and it doesn't take long for them to discover the door. They know they've got something good. But the stakes are higher now, they have time for reflection and they urge each other back into the maze.

Flashes of inspiration lead them to Exit Four. They've never been here before and the lights of glory beckon. It would be easy enough to stop here and cash in on their efforts but they simply mark the spot and press on back into the darkness. Somewhere in there they know there's another exit, a place you don't get to many times in your career. It's so close they can almost taste it. Hours go by. Days go by. They circle back to Exit Four and regroup. They beg for more time and they get it.

Life continues. Everything around them suggests a way forward, a conversation overheard on a bus, a snatch of music from a child's bedroom, a documentary about crocodile farming, the idiosyncratic smile of the weatherman. They gather up these bits and pieces and head back into the maze. They begin to see connections that weren't there before. Doors open where there were only walls. The accidental push on a protruding brick opens a secret trapdoor. And suddenly they are there: Exit Five. Pulses racing, hearts pounding, they step out into the light. But instead of a welcoming committee showering them with roses there is empty silence, a vacant hall, the drip of rainwater into a bucket.

The doors are locked and the windows are closed. Fluorescent tubes flicker overhead. The creatives holler for attention and bang on the doors. No response. They fall asleep on the hard wooden benches.

They are awoken by the sound of someone fiddling with the lock. It's a junior account manager in search of printer ink. He's surprised to find them in there.

'Where is everybody?' they ask.

'At a conference somewhere,' she says. 'Venice, I think.'

*

The next time they venture into the maze it's at a different company, where ideas are valued and originality is cherished.

*

Organizational disinterest kills creativity by demeaning the best efforts of creative people, devaluing their status, undermining their self-belief and sabotaging their passion.

But it's worse than that because it allows expediency to set the standards of acceptability. Here's what I mean . . .

A bright young talent, fresh from a good school and a thorough apprenticeship, joins a creative sector company with high hopes and huge ambitions. It could be a design company, a publishing company, a fashion studio, an ad agency, an interior design firm, a television production company, it doesn't matter which.

She is thrilled to get her first assignment, a challenging task that will require real imagination and a lot of perseverance. She is naïve, misty-eyed, passionate, keen as mustard. But she is smart enough to make sure that the brief is crystal clear and the goalposts are firmly rooted in place.

She finds out everything she can about the project. She reads widely, questions everyone she knows who might be of help, looks at the history and the future trends, and does a thorough review of the entire domain. She is nothing if not diligent. Then she plunges into the maze.

She thinks about it day and night. It obsesses her. She dreams about it, and in her dreams she gets glimpses of the extraordinary possibilities that lie ahead. She uses the inspiration of her dreams to guide her. She is energetic, determined and fearless. The cul de sacs make her even more focused. She is not disheartened by the long empty passages that lead nowhere, that turn on themselves in torturous coils. She ignores the flicker of light from the easy exits. She doesn't care. She has nothing to lose. Obsession turns into compulsion, and compulsion drives her forward on her very first try she arrives at Exit Five. No one is there to meet her. She is confused. It must be the wrong exit. She turns back into the maze, still as determined as ever. She comes out at Exit Four. It is silent and empty. She turns back into the maze, disorientated and anxious. No one at Exit Three, no one at Exit Two.

Finally she stumbles out of Exit One.

'Brilliant!' says the senior account man.

'Great job!' says the junior account executive snatching the work from her hand.

'The taxi's waiting,' says the even more junior account person looking anxiously at her watch.

'You've saved our lives,' says the senior account man.

'What took you so long?' says the junior account executive, not without sympathy.

'The client just called,' says the even more junior account person even more anxiously.

'Tell her we're on our way,' says the senior account man giving the creative an affectionate kiss on the cheek.

'Thanks again,' says the junior account executive.

The taxi roars off through the traffic. The creative stands on the pavement. They seem to be very pleased with me, she thinks to herself, still dazed and confused. Shame they weren't at Exit Five.

The next time she goes into the maze she's a little wiser and a little less enthusiastic. She doesn't make it to Exit Five, but she's pleased with what she has at Exit Four. Again there's no one to be found. Same thing at Exit Three and Exit Two.

With real resignation she finds her way back to Exit One. Once again she is greeted with enthusiasm and much gratitude.

The next time she goes into the maze she saves herself the bother of looking for the other exits. She heads straight for Exit One.

This job is easier than I thought, she thinks as she watches the taxi roar off into the traffic.

Six months later she is called into a meeting with the VP that hired her. It's come-to-Jesus time.

'We're very disappointed,' he tells her. 'We expected much more of you. I'm sorry to tell you your work just isn't good enough.'

She walks the streets for a few months and then gets a lucky break. A friend of a friend of a friend gets her into one of the best companies in the field, with a reputation for outstanding creative work.

She's nervous when she gets her first project. She knows that they expect superb work from her. But it's been a while since she got to Exit Five, and she doesn't want to kill herself if they're waiting outside Exit One.

It's harder in the maze this time. Everything feels weird and distorted. She's done her homework in her diligent way, gathering the materials she needs to work the magic. And she's dedicated enough. But she's still confused about what happened last time.

It takes her some time to get her bearings, and to find her courage. On the first few attempts she loses her nerve and has to make her way back to the entrance. She can't sleep, and when she does her dreams are of solid white walls and blank corridors.

She goes back into the maze. It doesn't feel like an adventure anymore; it feels like a curse. Voices in her head tell her to get out of here and find a normal job. She could work in a museum or a night-club or a bank. By sheer force of will she keeps going. She remembers everything she ever learned during those years of apprenticeship. She remembers how the maze felt at her previous company those first few times. Her craft and her perseverance get her to Exit One. At least it's a start, she thinks.

But Exit One is closed. And she can see from the brickwork that it's closed for good, and has been for some time. She flees the maze in horror.

She's angry with everyone, and with herself. People at work keep telling her to relax, which makes her even angrier. One day her car breaks down and she can't find a bus to get to work. She abandons the car and walks towards the nearest train station. She has to pass through a tunnel under the railway line. It feels like the maze. She is suddenly overwhelmed by it all. She stands still, takes a deep breath and closes her eyes. And she realizes the moment she opens them that Exit One was closed deliberately to prevent bad work from getting out there. The door is not a barrier to success; it's a commitment to success.

That night in the shower she gets to Exit Two. Closed. She races on. She gets to Exit Three just as she falls asleep. She knows that it's closed and no longer bothers to check. By the morning she has reached Exit Four. It's not her best work, but she knows it's better than good. They're waiting for her there, of course, and the welcome is warm.

*

Good creative companies do that: they close off the easy exits to prevent bad work from leaking out. Bad creative companies don't care which exit you come out of as long as you have something to sell. It's easier to sell Exit One work because it looks pretty much the same as everything else out there. It's quicker too, so it's much more profitable than hanging around outside Exits Four and Five in the hope that something will eventually turn up.

Exit Five companies know that the work is everything and the expediency is the road to creative perdition. Exit Five companies have a culture that's strong enough and cohesive enough to keep Exits One, Two and Three closed at all times, no matter how tempting it becomes to open them up when the pressure gets too intense. The managers of Exit Five companies know how it feels to be in the maze, not just once in a lifetime, but every day. Many of them will have been in there themselves. Those that haven't will have a fine appreciation of what it calls for.

Exit Five companies understand the difference between creativity and craft. Creativity makes ideas, and ideas are things of immense and remarkable value. Craft must bend to the service of ideas. If clients and customers want only your craft skills there's no harm in selling them as a service. But if your reputation depends on the quality of your ideas then you had better make sure that the customer knows exactly what he is buying, and that you know exactly what you're selling. When you start selling creativity as a service you might as well pack it in.

Craftspeople have no use for the maze. They need lathes, wheels, Apple Macs, studios, Magic Markers, good lighting and a steady hand.

*

Seven or eight months later the senior account man and the junior account executive and the even more junior account person are having lunch.

'Whatever happened to what's-her-name?' says the even more junior account person. 'You know, the one with the dirty fingernails?'

'Apparently she's doing great things over the road,' says the junior account executive.

The senior account man holds his glass of Pinot Grigio up to the light and studies it intensely. 'Everyone gets lucky at least once,' he says.

*

The flip side of organizational disinterest is good project management, second after freedom on Amabile's list of 'work environment stimulants to creativity'.

Good project management in creative companies means doing everything it takes to help creative people get to Exit Five – which means maximizing intrinsic motivation and being constantly on the alert for creativity killers.

Matching the right people to the right project is crucial. Creative people need to feel challenged, or 'stretched', as Amabile says. 'Not so little that they feel bored but not so much that they feel overwhelmed and threatened by a loss of control.' Repetition is a creativity killer, which is why the current practice of assigning creative people to specific clients or to specific types of projects is so deadly. Where's the excitement of getting through the maze if you already know the way?

We have touched on the importance of clear, transparent briefing. Companies that take creativity seriously will make sure that senior management is committed, and seen to be committed, to the objectives of every single creative brief. A brief is a covenant, an expression of collective faith in the honour of the mission, and a commitment to uphold and support the values for which it is undertaken. Briefs should be signed in blood by all the participants before any work begins. Failure to honour the contract should be punishable by excommunication, ostracism or death, whichever is legal in your country. There is hardly any crime more serious in a creative organization than redesigning the shape of the maze while people are still inside it. Changing the parameters of a brief, fiddling with resources, adding additional constraints or expectations half way through the process, and the notorious practice of giving creative people artificial deadlines in the belief that they will be more efficient, are manipulative, counterproductive and unforgivable.

Organizational cultures that allow anyone and everyone to have an opinion about the work that emerges from the maze are as lethal to creativity as constraint, organizational disinterest and poor project management. In those first few days after an idea is born it needs to be screened from the harsh light of public scrutiny and the cool breeze of gossip. One of the reasons why creative people are so notoriously hostile is because others keep on trying to take their babies away from them before they're ready to stand up for themselves.

Newborn ideas must be loved and fed and nurtured. If they survive the first 48 hours you can begin to play with them, but gently at first, and strictly behind closed doors. When they're robust enough to begin crawling about you can prod them and tease them and stretch them and turn them upside down. You need to see if they can jump through all the hoops and withstand all the knocks they're likely to get in the outside world. Then, and only then, should you expose them to others, but only to the 'judicious', as James Webb Young advised. It is essential that these colleagues stand shoulder to shoulder in support of the idea before it goes any further. If there are questions or problems that you didn't anticipate during the hoop-jumping stage, you might need to take them back into the maze for refinement.

Negative comments are highly infectious. Once they're expressed it's impossible to put them back in the bottle. Amabile calls this real and present danger 'evaluation'.

In one of the companies she studied, code named National Houseware Products, she found all of these creativity killers working in concert:

> [M]anagers undermined autonomy by continually changing goals and interfering with processes. At one quarterly review meeting, for example, four priorities that had been defined by management at the previous quarterly review meeting were not even mentioned. In another instance, a product that had been identified as the team's number one project was suddenly dropped without explanation.
>
> Resources were similarly mismanaged. For instance management perennially put teams under severe and seemingly arbitrary time and resource constraints. At first, many team members were energised by the fire-fighting atmosphere. They threw themselves into their work and rallied. But after a few months their verve had diminished, especially because the pressures had proved meaningless.
>
> But perhaps National's managers damaged creativity most with their approach to evaluation. They were routinely critical of new suggestions . . . Through its actions, management had too often sent the message that any big ideas about how to change the status quo would be carefully scrutinised. Those individuals brave enough to suggest new ideas had to endure long – often nasty – meetings, replete with suspicious questions.

Evaluation in creative companies may not be as obvious as it is in Amabile's example. It will be much more sophisticated. Hilarious comments disguised as witticisms, back-handed compliments or astute, strategic observations can be more spiteful than outright scorn. Evaluation is being pecked to death by very small ducks. Exit Five companies go to great lengths to ensure that ideas are protected and supported all the way through the elaboration phase, and that any issues encountered along the way are dealt with in a way that is devoid of personal criticism. Ideas can and do die even with the most solicitous care and attention. That's just a fact of life. But Exit Five companies bury them with honour and dignity.

Encouragement and recognition are the antidotes to evaluation. And neither of them costs a cent. Encouragement, in Amabile's words, is 'management enthusiasm for new ideas, creating an atmosphere free of threatening evaluation'.

There is a story of a brilliant but irascible research scientist working at a famous American university. Not even his supervisors understood what he was working on, but he had a track record of producing extraordinary breakthroughs in his field. The university made a policy of sending young graduate students to the mad scientist's office two or three times a week to tell him how brilliant he was and how much they were looking forward to seeing the results of his new project. This encouragement kept him going through years and years of difficult and tedious research, and he ended up rewarding the university with more stunning accomplishments.

Encouragement does exactly what it says on the tin – it gives courage. Courage is what keeps you going in the maze when nothing else will.

Recognition is very different from encouragement. If it's used in the right way and at the right time it can be an even more powerful creative aphrodisiac. But few managers know how to use it except as a cheap substitute for a cash bonus.

Recognition works the way dog biscuits work, providing instant reinforcement for the right kind of behaviour. So timing is everything. If the dog sits when you say, 'Sit!' you give the dog a biscuit. It isn't going to work if you save your biscuits until the dog has obeyed you 20 times in a row. The biscuit must be associated as closely as possible with the behaviour you want to reward. If the behaviourists were right about one thing it's the power of conditioning. And there's no shame in using it to reward creative people as long as – and here's the really important caveat – you use it to reward the behaviour and *not the result*.

Not every good idea finds fulfilment in fame and fortune. Some of them lie idle for years before they are recognized for what they are. Some of them fall on rocky ground. There's nothing natural about the natural selection of the creative marketplace: it's not the best ideas that survive, it's the fittest. Which means that a bad movie with a big marketing budget will trump a great move with a small one every time. The qwerty keyboard, the VHS format and George W. Bush didn't survive because they were the best ideas. They survived because they had the most muscle behind them.

Only the most cynical of managers will wait until an idea finds favour before showering the creative team with recognition. Exit Five managers recognize the effort that it takes to get through the maze; they recognize the persistence and the imagination that led to Exit Five – irrespective of the fate of the idea in the marketplace. Waiting to see whether a client likes an idea before rewarding the creative team is not only an unforgivable abdication of managerial responsibility, it sends a loud and clear signal to the creatives that their job is to deliver to the expectations of the client rather than to the quality standard of the company.

By rewarding the result of the creative effort in place of the creative effort itself, delayed recognition creates a downward spiral of expectations. Before long Exit One will begin to look like Exit Five. You're back in the service business and you can close the maze for good.

*

Every maze is as unique as the project that shapes it, and as individual as the person who enters it. But all mazes have three things in common: a library, a playground and a cellar. The library is stocked with your memories and your knowledge. Every time you go back into the maze you take in more books and scraps of information to add to the store. Usually it's the first place you go to in search of ideas. There's a special place in the library called The Bottom Drawer that is full of all the ideas from previous expeditions that never made it out of the maze. If you're in a hurry you'll go straight to The Bottom Drawer and dig out something that is more or less suitable for the project at hand. The playground is not far from the library. When you haven't been into the maze for a long time the playground gets rusty, the wheels don't turn, and the swings and seesaws squeak for oil. You can never quite remember where to find the door to the cellar, but you will only need to find it in emergencies anyway.

Einstein's maze had a library stocked with thousands of patent applications and a well-thumbed copy of *Principia Mathematica*. His playground had a life size train set, complete with platforms and passengers, and a large machine for generating beams of light that he could ride on anytime he liked. We don't really know what was in his cellar because he never told us. But we can guess that it was full of hatred for the short-sightedness of politicians.

Donatello's library had a gallery rich in the masterpieces of International Gothic, with vivid examples of recent work by Gentile de Fabriano, Lorenzo Monaco, Pisanello and Masaccio. Next to his playground he had a sculpture garden displaying pieces by his rivals Ghiberti and Brunelleschi. Branching out from there was a well-trodden path that led to the font in the Siena Baptistry, the dramatic bronze doors for the Old Sacristy in San Lorenzo, and other pieces from the same period.

Conscious that his maze needed refurbishing, Donatello spent two years in Rome absorbing the grandeur of classical antiquity. The patronage of Cosimo de Medici gave him all the free time and resource he needed. The recognition he received from an admiring Florence gave him the confidence to push deeper and further than any sculptor since Roman times. And a climate of experimentation and tolerance that allowed him to indulge his homoerotic genius – despite the church and the infamous 'Courts of the Night' – all combined to produce his *David*, argu-ably the single most influential piece of sculpture of the entire Renaissance.

Depending on what kind of business you're in, you're going to have a lot of knowledge in your library that is dedicated to your specific field. And your playground is going to be populated with the kinds of things you most enjoy playing with. Sometimes, for particular projects, you'll need new stuff to put into your playground and new information to add to your library. If you can't construct them out of memories or imagination you'll have to get them from the physical world outside. This can involve money.

'The two main resources that affect creativity are time and money. Manag-ers need to allot these resources carefully. Like matching people with the right assignments, deciding how much time and money to give to a team or project is a sophisticated judgement call that can either support or kill creativity.' With regard to physical and financial resources Amabile continues:

> Interestingly, adding more resources above a 'threshold of suf-ficiency' does not boost creativity. Below that threshold, however, a restriction of resources can dampen creativity. Unfortunately, many managers don't realise this and therefore often make another mistake. They keep resources tight, which pushes people to channel their creativity into finding additional resources, not in actually develop-ing new products or services.

Scientists need stuff to experiment with. People working in the creative sectors need stuff to play with. For a software developer it might be an expensive new mainframe.

For a theatrical director it might be the funds for a bigger ensemble. For a creative team working in an advertising agency it might be a trip to Morocco.

In 2002 Amabile and her colleagues Constance Hadley and Steven Kramer dedicated a special research project to the study of the effects of time on creativity, publishing their results in a *Harvard Business Review* article called 'Creativity Under the Gun'. Their results were unequivocal – time pressure kills creativity. There is only one rare exception, and that is when people feel as if they're on a mission.

There are certain times in creative sector businesses when a project takes on a significance way beyond the norm. Typically they will be times when the entire business is facing a critical challenge such as a new business pitch or a desperate attempt to save a very important account. At these times of extreme peril or extreme challenge it is possible to get creative people to do extraordinary things under the kind of time pressure that would normally kill a creative expedition before it begins. Not coincidentally, these are also the times when management is most focused on the need for exceptional ideas. Organizational interest in creativity peaks. All the resources that are not normally available for day-to-day projects are suddenly and miraculously available. Constraints are removed by slicing through the Gordian Knot of process. Mutual encouragement, fuelled by adrenaline and the camaraderie of the trenches, turns sworn enemies into the best of friends and the excitement of the challenge prevails over petty resentments and historical jealousies.

It happened in 1970 when NASA engineers were given only a few hours to save the crew of Apollo 13 from dying of carbon dioxide poisoning. It happened at Bletchley when British code breakers knew that the outcome of the Second World War would depend on whether or not they cracked the German Enigma machine. It happened in Athens in 2004 in the last desperate months of panic before the opening of the Olympic Games. It happens, interestingly, with the artificial deadlines imposed by major artistic competitions, such as the design for Chicago's magnificent Tribune building or before the first show of the haute couture season in Paris. But these are the exceptions, the mission-critical moments that make or break companies and careers.

The first three examples have more to do with problem solving than with creativity in the strictest sense. In mission-critical situations the maze is circumvented entirely. The individual is replaced by the team, and the focus is on the accomplishment of a physical – or mathematical – challenge. The solutions may be 'novel and appropriate' but they rely on group intelligence rather than on individual imagination. But they do capture the dynamic that comes into play at these win–lose moments.

Some companies, like Ideo and Apple, are famous for being able to sustain a mission-critical atmosphere for months at a time. Charismatic leadership that ruthlessly eliminates the obstacles to creativity is a vital factor. But the usual consequence of time constraints that are applied in the hope of eliciting mission-critical creative behaviour is burnout.

> There's no doubt that creative thinking is possible under high – even extreme – time pressure. But this seems to be likely only in a situation that, research suggests, is not the norm in modern organisations: being able to become immersed, and stay deeply immersed, in an important, urgent problem. Given the demands in most organisations for communication and process checks, as well as the prevalence of highly interdependent work roles, protected creativity time does not occur naturally.

The authors go on to warn creative sector managers: 'Don't be fooled into thinking that time pressure will, in itself, spur creativity. That's a powerful illusion but an illusion nonetheless. Complex cognitive processing takes time, and, without some reasonable time for that processing, creativity is almost impossible.'

So how much time is a reasonable amount of time? This is the question that obsesses those procurement managers charged with buying creativity more efficiently from their suppliers. More in the habit of buying beans than statues, they involve you in bizarre attempts to pin down a productivity formula for creative projects.

If one copywriter takes three days to write a radio commercial for a brand of mayonnaise in a handy new flip-top bottle, how many days will it take two copywriters to write a website for a caravan park?

When all you can hear in the maze is the sound of a ticking clock, all you can think of is getting out at the first exit. Head for The Bottom Drawer, avoid the playground, ignore the cellar, do not pass Go.

Exit Five companies understand the importance of time and know how to manage it. It's a combination of experience and instinct. Such rules as exist are counterintuitive. More experienced creatives need more time, not less. So much of the maze is already familiar to them and it takes more time to find the nooks and crannies where treasure lies undiscovered.

The more time matters, the more time you need. And the less time matters, the less time you need. A good idea can happen in a second or in a year. The space–time continuum of the maze is infinitely compressible and infinitely elastic. Time itself means nothing, but the management of time means everything.

*

As they say in the ad business, there's never the time to do things properly but there's always the time to do things again.

*

The most sacred word in the free market bible is 'competition'. Competition is the great regulator of all things good and fair, the conscience of industry, the beating heart of enterprise, the scourge of exploiters and monopolists, the all-seeing Aleph of production and consumption, the holy spirit of liberal democracy, the invisible hand of peace and plenty.

So it smacks of vile blasphemy to suggest, as Amabile does, that competition is an *obstacle* to creativity. She is somewhat embarrassed by her own findings, but she shouldn't be. Even the most cursory survey of popular culture reveals that market forces are peculiarly inept at telling the difference between good ideas and bad ones, as we saw earlier. Competition has the perverse effect of driving down the quality of creative thinking while driving up the quality of craft skills.

The most obvious reason for this is dramatically illustrated in the story of Donatello and the merchant. Unlike beans, which will fluctuate in value according to the principles of supply and demand, creative ideas can simultaneously be worth nothing and everything, which is where the word 'priceless' comes from. Donatello's sculpture doubled in value the instant it was smashed into a thousand pieces.

In separate studies Amabile found that competition had a negative effect on creativity, ascribing the result to 'a combination of several social factors: evaluation, reward, and an additional win–lose aspect: this is unique to competitive situations.' We know that evaluation, and the threat of judgement that it implies, limits creative exploration by dampening intrinsic motivation.

Reward, and the way reward is managed, has its very own set of dangers. Amabile has shown that the promise of financial reward for completing a creative task has the apparently contradictory effect of restraining creative ambition. The psychology of the maze reveals why. Creative people want money just as much as everyone else does. But the promise of money is an extrinsic motivator, which actively interferes with the kind of carefree abandon that is so important for exploring the maze.

Richard Florida found that money was only the fourth most important factor in the list of priorities for creative people. Far more important are 'challenge', 'flexibility' and 'stability'. Creative people want the excitement of doing things they've never done before. They also want to be able to determine for themselves when and how they work, the autonomy of process that is the opposite of constraint. Stability is interesting because it contradicts the perception of creative people as reckless experimenters who love living on the edge. The truth is that creative people don't want to have to think about the mundane practicalities of knowing where the next meal is coming from. The more they have to think about money, the less they can think about the work. The chaos of the maze is all the chaos they need and want.

Far from encouraging creative people to make that extra effort needed to get to Exit Five, the incentive of a financial reward will steer them post-haste to Exit One. Managers who don't understand this will continue to use incentives in the hope of stimulating creative productivity. Managers who do understand this will often use it to manipulate creative people, exploiting their love of the job as a way of paying them less than they deserve, which is even worse.

Creative people need to feel adequately compensated for the imaginative effort required to get through the maze. But because imaginative work is invisible, and because it can take a month or a minute to have a good idea, even good managers find it notoriously difficult to put a value on creative time. Pay them too little and they will put their creative effort into finding extra cash. Pay them too much and they will immediately feel the pressure of having to justify their worth with every project. Bonus them on the basis of their results and they will feel as if they are being bribed.

This is one of the great conundrums of managing creativity. The carrot isn't any better than the stick. Both are loaded with the kind of extrinsic pressure that will have the creative person heading for the nearest exit, though for very different reasons.

There is a way to incentivize creative people with money, but you need the tact and wisdom of the 'Consuls and Overseers' who commissioned Michelangelo's *David*. First, they made sure that the base contract was generous enough to make it worth his while. All his tools and materials would be paid for, his board and lodging would be taken care of, and his monthly stipend would be enough, with good husbanding, to accumulate a tidy profit by the time he finished. Then came this remarkable codicil: 'When the said work and the said male figure of marble shall be finished, then the Consuls and Overseers who shall at that time be in authority shall judge whether it merits a higher reward, being guided by the dictates of their own consciences.'

There are three principles worthy of note. The first is the guaranteed monthly payment that gives Michelangelo the comfort of knowing that he won't have to look for extra work to pay his bills while working on the statue. This removes any of the extrinsic factors likely to distract him from the task. The second is the absolute faith in his ability, so he doesn't have to look over his shoulder in fear of competition. And the third factor, beautifully phrased so as not to become a bribe, is the consideration of an extra bonus if the work is thought to be especially remarkable upon completion. The size of the bonus is not mentioned, for very good reason. If it were significantly bigger than the amount paid for the contract itself it would clearly distort the intrinsic/extrinsic balance. If it were trivial it would be an insult. In the back of his mind he knows there will be an extra reward for doing a particularly good job. But since the amount is undisclosed, and completely discretionary, it makes no difference to the substance of the contract.

It is common practice in creative sector companies to get different creative groups or individuals to compete against one another *on the same task* in the hope that it will result in faster, better ideas. This is always a mistake. The only thing it serves to achieve is to undermine the confidence of the creative people by implying to them that you do not have faith in their abilities, to create a false time frame that exacerbates extrinsic pressure, and to distract the focus of attention from the intrinsic pleasure of exploration to the extrinsic reward of winning. Instead of producing one great piece of work from Exit Five, competition between creatives on the same task will produce an abundance of work from Exit One.

Competition between creative people working *on different tasks* will be beneficial if – and only if – they are embedded in a culture that prizes highly creative work, that tolerates nonconformity, values self-expression and embraces indeterminacy. Exit Five companies do all of these things, just as they trust the people they employ to produce the very best work.

There is, however, one exceptional case in which competition on the same task can produce great work, even in Exit One cultures. We can call this the 'what-the-hell' scenario. It is the case that applies to public competitions such as the one that was held to solicit designs for the rebuilding of Ground Zero in New York.

They occur regularly in the world of art and literature, often with juicy cash prizes as bait. Theoretically they shouldn't work at all. They have artificial time constraints, the extrinsic motivation of financial reward, the detrimental effect of evaluation, and the negativity that competition on the same task produces in other circumstances – all the ingredients of a creative catastrophe.

But the Sydney Opera House, the Tribune building and other great landmarks testify that they can and do produce results, occasionally brilliant ones. And they work for a very simple reason – there is nothing to lose. Public competitions, whether they're attached to prizes or not, give creative people the opportunity to go to the extreme ends of experimentation without risking a thing. If they lose, well, what the hell. It's the 'no loss' condition that removes all constraints, that frees the creative mind to risk everything – and absolutely nothing – on the outside chance of spectacular success. There can be no failure because the adventure itself is its own reward.

*

Amabile lists two more obstacles to creativity that require scant elaboration. For the sake of completeness they are 'overemphasis on the status quo' and 'surveillance'. The first refers to the inertia of habit, which we have discussed at some length. The status quo is particularly prone to become hyperstasized in commercial bureaucracies because of the emphasis on systems, processes and hierarchy. Groupthink, constraint and evaluation are the direct consequences of organizations petrified by the prospect of change and creative indeterminacy.

The surveillance of employees, which now seems to be taken for granted as a fact of life in an organization, is clearly lethal to creative autonomy, the single most important stimulant on Amabile's list of intrinsic motivators. Surveillance now extends to the tyranny of email and web monitoring, and all the indignities that result from the constriction of time and space in the toxic workplace. Surveillance, in turn, has led to 'presenteeism', that sense of obligation to remain at your desk, or looking busy somewhere in the office, whether you have anything useful to do or not.

*

Of all of my achievements at J. Walter Thompson the one of which I am most proud is The Idea Hotel. At the time of writing it was still thriving and still turning out a steady stream of exceptional work that has been lauded year after year at the major advertising awards festivals. It was run by an exceptionally talented manager and an exceptionally gifted creative director.

Whether it continues to survive and flourish will depend on how well it defends itself from creeping bureaucratization, on the one hand, and from the political jealousies of corporate headquarters on the other. That the model for its success is replicated in the rest of the company, in the rest of the industry, and in the other creative sectors, is the earnest hope of this book.

The Idea Hotel is a physical manifestation of the wisdom of the maze. It is predicated on the belief that creative people are different and special, and that very creative people are very different and very special. It is unashamedly elitist. It takes the demarcated strategy of creative organization to its logical extreme by physically separating the most talented creative people, by a distance of several cross-town miles, from the stress and politics of the agency's commercial hub. It is located in a villa, not an office. But it could be a barn, a warehouse, a shed or a farm. The physical layout of creative space matters far less than the design consultants would have us believe. If the psychological space is right, creative people can work out of a shoebox in the middle of the road.

The Hotel is managed on the principle of maximum autonomy. There is no surveillance, no counting of hours, and no monitoring. Projects are selected from the full spectrum of clients, and from the entire region, on the basis of their significance to the company, their degree of challenge, and the opportunity they represent for creative expression. Deadlines are negotiated by the mutual agreement of the creative staff, the client and the 'concierge'. This last role is crucial. It combines the traditional traffic role with art buying and resource management. Budgets for experimentation are generous. Other resources, such as freelance assistance from suppliers with special craft skills, are shaped around creative outcomes. The structure is fluid and creative-centric. The concierge manages all practical considerations, shielding the creative people from all administrative and management concerns. The competitive frame is defined by the best work done, by the best agencies in the world, as judged by the best creative people in the world at the most famous awards festivals in the world. All other criteria for evaluation, including those of the client, are secondary.

Two other conditions are required for ongoing success: location and diversity. Contrary to the belief of people who spend their time looking down at the world from the windows of a first class cabin, geography is not dead. Most mortals, and that includes creative people, need to live in real homes, in real cities and in real cultures. The nature of these places will impinge dramatically on the lives of creative people, determining, to a much greater degree than the globalists think, the imaginative content of the maze.

The Idea Hotel is located in one of the most culturally vibrant cities in the world. The fact that it is fraught with economic and political instability serves only to sharpen the creative appetite, just the way the political uncertainties of Quattrocento Florence loosened the shackles of artistic constraint.

It is asexually liberated city, and highly tolerant of nonconformity. Like Periclean Athens it is marked by deep divisions of wealth and class. But it is, linguistically at least, a monoculture, and it is certainly not as global as it once was. So the lack of cultural diversity could be a problem.

The 'hotel' concept is designed to remedy this. Creative teams from different parts of the world are invited to stay in the villa two or three weeks at a time, ensuring a constant flow of different cultural influences and points of view. These teams bring their own projects to work on, and they are encouraged to develop their ideas under the aegis of the resident creatives. Each of the exotic projects brings a different challenge, and different cultural considerations. The constant traffic of visitors means that both resident and alien creatives are exposed to a significant diversity of style and stimulation.

The concierge has another important role in this regard. At least once a week, he or she must invite an interesting or eminent person from a different creative field to visit the hotel to share lunch or dinner with the resident creatives. It could be a poet, an architect, a stand-up comic, an acrobat, a striptease dancer or a professor of entomology. The point isn't to teach or lecture, but simply to expose the creatives to different kinds of skills, different obsessions and different perspectives. Teaching goes to the brain; osmosis goes to the maze.

This isn't a dream or a fantasy. The Idea Hotel simply does what all creative sector companies are there to do – to produce the very best ideas in their particular domain. Nor is it unique. Around the world, in one sector or another, there are companies that excel at managing their creative people to deliver Exit Five ideas with remarkable consistency. Examine any one of them and you'll find that they are applying, with only minor variations, the same principles and practices as The Idea Hotel.

The great irony is that you can't make an Idea Hotel out of ideas alone. The most fundamental of all requirements is not the location, the etiquette, the culture or even the theory of the maze: it is at least two flesh and blood individuals, in the manager and the creative, with the vision, talent and passion to make it work.

I was lucky. I had Cosimo de Medici and Donatello.

CHAPTER 17

The guardians of the maze

> The game of artist-manager is a very tricky game . . . the manager
> doesn't have a union. He is a manager only because he and his talent
> say he is. He doesn't have any other qualification. It's a bastard art.
>
> Jon Hartmann, sometime gofer for Colonel Tom Parker

There is no more reason to admire creative people for being creative than there is
to admire left-handed people for being left-handed, or to admire blondes for being
blonde. Nature deals out the cards. Fate determines the rules of the game. Left-
handers have an advantage in certain games. Blondes have an advantage in others.
But it is clear from all the evidence we have, from both historical and contemporary practice, that when societies or organizations care about creativity it is much
more liable to happen. And the more deeply they care about it, the better it gets.

At certain times and places in history creativity has been especially valued.
And when it has been valued, it has flourished. Peter Hall quotes the examples of
the Athens of Pericles, Quattrocento Florence, Elizabethan London, Vienna in the
late 18th century and at the end of the 19th, Paris at about the same time, and
Berlin between the wars. Common to all of them, as Hall points out, are several
necessary, but not sufficient, features that promote creative excellence.

All of them were big, though not all of them were the biggest in their region
or at their time. So let's say all of them were big enough. If they weren't all great
global traders, they were certainly all at a crossroad of global traffic. Most of them
were capitalist, although in almost every case there were strong pre-capitalist
influences such as the guilds and the studios. They were all cities in transition,
breaking away from the conservative values that had glued them together in the
preceding centuries. They were all wealthy, or rather, there was a strong concentration of wealth among the aristocracy and the merchant classes, the 'bourgeoisie'

of Marxist analysis. All of them attracted talent from beyond the urban and national borders, and all of them were intellectually and culturally turbulent. All of them shared the excitement of discovering the worth of individual talent, a sense of enlightenment in an age of darkness. All of them needed something to react to, an establishment to push against. If Hall had read Richard Florida he might also have added a significant gay population or, at least, a social milieu that was tolerant of sexual ambiguities, a high degree of tolerance for nonconformity and self-expression, and a progressive attitude towards social values.

The way these factors interact with one another is clearly far too complex to provide us with a top 10 list of things you need to do to make you own creative crucible. And it would be reductive and dishonest to try. It wasn't a simple question of supply and demand, nor can it be fitted into a Marxist framework, as Hall freely admits. But shining through all of these creative places, both the historical examples of Peter Hall and the contemporary creative cities of Richard Florida, is one illuminating principle that sets them apart from the rest. Hall touches upon it here:

> A creative city will . . . be a place where outsiders can enter and feel that state of ambiguity: they must neither be excluded from opportunity, nor must they be so warmly embraced that the creative drive is lost.
>
> They must then communicate their avant garde notions to at least a section of the class that patronises them: they must communicate their uncertainties, their sense that there is another way of perceiving their reality of the world. That demands a wide spread social and spiritual schism in the mainstream society, wide enough to provide at least a minority of patrons for the new product.

There would have been no Greek drama or philosophy without an enthusiastic audience of Athenians. There would have been no renaissance without the commissions of a few Italian merchants. There would have been no Shakespeare without the royal playhouses and the galleries at the Globe. The same applies to 'the Viennese concert goers who embraced romanticism or their great-grandchildren who eagerly read *Die Fackel*, the Parisian bourgeoisie who bought Manet and later Picasso, and their Berlin equivalents who flocked to the Schiffbauerdamm to hear their values parodied and attacked'.

Without Cosimo there is no Donatello.

*

Donatello's *David* was the first free-standing male nude sculpture for well over a thousand years. Many art historians regard it as the work of art that presages the extraordinary intellectual and artistic accomplishments on the High Renaissance, of Michelangelo, da Vinci, Bellini, Raphael, Copernicus and Galileo, which laid the foundation, in turn, for the Enlightenment and the way we have come to regard ourselves in the modern age. In *The Art of the Renaissance* Peter and Linda Murray state:

> The *David* is . . . evidence of the rebirth of the classical past, and of the final emergence of the new spirit which was to inform the Renaissance: the sense, not of a lesson learned by rote, not of a model to be imitated, but of a parity of creation, of equality with the tradition that inspired it, of continuity of thought and feeling, even though the purpose to which the art was dedicated was entirely different.

John R. Hale, in *Renaissance*, says it exemplifies 'an unabashed delight in the human form', the 'vital optimism of the time', and a new sense of man's place in the universe, put into these words by Count Pico della Mirandola: 'God the Father endowed man, from birth, with the seeds of every possibility and every life.'

One shouldn't make too much of this, I suppose. It's just one bronze sculpture. You can find turning points in anything if you try hard enough. But think about this:

When Cosimo de Medici made his triumphal return to Florence in 1434 to begin his 30-year reign as the undisputed champion of the republic, the entire population of the city was around fifty-five thousand strong. That's smaller than the number of fans who turn out to see Arsenal playing Spurs on a rainy afternoon in January. Which invites us to wonder – given all the time and money in the world – what we would need to do to get that football crowd to produce a cultural renaissance half as interesting as the one produced by the fifty-five thousand people who populated Florence in the 15th century.

Perhaps it's unfair to start with Arsenal fans. So let's take a creative sector company that employs about the same number of people. Exclude the children and the women and grandparents who have to look after them and you get around twenty thousand, roughly the size of the BBC. So it could be a national broadcaster, a Hollywood studio, or a software company. It could be any similarly sized company with a significant stake in one of the 15 creative sectors.

A company with a good creative reputation will attract talent from far and wide, just as Florence did. It will operate in a global market, with access to foreign capital and the international markets, just as Florence did. It will have complete financial, bureaucratic and management control over the behaviour of its employees, possibly even more than the Medicis had. It will have double-entry bookkeeping, and rigorous systems of weights and measures, just as the Florentines had.

It will have the same sort of distribution of wealth and power. Historians estimate that the top 1% of Florentine households controlled around 30% of the available equity, which makes them look positively generous when compared to the proportion of equity held by the management stratum of the modern corporation.

In all other respects our modern creative sector company clearly has the means to more than match the remaining Hall–Florida criteria for successful creative cities. It can employ the requisite number of gay people. It can promote self-expression and cultivate a tolerance for nonconformity. It can, with a little imagination, create a culture that's as intellectually turbulent as it chooses. It can grant autonomy of process to its workers and thereby sustain the excitement of self-discovery and self-fulfilment.

It has the advantage over Florence of resources, both technical and creative, utterly unimaginable to the merchants and studios of that time. It has all the machinery for instant communication between all twenty thousand staff, and multimedia platforms that allow for the exchange of all sorts of conceptual material. Unlike Florence, it can choose the location of its corporate headquarters, and it can manage the work–life balance of its staff with the help of nutritionists, life coaches and fitness experts. Its artists won't be ingesting arsenic and mercury in search of the right shade of blue.

But surely the most important advantage we have over Florence is the wisdom of half a century of history, the perspicacity of hindsight, and the accumulated learning of the best research and the best thinking on the subject of creative productivity. Armed with this knowledge, and spurred on by the obvious failure of current systems of creativity management, what is there to get in the way of shaping the creative corporation of the future except blind obduracy and a lack of will?

Sitting down with a blank piece of paper, an open mind, and an agenda cleansed of all the mythology, the prejudices, and the mumbo-jumbo that surround the subject of creativity in organizations, we can now jot down the highlights of what we have learned so far. They will provide the guidelines for our new corporate strategy.

But first we must define our values, or at least our *raison d'être*, because we have seen how easily strategic objectives can fall apart if they're not glued together by something to believe in. It could be a call to arms, a rallying cry, a proclamation of intent, a covenant or anything else that hasn't been completely devalued by the corrosion of excessive exposure to PowerPoint. Whatever one calls it, it is certainly much more than a positioning, a set of goals or a commitment to enhance shareholder value.

We will arrogate for ourselves, since we are talking of ideals, the motto of the Medici family crest, 'Col nome di Dio e di Buonaventura', in the name of God and Good Fortune, where the latter stands for the risks that attend any great adventure, and God stands for all the incandescent powers of the creative imagination.

Our values derive from that: art for art's sake, money for God's sake.

As for strategy, we have a lot of the answers already. We have come across them in the peculiar biology of the creative brain, in the distinctive personality traits of creative people, in clues from evolutionary psychology, in the politics of pragmatism, in the characteristics of creative environments, in the notions of intrinsic motivation and self-consummatory behaviour, in the work stimulants to creativity and in the metaphor of the maze. We have seen it in the difference between problem solving and true creativity, and in the difference between craft and originality.

The macro issues are already in place. We have chosen a vibrant and diverse location that's as interesting to live in as it is to work in. Creative people flock to this place like bees to honey. It is global, dynamic, diverse, expressive, tolerant and cool – everything that Hall and Florida recommend it should be. It is not Stockholm, Canberra, Houston or chewing gum-free Singapore.

Internally we will take heed of the advice of Davis and Scase, making sure that the creative functions are clearly demarcated, pretty much the way they were in Florence. All designated creative people will have to undergo intense training in their craft with suitable apprenticeships at the feet of the acknowledged masters of their discipline. They will be managed according to Amabile's laws of intrinsic motivation, with autonomy of process management support and interest, clear project objectives, encouragement and recognition, and the appropriate levels of time and resource. We will acknowledge the principles of redundancy, keeping faith with our chosen creative people even after successive failures.

We will remind ourselves of the '10-year rule'.

We will pay them salaries that keep them comfortable. Occasionally we may give them bonuses that acknowledge work of exceptional brilliance, but these will always take the form of things that enhance creative learning or increase creative challenge, and they will never be linked to results.

We will make sure they never have to think about time or money.

Central to our new management approach will be the concept of the maze and all that it demands of us in both attitude and structure. We will incorporate the learnings of the Idea Hotel, though clearly they would be scaled up to suit our objectives.

We will be vigilant for signs of creeping bureaucracy, for systems and processes and for any other factors that could create extrinsic motivations.

We will never work in teams unless they arise organically out of personal preferences or interpersonal chemistry.

Every day, more or less at noon, we will burn an effigy of Stephen Covey on a bonfire of books by Edward de Bono. Attendance will be voluntary. Once a month we will sacrifice a strategic planner to the gods of chaos, in the method of the ancient people of Tenochtitlan.

Nothing will be sacred except the laws of the maze. Apostasy will be punished by PowerPoint.

*

There is one other critical ingredient for success. We have touched on it, but only obliquely. Without it, none of the rest of this will work – not the maze itself, nor any amount of passionate creative devotion. This is the Cosimo factor: the power of patronage.

Given the vital role played by patrons and patronage since the very beginning of the recorded history of creative achievement, it's more than a little surprising to discover that there is not a single reference to it in any of the contemporary literature on the psychology of creativity. Any close reading of a biography of a famous writer or artist or scientist will reveal the figures who helped nurture creative talent to success, sometimes with cash, but most often with encouragement, emotional support, praise, criticism, inspiration, guidance or just cups of tea. Yet for some inexplicable reason this notion of creative facilitation disappeared abruptly from the academic discourse just as soon as creativity was deemed worthy of serious study.

Perhaps the word had something to do with it. 'Patron' sounds archaic and dusty. And of the five possible meanings of the verb 'to patronize' the pejorative sense has raced clear of the pack. Two of the meanings, 'to defend' and 'to father', were declared obsolete by Webster's in 1953. By 1999 Oxford had demoted the meaning we're interested in, 'to act as a patron', which was the primary meaning only 46 years earlier, to a distant third. By the end of the century the neutral sense, 'to frequent (an establishment) as a customer', trailed in second place. But the outright winner, by several lengths, was 'to treat with an apparent kindness which betrays a feeling of superiority'.

Perhaps the beneficent sense of 'patronize' fell victim to the unstoppable tide of political correctness that swept the language clean of all suggestions of implied inequality. If it were able to stigmatize such commonplace words as 'he' and 'she' then 'patronize', loaded with its underlying sense of patriarchy, power and wealth, would have been among the first to drown. It has been replaced, to some extent at least, by 'sponsorship', which suggests a much more reciprocal arrangement as in we're happy to pay for your bowls tournament as long as you wear our logo on your hats. This is a shame, not only because we've lost a useful word, but because the practice succumbed in the process. To be a patron in the current social climate is to expose yourself as someone with too much money and not enough to do.

It's odd that the words 'rich' and 'poor' didn't suffer the same fate as 'he' and 'she', but that's another discussion. And Hall points out that patronage can only survive in the schism between wealth and poverty, so perhaps there is yet room for redemption.

There is another obvious problem with patronage that has nothing to do with the politics of language. We think about it only in its narrow historical sense, and most often in the context of people like the Medicis and the other great aristocratic families of the succeeding centuries. It feels old fashioned and irrelevant, an antiquated practice that exchanged charity for prestige, that made of the artist an indentured slave, indebted forever to the magnanimity of the patron. Clearly this is an arrangement out of sorts with the modern labour contract, which invites you to give a life of labour to a wealthy corporation in exchange for just enough money to pay the mortgage.

But patronage, in the sense that I now wish to reinstate it, has always come in many forms, not all of them as obvious as the Medici variety. In fact, the most common and useful forms of patronage have nothing to do with money or even with power. In its purist form, patronage appears as a set of skills just as rare as the creative talents they help to groom, skills that are vital to the successful management of creative sector companies.

First, we must make a clear distinction between patronage and commissioning, and separate out at the same time the very different role of the collector. Corporations or wealthy people that commission creative activities, either for themselves or for the sake of great public works, will tend to do so with a result in mind, something that can be shown or displayed or paraded as a function of their generosity, their faith or their public spiritedness. It is clearly a part of patronage, and a very useful one too. It gave us the Sistine Chapel, Holbein's portraits of royalty, most of Velasquez, and a host of other great works of art and architecture that are central to our western cultural legacy. But commissioning tends to happen only once the creative person has already established some sort of reputation. It tends to exclude that part of the patron/artist relationship that occurs in the early experimental days long before there are any guarantees of extraordinary accomplishment. This is the sense that Dr Samuel Johnson was referring to in his letter to Lord Chesterfield in 1754: 'Is not a patron, my lord, one who looks with unconcern on a man struggling for life in the water, and when he has reached ground, encumbers him with help?'

Collectors can be patrons too, but again only in a limited sense of bestowing their favour on those creative souls who fall within the realm of their grace. Charles Saatchi does a spectacular job of this, dispensing celebrity on a charmed circle of creative hopefuls, and blessing them with the credibility of his Midas touch. The patronage of the collector is to be admired for bringing new work to the attention of the public and giving avant-garde artists the courage to pursue their ideas with the knowledge that they might be accepted and appreciated by a social elite sheltered from the cold winds of mainstream criticism. But collectors usually need some wealth and prestige to start with; without it they cannot dispense the stardust of fame and fortune. Think of Penny Guggenheim or Pope Leo X.

Money is always good, but it's seldom the most important thing. In the case of Tchaikovsky and his benefactress, Nadezhda Fillaretovna von Meck, six thousand roubles a year, with no strings attached, was enough to allow him to give up his very distressing teaching career and concentrate instead on pursuing his musical ambitions. But it wasn't the money that made such a significant difference to the composer's career.

Tchaikovsky, by all accounts, was a weird, neurotic, sexually ambivalent mess. Von Meck was the widow of a wealthy railway engineer with a genuine interest in new Russian music in general, and a particular interest in the promising early work of Tchaikovsky. She decided from the very beginning that they should never meet, which was probably a blessing for both of them. So for 20 odd years they corresponded by letter, leaving an invaluable collection of pickings for biographers and musicologists. She was an excellent listener, if that's the right word. And she provided the perfect sounding board for his relentless stream of hopes, fears, aspirations, beliefs, opinions, neuroses, diatribes and confessions. It was the perfect arrangement for Tchaikosvsky's unstable psychology. More than anything else it was von Meck's tireless encouragement and emotional support, and her unshakeable belief in his abilities, that accounted for his most productive years and his greatest work.

Stories like these are legion in the lives of creative individuals, though they're seldom quite as vivid as the von Meck example.

Families often make good early patrons, sometimes actively, but sometimes simply by not getting in the way. Chagall's case is typical:

> His mother had yielded to the child's desire to become a painter – a strange desire, which could hardly have been induced by anything in his home environment. But his mother was a kindly woman with an alert and positive mind, and after her initial reaction of utter dismay she resigned herself to the situation. His uncle Pissanewsky, an enlightened man with a number of contacts in the outside world . . . supported him in his decision.

Jewish families seem to be particularly good at nurturing early talent. Creative people born into Protestant families seem to have to rebel against them to get anywhere in the world. Catholic families are good at providing the early anguish necessary for creative neurosis.

Friends, colleagues, teachers, university professors, curators, collectors, publishers, dealers, mentors, lovers – any of these could provide the support, the encouragement, the nurturing or the challenge so influential in drawing out the special talent of a given creative individual. For Basquiat it was the eccentric Diego Cortez who encouraged him to paint, bought as many of his drawings as he could afford, and arranged the 'Times Square Show' that brought Basquiat to the attention of the New York intelligentsia. For W.H. Auden it was Elizabeth Mayer who gave him unconditional friendship and the mother-figure he so desperately craved.

Every writer and artist and scientific genius has one, a special individual, or a special cluster of colleagues or friends or supporters, who provides that special stimulus to great achievement. Sometimes we know their names – Sam Phillips, Lorenzo the Magnificent, Ted Hughes, MIT, The Royal Academy, George Martin; just as often we don't. They can be creative themselves, or have creative aspirations, but they don't require either. They can be publicity seeking or publicity shy. They can be wealthy entrepreneurs or bank clerks grinding away at a job they hate.

You wouldn't know them by looking at them, or by diagnosing a pattern in their biographies. You wouldn't be able to pick them out in a crowded room, or deduce from their behaviour one notable sign that marks them out as belonging to this rare and remarkable breed. Some of them would not even be conscious of this peculiar gift they have, regarding themselves as entirely ordinary in all respects.

These are the men and women who do small things to create big things. They would remember to pass on a telephone number of a friend of a friend who might be helpful. They might send you the book you never knew existed that fits together the final piece of your puzzle. They will buy your painting on a whim and someone will notice it and want to buy another. They will email you unexpectedly with a chance thought or a chance connection. They will have dinner parties to introduce interesting people to other interesting people. They are networkers, influencers, godmothers. They are connectors, facilitators, empathizers.

Famous or not, wealthy or not, influential or not, it hardly matters. What unites them is their love of seeing new things unfold, new talents being revealed, new ideas emerging where once there was nothing. They have deep intuitions about creative people and what they need to progress. They understand creative people better than creative people understand themselves. They are translators, therapists, catalysts. They can make right-handers feel like left-handers and vice versa. They are coaches and caretakers. They have the rare gift of being able to walk in other people's shoes, and to see with other people's eyes.

A patron is someone who stands outside of Exit Five while everyone else is standing outside of Exit One.

Patrons are the guardians of the maze.

CHAPTER 18

The new patronage

Effective leaders allow great people to do the work they were born to do.

Warren Bennis and Patricia Ward Biederman,
from *Organizing Genius*

I see people who make space for the work. Because they care about it. They make space in the minds of conservative or unwilling clients, they help make space in our own organisations for the work to be done, they fight for time, they fight for money, they fight for resource. They navigate difficult teams and precious planners through the maze of client politics. They protect our thinking and they protect our newborn ideas. They make space in client organisations for our creativity and cleverness and mop up the mess when we're truculent. Or late. Or crap. I see people who open up the eyes of clients to the power of creativity. I see people who work to get them to take their heads out of their asses and have ambition and vision. And for all that they have to put up with being called asskissers, flunkies, and empty suits.

A blogger known as 'crankyoldbugger' writing on scampblog.
blogspot.com

The cult of celebrity has distorted history's perspective of creative achievement. By shining such a bright spotlight on the star of the show, the men and women who made genius possible have been relegated to the shadows of memory.

Roy Disney carved out the space and the resources that gave Walt the freedom to express his genius. General Leslie Groves did it for Robert Oppenheimer and the other brilliant scientists of the Manhattan Project. Kelly Johnson joined the Lockheed board of directors to protect the Skunk Works from bureaucratic interference. Jobs did it for Pixar and Apple. 3M's 15% rule does it for a culture of innovation.

Without a Doyle and a Dane there might not have been a Bernbach. Without a Bernbach there might not have been a Krone. And without the patronage of Audi and Polaroid, who were prepared to work with him when he had become too irascible and intractable for DDB's other corporate clients, we wouldn't have had the extraordinary art direction of Krone's last creative years.

Without a Lascaris there might not have been a Hunt. Without a Mather there might not have been an Ogilvy. You will think of many other examples, the unsung heroes whose names and faces have been skilfully airbrushed from the official stories of creative achievement. There should be a monument to them: the Tomb of the Unknown Suit.

Wieden + Kennedy produced the work, but Nike were the patrons. The Alaskan Airlines client gave Joe Sedelmaier the freedom to develop his unique directorial style. Behind every story of creative accomplishment in the advertising business you'll find a patron lurking in the shadows. It could be a marketing director, an agency CEO, an account director, a planner. Few of them are as visible as Charles Saatchi who translated his agency skills into a Medici-like patronage of young British artists.

Great film producers do it for great directors. Great publishers do it for great writers. How many of us know the name of the literary agent who had enough faith in the first Harry Potter manuscript to continue trying to find a publisher after having it turned down 12 times? How many of us know the name of the editor at Bloomsbury who decided to take a chance on it?

The great patrons of the past had the money or the influence to nourish creativity to fruition. The new patrons are those rare creatures who will risk their careers by challenging the inertia of commercial bureaucracies to back something or someone they believe in.

The guardians of the maze connect the outer planets of creativity to the contingent world of our daily experience, the world of sham, drudgery and broken dreams. Without them all ideas would seem alien and irredeemable.

They're the people in the meeting who surprise you by saying 'Why not?' when everyone else is wearing frowns and saying 'Why on earth . . .?'

Creative sector companies cannot function without them.

They can come from any discipline, which is why it is so difficult to identify them. In advertising agencies they would typically be account directors or strategic planners or senior managers who love the work more than they love their own careers. They are the ones who gravitate to the creatives in the bar. They are the only people that creatives will buy drinks for. There are never more than a handful of them in any company.

They wear their disguises well. You would never know that they were different from the other account directors, strategic planners or senior managers unless you happened to be in that meeting when they saved your idea from certain death.

They are immune to groupthink.

They are not to be confused with the star-fuckers, the groupies who hang around the creatives in the hope of rubbing up against some magic dust. They are far too independent-minded and objective for that.

They don't like creative people because they are creative. They like the ideas that the good ones produce, and nothing more and nothing less.

They are politically neutral. They have the courage of their convictions.

They have a natural understanding of the maze and how it works, even if they've never ventured into it themselves. They are the ones who, against all the advice of the management levels above and below them, and in the face of nagging and threatening clients who want their work and want it now, will find a way to buy more time to complete the creative process. They will tolerate the most absurd and extreme behaviour from creative people if they have faith in their ability to deliver great ideas.

They are the tacklers that prevent the defence from getting to the quarterback. They will clear the maze of constraints before the work begins. They will create a zone of maximum freedom around the maze and guard it with their lives.

Very few people who can resist the temptation enter the maze in the deluded belief that they can be of some assistance. They'll be the ones stumbling around in the dark and shouting 'There might be something interesting over here!' and 'Have you tried going left after the red curtain?' Or they'll be the ones who open the door at Exit One, from the outside, flooding the maze with a blinding light, just the way an inexperienced cook will open the oven door before the cake has risen.

The guardians will make sure no one gets close. They will patrol the perimeter for signs of intrusion. They will make sure that Exits One to Three remain firmly locked at all times.

Inside the creative sector company they are the true patrons of good ideas. They will demand, persuade or beg from the holders of the purse-strings enough money to prevent the creatives from having to think about it. So the first side of the von Meck equation is taken care of. Now the guardians are free to provide the rest, the listening, the support, the encouragement and the insulation from outside distractions. Indeed, liberated from the obligations and conditions that always go hand in hand with managing money, their relationship with the mazers can focus exclusively on providing the stimulants to, and removing the obstacles in the way of, creative success.

They are patrons in other ways too. When the mazers get stuck or tired or frustrated they bring them sustenance in the form of interesting things that may or may not be related to the project at hand. A reel of interesting news ads or animation techniques, the soundtrack from a weird Danish film they saw on TV last night, a magazine article about Ndebele wall paintings, a collection of photographs taken on the set of *Nosferatu*, two tickets to see the Red Sox. They take them to lunch and introduce them to someone who makes dresses out of garbage bags, or someone who had her leg blown off by a landmine in Mozambique.

They are interested in everything, so they find things of interest even in the dullest of domains and situations. They are like magpies. They search for shiny things and bring them back to the courtyard outside the entrance to the maze. They don't much care if they are used or stolen. Patrons collect things for their intrinsic worth, for their interest in the object itself. If they make money out of their collections, well and good, but that's secondary.

Like Cosimo de Medici waiting to see what Donatello would do with all that bronze, the guardians of the maze wait patiently outside of Exit Five, reading endless newspapers and doing all the crossword puzzles. They also serve those who only stand and wait. Perhaps this is their most important role – simply to wait with an open mind. And when the creatives finally come staggering out into the open, their eyes screwed up against the light, the guardians will continue to wait with the patience of saints.

They won't judge, they won't evaluate, they won't anticipate, they won't grab; they will accept. They will wait for the mazers to reveal their treasures in the time and place of their own choosing. It might be something tiny, wrapped in cotton wool, still bleeding. They won't be shocked or confused. It might be something with flashing lights that makes the noise of a thousand engines that screams obscenities in alien accents. They won't take much notice. What they're interested in, right now, is the glow of satisfaction. That will be the first sign.

There is a look and a feel about people who know they have achieved something extraordinary. They behave like mothers and fathers after the birth of a firstborn child. There is pride, but there is also bewilderment. There is relief and a profound sense of accomplishment. Overshadowing all of it is the awe of having been part of something mysterious, incomprehensible and deeply significant.

Before they look at the idea itself the guardians will seek out the distinguishing marks of passion. Passion will feed the idea through these first vulnerable days. Passion will provide the amniotic fluid that contains the antibodies against the evaluation of the injudicious.

Now the guardians will become advocates. While the idea is gaining the strength it needs to survive, the guardians will begin to herald its arrival, with subtlety and discretion at first, and always with the utmost tact. They know that it will soon take on a life and momentum of its own, and that there will be a time for conspicuous celebration.

They must also protect it from its creators.

Creative people can't stop fiddling. In the flush of triumph they cannot be trusted to leave it well alone. Nor can they be trusted not to compromise its worth by reshaping it and re-engineering it to fit the expectations and concerns of the outside world. That is why creative people should never have to manage their own creations across the threshold of the maze's perimeter.

Soon everyone will want a piece of it. The people who paid for it will want to put their indelible stamp on it. The people who briefed it will want to claim it as their own, disfiguring it in the process. The people who have to work with it will want to adjust it to conform to their own expectations or level of understanding. Even when the battle for survival has been won, the battle for integrity will continue. Only the guardians can fight that cause. They know how quickly passion can turn to cynicism. When the creatives begin to think that the idea has been taken away from them they will turn on it in scorn, destroying it themselves rather than giving it over to the callous disregard of the technocrats.

The guardians must be at once extraordinarily passionate and extraordinarily dispassionate. They must be able to separate the idea from the politics of power and personal preference. They must side with the idea and the idea alone. They must see its merits and be conscious of its weaknesses. They must defend it from its detractors and protect it from the enthusiasm of its supporters, who are often much more dangerous.

There is hardly anything in this world as offensive to most people as an idea they haven't thought of themselves. And this, with all its implications, is the ultimate challenge of the guardians of the maze.

*

But where to find them, and where to put them? If you can't already recognize them from the description we have thus far, ask the creative people. They will know exactly who they are. They should be project managers, but with staff – not line – positions. Like the creatives themselves they must be exempt from the measures of time, money and productivity. They should be sergeants, not officers; the foremen, not the men in glasses looking down on the factory floor. They must work, by perforce of standard company protocols, within the hierarchy of the management system, but they must have a direct line to the most senior management that frees them from the direct authority of their immediate superiors.

They are the concierges of the Idea Hotel. The curators of the gallery of the imagination.

Nothing in our creative sector company will be more important than the quality of the work. The guardians of the maze will be entrusted to manage it the way that only they know how.

*

Only the long view of history can decide with any certainty whether ideas are good or bad or irrelevant. In the meantime we must do the best we can with the judgement we have. Even great artists and thinkers make stupid mistakes and terrible errors of judgement. There is no certainty in the business of creativity except this: that more ideas are better than fewer ideas, and that it is now within our power to increase the chances of producing better ones, and reduce the chances of getting bad ones. Systems and processes won't do it. The only thing that will is the judicious management of the maze by people who know how it works.

What is required for creative success in this age of instrumentalism is nothing short of a radical revision of the way we manage the productions of ideas. The idea-generating machine will not be a factory producing repetitive work to specifications designed to minimize cost and maximize productivity. They will be 'unfactories', producing work that defies precedent, defeating habit by originality, reshaping our world and our lives in a way that's as free of ideology as it is rich in complexity.

The unfactory is a revolution in the management practice of creative sector companies, but it is not new. It is based on the way great ideas were generated in the past, in the great cities and the great societies, and the great companies of men and women who valued novelty above habit, who would rather suffer the embarrassment of a risk that failed than the shame of a risk not taken.

Bibliography

Amabile, Teresa M., 1998, How to Kill Creativity, *Harvard Business Review*.

Amabile, Teresa M., Collins, Mary Ann and Regina, Conti, 1996, *Creativity in Context*, New York, Westview Press.

Amabile, Teresa M., Hadley, Constance N. and Kramer, Steven J., 2002, Creativity Under the Gun, *Harvard Business Review*, August.

Anderson, Walter Truett, 1990, *Reality Isn't What It Used To Be*, New York, Harper Collins.

Arden, Paul, 2003, *It's Not How Good You Are, It's How Good You Want To Be*, London, Phaidon.

Bazin, Germain, 1968, *A Concise History of Art*, London, Thames and Hudson.

Bennis, Warren and Biederman, Patricia Ward, 1996, *Organizing Genius*, Reading MA.

Boden, Margaret A., 2003, *Computer Models of Creativity*, in R.J. Sternberg (ed.) *Handbook of Creativity*, Cambridge, Cambridge University Press.

Brockman, John, Ed., 2006, *What is Your Dangerous Idea?*, New York, Simon & Schuster Ltd.

Bullmore, Jeremy, 2003, *Behind the Scenes in Advertising (Mark III)*, Henley on Thames, World Advertising Research Center.

Bulwer-Lytton, Edward, http://www.brainyquote.com/quotes/authors/e/edward_bulwer-lytton.html.

BusinessWeek Online, August 28, 2000, Issue, www.businessweek.com/2000/00_35/63696002htm.

Calvin, William H., 1996, *How Brains Think*, London, Phoenix.

Campbell, Joesph, 2003, *The Hero with a Thousand Faces*, in R.J. Sternberg (ed.) *Handbook of Creativity*, Cambridge, Cambridge University Press.

Carpenter, Humphrey, 1983, *W.H. Auden, a Biography*, London, Unwin Paperbacks.

Cassou, Jean, 1965, *Chagale*, London, Thames and Hudson.

Cosmides, L. and Tooby, J., 1992, *Cognitive Adaptations for Social Exchange*, in J.H. Barkow, L. Cosmides and J. Tooby (eds) *The Adapted Mind: Evolutionary Psychology and the Generation of Culture*, New York, Oxford University Press.

Courtney-Clarke, Margaret, 1986, *Ndebele*, London, Thames & Hudson.

Creative Knowledge Company UK, Peter Feroze, promotional flyer.

Csikszentmihalyi, Mihaly, 1997, *Creativity*, New York, Harper Collins.

Csikszentmihalyi, Mihaly, 1991, *Flow, the Psychology of Optimal Experience*, New York, Harper Collins.

Davis, Howard and Scase, Richard, 2000, *Managing Creativity*, Buckingham, Open University Press.

Dawkins, Richard, 1976, *The Selfish Gene*, 3rd Revised Edition, Oxford, Oxford University Press.

de Bono, Edward, 1990, *The Mechanism of Mind*, new edition, Penguin Books Ltd.

Delavigne, Kenneth T. and Robertson, Daniel J., 1994, *Deming's Profound Changes*, Prentice Hall PTR, Facsimile Edition.

De Tocqueville, Alexis, 1994, *Democracy in America*, London, David Campbell Publishers.

Diaz, Porfirio, Quote from www.thinkexist.com/quotes/porfirio_diaz.

Donkin, Richard, 2001, *Blood, Sweat & Tears: The Evolution of Work*, London, Texere Publishing.

Dryden, John, 1681, *Absalom and Achitophel* (poem).

Einstein, A., attributed, source unknown.

Emmerling, Leonhard, 2003, *Jean-Michel Basquiat*, Cologne, Taschen.

Feist, Gregory J., 2003, The influence of Personality on Artistic and Scientific Creativity, in R.J. Sternberg (ed.) *Handbook of Creativity*, Cambridge, Cambridge University Press.

Florida, Richard, 2002, *The Rise of the Creative Class*, New York, Basic Books.

Freeman, Walter J., 1999, *How Brains Make up Their Minds*, London, Phoenix.

Gardner, Howard, 1997, *Extraordinary Minds*, London, Phoenix, Orion Books.

Ghiselin, Brewster, Ed., 1985, *The Creative Process*, Los Angeles, University of California Press.

Gleick, James, 1998, *Chaos*, London, Vintage.

Hale, John R., 1966, Renaissance, *Time Life*.

Hall, Peter, 1999, *Cities in Civilization*, London, Phoenix, Orion Books.

Heller, Robert, 1998, *Motivating People*, London, Dorling Kindersley.

Hirschberg, Jerry, 1998, *The Creative Priority*, Collins.

Hofstadter, Douglas R., 1999, *Godel, Escher, Bach: An Eternal Golden Braid*, Basic Books.

Hunt, John W., 1992, *Managing People at Work*, Maidenhead, McGraw-Hill.

Jacobs, Lewis, 1994, quoted in Tom Gunning *D.W. Griffith and the Origins of American Narrative Film: The Early Years at Biograph*, University of Illinois Press.

Janis, Irving, 1982, *Groupthink: Psychological Studies of Policy Decisions and Fiascoes*, Houghton Mifflin.

Johansson, Frans, 2004, *The Medici Effect*, Cambridge MA, Harvard Business School Press.

Jung, C.G., 1939, *Psychological Aspects of the Mother Archetype*, in CW9, Part I: The Archetypes of the Collective Unconscious, p. 187.

Keirsey, David West, 1978, *The Sixteen Types*, B&D Book Co.

Kierkegaard, Søren, 1959, Journal entry 1843, *The Journals of Kierkegaard*, Alexander Dru, Harpers & Row.

King, D. Brett and Wertheimer, Michael, 2005, *Max Wertheimer and Gestalt Theory*, New Brunswick, NJ, Transaction Publishers.

Koberg, Don and Bagnell, Jim, 1991, *The Universal Traveler: Soft-Systems Guide to Creativity, Problem-Solving and the Process of Reaching Goals*, Crisp Publications Inc.

Koestler, Arthur, 1989, *The Act of Creation*, London, Arkana.

Kracauer, Sigfried, 1973, *Theory of Film*, New York, Oxford University Press.

Lessig, Lawrence, 2001, *The Future of Ideas*, New York, Random House.

Lombroso, Cesare, 1895, The Man of Genius, Walter Scott quoted by Martindale.

Lumsden, Charles L., 2003, *Evolving Creative Minds: Stories and Mechanisms*, in R.J. Sternberg (ed.) *Handbook of Creativity*, Cambridge, Cambridge University Press.

Marcus, Carmen, 2005, *Future of Creative Industries: Implications for Research Policy*, European Commission, Foresight Working Document Series, April, www.heranet. info/Admin/Public/DWS Download.aspx.

Martindale, Colin, 2003, *Biological Bases of Creativity*, in R.J. Sternberg (ed.) *Handbook of Creativity*, Cambridge, Cambridge University Press.

Melly, George, 1972, *Revolt into Style*, London, Penguin Books.

Menand, Louis, 2001, *The Metaphysical Club*, New York, Ferrar, Straus, Giroux.

Mendelson, Edward, Ed., 1976, *W.H. Auden Collected Poems*, London, Faber and Faber.

Murray, Peter and Linda, 1971, *The Art of the Renaissance*, London, Thames and Hudson.

Nickerson, Raymond S., 2003, *Enhancing Creativity*, in R.J. Sternberg (ed.) *Handbook of Creativity*, Cambridge, Cambridge University Press.

Nietzsche, Friedrich, 1979, *Ecce Homo*, London, Penguin Books, p. 102.

Nietzsche, Friedrich, 2003, quoted in Schner, George P. and Ziegler, Philip Gordon, *Essays Catholic and Critical*, Ashgate Publishing, Ltd.

Osborn, Alex F., 2001, *Applied Imagination*, New York, Creative Education Foundation Press.

Paglia, Camille, 1991, *Sexual Personae: Art and Decadence from Nefertiti to Emily Dickinson*, Vintage Books.

Parnes, Sidney J., Ed., 1992, *Source Book for Creative Problem Solving*, New York, Creative Education Foundation Press.

Pfeffer, Jeffrey, from an interview in *Fast Company*, www.fastcompany.com/magazine/19/toxic/html.

Pinker, Steven, 1998, *How the Mind Works*, London, Penguin Books.

Plsek, Paul E., 1997, *Creativity, Innovations and Quality*, Irwin.

Plsek, Paul E., http://www.directedcreativity.com.

Plucker, Jonathan A. and Renzulli, Joesph, S., 2003, *Psychometric Approaches to the Study of Human Creativity*, in R.J. Sternberg (ed.) *Handbook of Creativity*, Cambridge, Cambridge University Press.

Runco, Mark A. and Sakamoto, Shawn O., 2003, *Experimental Studies of Creativity*, in R.J. Sternberg (ed.) *Handbook of Creativity*, Cambridge, Cambridge University Press.

Simonton, Dean K., 2003, *Creativity from a Historiometric Perspective*, in R.J. Sternberg (ed.) *Handbook of Creativity*, Cambridge, Cambridge University Press.

Stein, Morris I., 1990, *Creativity Programs in Stochastical Context*, in Sidney J. Parnes (ed.) *Source Book for Creative Problem Solving*, New York, Creative Education Foundation Press.

Steiner, George, 1978, *On Difficulty and Other Essays*, quoted by William Calvin, *How Brains Think*, London, Phoenix.

Steiner, Rudolf, 1964, *The Philosophy of Freedom*, London, Rudolf Steiner Press.

Stengel, James R., 2003, *We're going to Cannes to learn*, *New York Times*, Business section.

Sternberg, Robert J., Ed., 2003, *Handbook of Creativity*, Cambridge, Cambridge University Press.

Sullivan, Luke, 1998, *Hey Whipple, Squeeze This*, New York, John Wiley & Sons, Inc.

Swift, Jonathan, 1726, *Gullivers Travels*.

Taylor, Derek, 1987, *It Was Twenty Years Ago Today*, London, Transworld Publishers Ltd.

The Economist (US edition), 2003, *Lights! Camera! No Profits!*, January.

The Guardian, 2006, Organgrinder website, comment by Jughead no. 231258, 19 July, http://blogs.guardian.co.uk/organgrinder/2006/07/post_8.html.

Thompson, Mark, 2006, in an address to BBC staff, 19 July, www.bbc.co.uk/pressoffice/speeches/stories/thompson_future.html-60k.

Tumin, Melvin, 1962, *Obstacles to Creativity*, in S.J. Parnes and H.F. Harding (eds) *A Source Book for Creative Thinking*, New York, Scribners.

Vance, Mike and Deacon, Diane, 1995, *Think Out of the Box*, Franklin Lakes, NJ, Career Press.

Venturelli, Shalini, *From the Information Economy to the Creative Economy*, Center for Arts and Culture, 401F Street, NW, Suite 334, Washington, DC 20001–2728, www. culturalpolicy.org/pdf/venturelli.pdf.

Vinacke, W. Edgar, 1952, *The Psychology of Thinking*, McGraw-Hill Book Co.

Wallas, Graham, 1926, *The Art of Thought*, New York, Harcourt Brace.

Weisberg, Robert W., 2003, *Creativity and Knowledge: A Challenge to Theories*, in R.J. Sternberg (ed.) *Handbook of Creativity*, Cambridge, Cambridge University Press.

Whyte, David, 1994, *The Heart Aroused – Poetry and the Preservation of the Soul in Corporate America*, New York, Currency Doubleday.

Wilson, Edward O., 2001, *Consilience: The Unity of Knowledge*, London, Abacus.

Wilson, Jim, 1999, *How a handful of men broke the rules and created the worlds most amazing high-tech weaponry*, Popular Mechanics, September, http://www. popularmechanics.com/science/air_space/1280596.html.

Wiseman, Richard, 2007, *Quirkology: How We Discover the Big Truths in Small Things*, Basic Books.

Young, James Webb, 1991, *A Technique for Producing Ideas*, Chicago, NTC Business Books.

Zappa, Frank, 2008, quoted in *The Vancouver Sun*, 12 February.

Zukav, Gary, 1980, *The Dancing Wu Li Masters*, New York, Bantam Books.

Further reading list

Allan, Dave, Kingdon, Matt, Murrin, Kris and Rudkin, Daz, 2001, *?What If!*, Oxford, Capstone.

Backer, Bill, 1993, *The Care and Feeding of Ideas*, New York, Times Books.

Braudrillard, Jean, 1996, *The Transparency of Evil*, Paris, Editions Galilee.

Campbell, Joseph, 1988, *The Power of Mythe*, New York, Anchor Books, Doubleday.

Catling, Tina and Davies, Mark, 2002, *Think!*, Oxford, Capstone.

Dru, Jean-Marie, 1996, *Disruption*, New York, John Wiley & Sons.

Earls, Mark, 2002, *Welcome to the Creative Age*, Chichester, John Wiley & Sons.

Foster, Jack, 1996, *How to Get Ideas*, San Fransisco, Berrett-Koehler Publishers.

Schacter, Daniel L., 2001, *The Seven Sins of Memory*, New York, Houghton Mifflin.

Schumpeter, J.A., 1996, *Capitalism, Socialism and Democracy*, London, Unwin University Books.

Trilling, Lionel and Bloom, Harold, 1973, *Victorian Prose and Poetry*, New York, Oxford University Press.

Index